(Mis) Understanding Families

LEARNING FROM REAL FAMILIES IN OUR SCHOOLS

(Mis) Understanding Families

LEARNING FROM REAL FAMILIES IN OUR SCHOOLS

Edited by

MONICA MILLER MARSH
TAMMY TURNER-VORBECK

TEACHERS COLLEGE PRESS

Teachers College, Columbia University
New York and London

Published by Teachers College Press, 1234 Amsterdam Avenue, New York, NY 10027

Library of Congress Cataloging-in-Publication Data

(Mis)Understanding families : learning from real families in our schools / edited by Monica Miller Marsh, Tammy Turner-Vorbeck.
    p. cm.
  Includes bibliographical references and index.
  ISBN 978-0-8077-5037-7 (pbk. : alk. paper) -- ISBN 978-0-8077-5038-4 (hard-cover : alk. paper)
  1. Education--Parent participation. 2. Active learning. 3. Child rearing. I. Miller Marsh, Monica, 1965- II. Turner-Vorveck, Tammy. III. Title: Misunderstanding families. IV. Title: LB1048.5+.
  LB1048.5.M57 2010
  371.19'2--dc22

                                                       2009030507

ISBN 978-0-8077-5037-7 (paper)
ISBN 978-0-8077-5038-4 (hardcover)

Printed on acid-free paper
Manufactured in the United States of America

17 16 15 14 13 12 11 10   8 7 6 5 4 3 2 1

We dedicate this book to our steadfast partners,
Jeff Marsh and Dave Vorbeck,
whose unwavering commitment and devotion to others,
to our children, and to us, sustain and inspire us every day.

Contents

PART II: FAMILY-SCHOOL COLLABORATIONS

Acknowledgments

We owe special thanks to our editor, Marie Ellen Larcada, and to Alice Debus for their guidance, insights, and thoughtful questions throughout this process. Our work is much stronger because of them.

Introduction

Monica Miller Marsh
Tammy Turner-Vorbeck

There is a well-established line of scholarly work that explores family-home-school collaborations. There is also a growing body of literature that examines representations of families in schools. The work of the authors included in our first coedited book, *Other Kinds of Families: Embracing Diversity in Schools* (Turner-Vorbeck & Marsh, 2008), fits squarely into this second category of emerging scholarship. However, a text that critically examines representations of families and applies that information to forging stronger, more successful relationships among families and educators had yet to be made available. This book attempts to fill that void. *(Mis)Understanding Families: Learning from Real Families in Our Schools* has been written to inform prospective and practicing teachers, school personnel, and teacher educators about ways to effectively and inclusively identify, address, and meet the needs of diverse forms of families represented in today's classrooms.

The chapters in this text examine how relationships among families and teachers are defined by discourses that circulate through formal and informal curricula, and explore how educators can learn from the discourses that circulate through families and communities. Our hope is that through collaboration, families and educators can reconceptualize the discourses of family that currently dominate informal and formal curricula to become co-constructors of positive educational experiences for all children.

Children begin their schooling in the contexts of their families and communities. They enter formal school settings holding knowledge that arises within these contexts. When educators in formal school settings fail to seek out the knowledge that resides within families, they fail to acknowledge a significant part of a child's identity. Identity formation is a complex process that involves incorporating other peoples' evaluations of us into the way we think and feel about who we are (Bakhtin, 1920/1990).

Bakhtin (1920/1990) explains that self-identity is never formed in isolation. Rather, it is always forming in response to others. We fashion our identities by piecing together all the verbal and nonverbal messages we receive from others. With this in mind, our goal as educators should be to develop and implement curricula that include a variety of discourses in which strong, positive images are present and can be drawn upon by all children as they attempt to craft their identities. The chapter authors in this book present a diversity of discourses from which to draw, using pseudonyms for all people and places, unless otherwise noted.

In Chapter 1, an introductory chapter, Debbie Pushor asks readers to challenge the assumptions and beliefs that underlie typical school practices and to interrupt those practices by positioning families and children at the center of school experiences. Subsequent chapters are divided into two distinct parts. In Part I the chapter authors analyze the portrayal of families as they appear in informal and formal curricula. In Chapter 2 Gerardo López and Kent Stoelting examine how Latino families are represented in discourses of professional development. In Chapter 3 Shirley Steinberg explores the contexts in which families have been depicted in the media. Tamara Lindsey and Linda Parsons, in Chapter 4, investigate images of families that are portrayed in books that have won the Newbery, King, and Printz awards during the past 3 years. Chapter 5 explores how teacher identities are shaped as the chapter authors, Janice Huber, Deborah Graham, Anne Murray Orr, and Nathalie Reid, trace their own family stories in an attempt to understand the complex ways in which diverse experiences in families and with families shape who teachers are becoming. Monica Miller Marsh and Tammy Turner-Vorbeck, in Chapter 6, explore stories of exclusion in formal and informal curricula that are shared by children who have been in foster care and have been adopted.

Part II of this book features researchers who are working in collaboration with families and teachers to share knowledge, create curricula, and design programs with the educational success of all children in mind. In Chapter 7 Elizabeth Graue and Margaret Hawkins explore the home-school relations of 13 parents from a diverse school community. Rochelle Brock, in Chapter 8, attempts to redefine the image of the urban family from the way it has typically been portrayed in teacher education courses. The challenges and successes of past and current school experiences of Native American parents and their children are discussed by Angela Jaime and Caskey Russell in Chapter 9. Guofang Li, in Chapter 10, draws on ethnographic studies on families of various social-class groups in diverse settings to discuss what social class means in a time of economic restructuring, especially for immigrant and minority groups in the United States. In Chapter 11 Simmee Chung and D. Jean Clandinin inquire into the intergenerational stories lived and told by one Korean parent and her daughter newly arrived to Canada and the teacher-researcher with whom they negotiated and lived curricula.

Through discussion questions located at the end of each chapter, readers are invited to examine the relationships they have already, and have yet to forge, with the families of the children with whom they work. When educators and other school personnel recognize the knowledge that families bring to the education of their children and work to integrate this familial knowledge into the curriculum, new possibilities emerge for successful home-school collaborations that benefit teachers, families, and most important, the children who are in their care.

REFERENCES

Bakhtin, M. M. (1990). Author and hero in aesthetic activity. In M. Holquist & V. Liapunov (Eds. and Trans.), *Art and answerability: Early philosophical essays by M. M. Bakhtin* (pp. 4–256, v). Austin: University of Texas Press. (Original work written ca. 1920)

Turner-Vorbeck, T., & Marsh, M. M. (Eds.) (2008). *Other kinds of families: Embracing diversity in schools.* New York: Teachers College Press.

CHAPTER 1

Are Schools Doing Enough to Learn About Families?

Debbie Pushor

I paused briefly in the faculty lounge the other day to eat lunch before my afternoon class. Jane Preston, a doctoral student, was at the table, and we soon began a conversation about her son Zachary's recent entry into kindergarten. She said, "Last night was Meet the Parent . . . I mean Meet the Teacher night . . . at Zachary's school." I was struck by Jane's slip in language. When she finished speaking, I noted aloud what an important reconceptualization she had caused me to consider. Why was that first interaction of the year a Meet the Teacher night? What, perhaps unconscious or taken-for-granted, assumptions and beliefs are at play that prompt educators to perpetuate a practice that centers the teacher as the focal point to schooling? How might a Meet the Parent—or a Meet the Family—night challenge them?

MEET THE TEACHER NIGHT

With these questions in mind, my conversation with Jane replayed in my mind along with my own first experience as a parent with Meet the Teacher night. The elementary school in which my eldest son, Cohen, attended kindergarten consisted of about 500 students from a middle-class suburban neighborhood.

> [My partner and I] went early to the school, having been told by our neighbor that if we wanted to get seats in the gym for the principal's welcome, we needed to be at the school at least half an hour early. As we walked across the field together, I observed the surge of parents coming from all over the neighborhood. . . . [Inside,] the school hallways were crowded and noisy as parents called greetings to one another or joined together on their way to the gym. As parents new to the school, we found ourselves falling in with the crowd, rushing toward a destination that seemed to be collectively understood.

Inside the gymnasium, chairs were stretched from wall to wall, lining the large room from front to back. Already the room was half-filled and parents continued to flow in from both doorways. . . . The crowd of parents settled and fell silent as the principal stepped to the microphone. It was [her] first year at the school and parents were interested in hearing her words. They listened as she introduced herself and the staff, both new and returning, and spoke words of welcome.

[She] then explained how the rest of the evening was organized. There would be two half-hour sessions for parents in classrooms. Parents were invited to move to one of their children's classrooms to listen to the teacher's presentation regarding curriculum and programming. . . . After half an hour, [she] would then announce it was time to change, and parents could move to a second classroom for a session with another teacher. The principal let parents know she would be in the open library area just outside her office if parents wanted to speak with her. . . .

In the session in Cohen's kindergarten, the teacher stood at one end of the "cozy corner." Because, perhaps, she wanted parents to see the physical organization of the classroom as it is when children are there working, there were no chairs set up for parents or places to sit other than on small chairs at learning centers. While she warmly invited us in, there was a sense of awkwardness, of really not knowing where to be or what to do. She talked through a handout containing her beliefs about kindergarten, and including information about the program and her expectations for children. . . . There were just a couple of minutes for questions before the principal announced it was time to move on.

. . . Walking home, I was filled with a sense of emptiness. We had been rushed in, we had been rushed out. There was no coffee, no time for conversation, no invitation to linger. . . . I wondered if we moved with any purpose and intention or if we simply followed a . . . path trodden before us. I wondered if [there would ever be an opportunity, as parents, to speak;] to bring our questions, our wonders, our hopes for our children's schooling to the conversation. (Pushor, 2001, pp. 14–16)

Interrupting the Taken-for-Grantedness

The institution of "school" and the practices of the institution have a long-standing and storied history. Over time and through contact with schools—whether positioned as students, educators, staff, parents, family, and/or community members—we come to know the patterns, the consistencies, the predictabilities inherent in and across schools. Meet the Teacher night, parent-teacher communication and conferences, concerts, sporting events, and home-and-school meetings are typical practices in many schools. While it may be handled differently from one school to another, the familiarity creates a taken-for-grantedness about school; we know these practices well enough to stop questioning them. When the taken-for-grantedness gets interrupted–as in my experience with Meet the Teacher night as a parent or when Jane inadvertently referred to it as Meet the Parent night—we begin to question or seek possibilities.

I use the term *interruption* very consciously (Pushor & Ruitenberg, 2005): "The word interruption [is] derived from the Latin *rumpere*, to break. . . . *Interrupting* . . . is breaking in on, breaking to put something else in the place of. Interrupting puts something in the place of what came before, as in 'We interrupt our programming for an important message'" (p. 4). Ruitenberg and I see interruption as a thoughtful, deliberate act to break in on well-known and well-rehearsed stories of school and of parents' positioning in relation to schools, to put new stories in their place–stories that arise from different assumptions and beliefs.

Making Visible Well-Known Stories of School

In my experience with Meet the Teacher night, we were irrelevant to the principal's words of welcome and to the teacher's prepared handout and her accompanying talk. That evening we were not individuals; we were part of a parent body. We were rendered invisible by the large number of people present; by not having the opportunity to speak, share our thoughts, or ask questions; by the small children's chairs or the floor on which to sit; and by receiving no gesture of hospitality. It was a night to see and hear the principal, to see and hear the teacher, and to see the classroom and hear about the program and the teacher's expectations of our children and of us.

When we become aware of the taken-for-grantedness of a common practice like Meet the Teacher night, what do we see? In the right-to-voice assumed by educators and the absence-of-voice given to parents and family members, we see a hierarchical structure and a unidirectional agenda at play. Educators are positioned as holders of knowledge: of curriculum and programming; of school policies, procedures, and practices; of children, teaching, and learning; and of appropriate expectations. Parents are positioned as recipients of this knowledge, which implies they are unknowing, or less-knowing, than educators. As holders of knowledge, educators set the agenda for the evening. Not surprisingly, their agenda foregrounds their knowledge, their voice, and their decisions about how the school year will unfold. Their agenda implies that the role of parents is to provide support: for their children, for the educators, for the goals of the educators, and for the plans the educators have outlined to achieve those goals (Pushor, 2001).

Making Visible Beliefs Being Lived Out in These Stories

What beliefs may underlie or be implicit in what we see? From the lack of request for parent voice, we see a belief that schooling is about children, outside of the context of their family and community. From the privileging of educators' knowledge and experience, we see a belief in expert or professional knowledge as the most important knowledge for teaching and learning. From the privileging of the school's agenda, we see a belief that the goals of the school take priority over any other goals for our children and their learning. From the focus on what happens in the classroom and in the school, we see a belief in the school as the central site for children's education.

Putting New Beliefs in Their Place

Let's interrupt these beliefs—break in on them—to put new beliefs in their place.

A belief in the presence of children's families and communities. When children come to us in schools, they are already living multiple identities: as a grandchild, a daughter or son, a sister or brother, a nephew or a niece; as orphaned, detained, or wards of the system; as situated in neighborhoods, reserves, on the streets, or in other geographical locations; as members of racial, cultural, religious, or economic groups; and as members of other chosen communities. When they come to school, they come with this multiplicity and contextuality, not independent of it. In both direct and indirect ways, they bring their families and communities with them. It is our role as educators to make space in our classrooms and schools for all those who accompany them.

Children's education begins when they are born and is well underway when they first come to school. Schooling adds just one more element to their education. While educators have goals and outcomes for students, mandated by departments of education, reflective of principles of child development, and representative of their own philosophical stance, parents and family members also have hopes and dreams for their children and the education of their children.

A belief in parent knowledge. Acknowledging that parents are constructors and holders of knowledge regarding their children, teaching, and learning is another critical piece in shifting parents' positioning on the landscape of schools, from the margins to the center, alongside teachers. We have long been cognizant of the "personal practical knowledge" (Clandinin, 1986; Clandinin & Connelly, 1986, 1995, 1996; Connelly & Clandinin, 1985, 1988, 1999, 2000) held and used by teachers. Personal knowledge—gained from lived experience in all aspects of life—and practical knowledge—gained through experiencing the dynamic interaction of persons, things, and processes in the situation or the environment of the classroom—enables the teacher to make thoughtful, contextualized decisions about practice in the complex and multifaceted unfoldings of the classroom (Connelly & Clandinin, 1988). Parents, too, have personal practical knowledge of their children, teaching, and learning, also shaped by their lived experience in all aspects of their children's lives, arising from their experiences of the dynamic interaction in their homes and the varied contexts in which they spend time as families. While parents have very different knowledge of their children than teachers, this knowledge can significantly inform their children's schooling experiences.

In a current study, funded by the Social Sciences and Humanities Research Council of Canada, in which I am exploring with three families what parent knowledge is and how it is held and used, many aspects of their parent knowledge are emerging. I see in the parents' knowledge, as an example, an intimate knowledge of self and how this knowledge both shapes and informs them as parents. I see their passions being pursued with their children and permeating all aspects of their home context. I see an intimate knowledge of children that reflects both what they know of their children and how they know it. I see principles they live by, principles that are sometimes explicit and sometimes implicit, which guide in broad and philosophical ways how they live with and parent their children. I see knowledge of their children's rhythms and patterns and an application of this knowledge in the responsive routines and structures they put in place in their families. I see intimate teaching occurring in all kinds of moments and places and an intimate understanding of teaching—of the teaching they believe is needed and of how they respond in the particular. These observations are just a beginning glimpse of what I see.

In our new stories of school, using parent knowledge alongside teacher knowledge to inform schooling decisions and programming moves us away from privileging expert knowledge as the most valued knowledge to recognizing there is also value in knowing children "big" (Greene, 1995), in all their particularity and specificity, up close and personal, as only someone living with them in the intimate environment of a home can know. It moves us away from a stance that reinforces the position of educators in the center of the landscape and parents in the margins to one that welcomes everyone into the center. It invites us to ask, "What richness is gained when we know children from multiple vantage points?"

A belief in parent engagement. Engaging parents in the core work of schooling—the work of teaching and learning—is integral to positioning parents on the school landscape.

"Engagement" . . . comes from en, meaning "make," and gage, meaning "pledge" —to make a pledge (Harper, 2001), to make a moral commitment (Sykes, 1976,

p. 343). The word engagement is further defined as "contact by fitting together; . . . the meshing of gears" ("Engagement," n.d.). The implication is that a person "engaged" is an integral and essential part of a process, brought into the act because of care and commitment. (Pushor & Ruitenberg, 2005, pp. 12–13)

Different from parent involvement, where parents typically fill the roles of "audience, spectators, fundraisers, aides, and organizers" (McGilp & Michael, 1994, p. 2), serving only the school's agenda by doing the things educators expect them to do (Pushor, 2001; Pushor & Murphy, 2004; Pushor & Ruitenberg, 2005), parent engagement enables a sense of mutual benefit for both the family and the school. Instead of being restricted to the tasks parents typically do in schools—laminating and photocopying, organizing hot-dog days and milk programs, or supervising field trips, parents share their knowledge with teachers as together they make decisions about children's programs, the homework policy, the school's continuous improvement plan, or classroom curriculum delivery.

Parent engagement enables us to acknowledge the part that parents play in their child's education off the school landscape, as well as attending to the part they play in their child's schooling on the landscape. Parent engagement recognizes that much of what parents do to support their children's education may not be visible to educators. Telling personal and family stories of success or failure, instilling values, buying clothes that enable their child to "fit in" at school, speaking a second language, traveling, playing games, working an extra job to have the money for school fees, are all examples in which parents are engaged in their children's education. Actions that create "an educationally oriented ambiance" (Jeynes, 2005, p. 262)—an attitude or an atmosphere that forms a sense of standards or support for the child— have been found to have a greater impact on student learning than the more general forms of involvement. Engagement, in its many and varied forms, creates this ambiance.

A belief in family purpose. An aspect of shifting parents' positioning on the landscape of schools from the margins to the center is ensuring that the ways in which we engage parents in schooling serves their family's purposes as well as the purposes of the school. When educators *involve* parents in schools, they do it because they are seeking ways to address their central agenda of enhancing student achievement. In addressing their agenda, they talk to parents about the parents' role in relation to schooling, they offer parent education classes, they establish and communicate to parents information on policies (e.g., homework), and curricular initiatives (e.g., literacy for life), and they work to build parent membership on school councils. When educators *engage* parents in schools, they ensure that there are reciprocal benefits for parents and families through their engagement, both within and outside of the boundaries of the school's agenda. We see reciprocity in the following things:

> the difference culturally appropriate programming makes to school attendance and participation, and to positive identity formation for both students and their parents; the influence of adult education classes on student engagement and retention and on parental success and well-being; the provision of easy and open access to computers, the Internet, newspapers, and resources in enhancing both school and home literacies; and the provision of opportunity for voice, for sharing [parent knowledge], and for influencing decisions of personal, family, and community consequence in strengthening students' and parents' sense of personal power and autonomy. (Pushor & Ruitenberg, 2005, p. 15)

Central to reciprocity is the intention that everyone—parents, family members, students, and educators—leaves their engagement feeling strengthened.

NEW STORIES OF PARENT POSITIONS IN SCHOOL

Let's return to my lunchtime conversation with Jane about Zachary and his entry into kindergarten, and imagine that the event she attended the night before had been a Meet the Family night. How might the evening have unfolded? The event I create for you, a fictionalized event in which Jane, her partner Tony, and her son Zachary are characters, is a composite story, drawing on field text from three narrative inquiries: my research on parents' positioning in relation to school landscapes at Gardenview School in Edmonton, Alberta (Pushor, 2001); on parent engagement and leadership at Princess Alexandra Community School in Saskatoon, Saskatchewan (Pushor & Ruitenberg, 2005); and from my current research on parent knowledge, also being done in Saskatoon (Pushor, 2007). Further, it will pull from my lived experiences as a parent of school-age children and as an educator, from literature I have read, and from possibilities I believe can be realized.

Meet the Family Night

In mid-August, Jane and Tony received an envelope in the mail from Zachary's school. In the envelope, there were four letters. There were two letters of introduction, one from the school principal and one from Zachary's kindergarten teacher, that were warmly and informally written. The third letter, also from Zachary's teacher, is written personally and directly to Zachary. The final letter in their package, addressed to all members living in the household, is an invitation to a "Meet the Family" night at the school in early September.

When Jane, Tony, and Zachary arrived at the school for Meet the Family night, there was quite a buzz of activity. As they made their way inside, they were drawn to a banner that read "Welcome . . . Friends live here!", where they were greeted by a senior student. He welcomed them and provided a map of the school and directions to where they can get something to eat or drink.

Making their way to the gym, Jane, Tony, and Zachary met the school principal. She was dressed casually, wearing a name tag with her first name on it. She smiled, gave them name tags to fill out, and invited them to introduce themselves. She spoke personally to Zachary, as well as to Jane and Tony.

Jane and Tony moved deeper into the room, getting themselves tea and juice for Zachary. An individual approached them, introducing himself as the school custodian, and said, "Let me introduce you to some other families." Once introductions were made, he moved on, making connections between other families. After some time, one of the senior students who had been greeting families earlier in the evening came by to signal to staff and families that it was time to move into gathering circles.

In the gathering circle in the kindergarten, the teacher invited everyone to take a seat at one of the tables, arranged in a circular manner around the room. She briefly introduced herself, indicating she had created a display about herself and her family that she would leave displayed through the early part of September while they all get to know one another. She invited families sitting at tables together to introduce themselves and gave them a few quick minutes to chat. She then explained that she had selected a story to read to them that she felt would lead them into telling family stories of their own.

The teacher then reads *The Memory String*, a beautiful and moving picture book written by Eve Bunting (2000), about a young girl who lives with her father and stepmother. The little girl has a string of buttons she carries with her everywhere, buttons taken from the clothing of family members, including special articles of clothing her mother wore before she passed away. The buttons represent important people and moments and they pull forward cherished memories. Particularly, they bring her mom closer to her and speak to her of family. As the story unfolds, both her mom and her stepmom are honored.

After reading the story, the teacher invited each family to take some chart paper and felt pens from the center of the table and to begin to note "button memories" that tell about who they are as a family and what is important to them. She invited the children to draw memories on the chart paper as well as their parents sketched images or wrote words. She also invited the children to take a piece of string and for each memory their family noted, to slip a button on the string. She told them they can wear their memory strings home at the end of the evening.

As the room filled with talk and the families recorded important moments or memories on their charts, the teacher moved around the room, chatting with people at each table, using the time to make personal connections and listen to storied moments. After 20 minutes or so, she invites each family to share one button memory from their chart with the other families. When every family who accepted this invitation had an opportunity to share, the teacher asks them to post their charts on the walls.

Just before she invited families to move around the room to visit each other's button memories charts, she noted the information they shared about their families would help shape the program for the year. She thanked them for their time, their stories, and their engagement. She said she hoped this will be just the first of many family gatherings where they would come to know one another better and work together in planning a rich and responsive program for their children.

SHIFTING THE ROLE OF PARENTS
WITH PURPOSE AND INTENTION

Choosing not to follow the path trodden before us—as the imagined staff did in the story of Meet the Family night—choosing instead to move with purpose and intention requires consciously articulating and then translating into lived action beliefs that create a new story of school, a story in which parents are centered on the landscape of schools alongside educators.

Build Trust and Relationships

A starting point for educators in creating such a shift in the parents' position is developing a sense of trust and relationship between educators and parents, of honoring the belief that each has much to learn from the other (Cairney & Munsie, 1992: Pushor, 2001; Pushor & Ruitenberg, 2005). The relationships in our personal and professional lives that are rich and meaningful to us are relationships in which there is a sense of mutuality and reciprocity in a multitude of ways—we both talk and listen, give and receive, teach and learn, lead and follow. These relationships are based on a trust that enables us to say what we think to each other openly, honestly, and sometimes with vulnerability and uncertainty. They give us a place to be proud, celebratory, and confident in who we are and what we do, and they provide support for us to continue to take risks as we learn and grow. They are relationships arising from time and contact, from knowing one another, from having many and varied shared or common experiences. Relationships with parents and families are formed in this same way. They, too, require this same investment of sustained time and contact.

In the new story of Meet the Family night we see the commitment of educators and staff members to be present and visible with families and to share themselves, their lives, and their families in personal ways. In doing so, they create an opening for connections to form: points of mutual interest, experiences in common, and a place to start a conversation. Teachers and staff members are no longer strangers expecting parents' trust but are invested individuals who are positioned to earn that trust.

Welcome Families and Extend Invitations and Hospitality

In this restorying we see invitations being extended to families multiple times and in multiple ways. Invitations arrive in the mail from both the principal and the teacher, including both text and photographs, addressed both to the parents and to the students. Invitations are extended in person in the school building to come in, find a place, get something to eat or drink, make introductions, get acquainted, tell stories of your family. These invitations are extended by the teachers and the principal and by senior students and other staff members. They can be repeated later in the year over the telephone or in notes home, and they can be varied to reflect the context of each family.

In the restorying, we also see elements of welcoming and hospitality (Pushor, 2001, 2007; Pushor & Ruitenberg, 2005). These elements become evident in the breadth of the invitations, extended beyond parents to include other family members and people important in the life of the child. We see it in the messaging—"Welcome . . . Friends live here"—and in the affect and the attention to the environment that says, "We care that you are here." We also see it in the hospitality: the food and beverages, the time dedicated to conversation, the invitation to linger, the introductions made by staff and those facilitated between families. We see it in more subtle ways as well, in the choice of casual clothing, which invites proximity rather than distance, and in the use of first names rather than formal titles and names. There is an implicit message in all of these actions: "We want to share this place of school with you."

Another aspect of the plotline of this new story of Meet the Family night is a sense of inclusiveness. The teacher shares that the families who were unable to attend that evening will be given the opportunity to record their own "button memories" at another time and that their charts will be posted for sharing as well. The teacher notes this is just the first of many family gatherings; she speaks of her plans to reflect families' lives in the "curriculum-as-lived" (Aoki,

2005) in the classroom; and she shares her hopes to work alongside families as they share their voice in the development of program plans.

In our new stories of school we see that moving away from "public, ritualistic occasions that do not allow for real contact" (Lightfoot, 1978, p. 27) moves us away from the hierarchical positioning of teachers and parents as polite strangers or, in some instances, as adversaries to a side-by-side positioning as friends or, at least, as members in a relational community. It moves us away from a stance that shames and blames parents for being "lesser" or "different from" those who are mainstream, middle class, or holders of expert or professional knowledge. It moves us away from a stance that insists on someone being right and someone being wrong, someone winning and someone being defeated. Instead, it brings us to a stance that asks, "How do we, together, use what we each know to make good decisions about children and their teaching and learning?"

SO, ARE SCHOOLS DOING ENOUGH?

The stories I have told of typical and taken-for-granted practices speak to us about how parents are often rendered invisible in schools and how their parent knowledge is overlooked as teachers privilege their own knowledge and prioritize the school's agenda over that of the parents. They speak to us about how children are often not viewed in the broader context of family and how educators' attention to parents is often focused on their involvement in the mechanics of schooling rather than in their engagement of teaching and learning. They invite us to consider how parents sometimes become storied as deficit or lesser, and how their families are judged when the context of their families is different from that of the often White and middle-class norm of the educators. My restorying of these practices brings forward a glimpse of what can be realized for children, parents, families, and educators when we challenge the assumptions and beliefs that underlie typical school practices, when we interrupt them to put new practices in place—practices based on beliefs that center families on the landscape of schools. My restorying raises questions important for each of us to address as we consider whether schools are doing enough to know the families of their students: How do we make it central to our work as educators to challenge our assumptions and beliefs, both conscious and implicit, regarding parents and families? How do we make it central to our work to interrupt the taken-for-grantedness of hierarchical and unidirectional school structures, which continue to silence and marginalize parents and families?

In this book, the authors, chapter by chapter and collectively, interrupt taken-for-granted conceptions of an ideal family. Through their research and their stories of experience, they awaken us to how our conceptions arise from our lived experiences in family, from families we know and are in relationship with, from families often very similar to our own. They awaken us to how conceptions of an ideal family are created and perpetuated in popular culture and in children's and adolescent literature. As they bring us into the lives of a diverse range of parents and families they interrupt our conceptions of an ideal family, and they provide us with the opportunity to see and know "family" in new ways. In every chapter, they beg us to ask, "Are schools doing enough to know *these* families?"

Discussion Questions

1. What assumptions and beliefs about parents and families are at play in typical and "taken-for-granted" school practices?
2. How might we, as educators, "interrupt" these assumptions and beliefs? Why is this "interruption" important?
3. What new school practices might we imagine to create a place for parents on school landscapes and a voice for parents in decisions that impact their children's schooling?
4. What knowledge do you see parents holding about children, teaching, and learning?
5. How might we use parent knowledge, alongside teacher knowledge, to make better programming and policy decisions for children and schools?

REFERENCES

Aoki, T. T. (2005). *Curriculum in a new key: The collected works of Ted T. Aoki* (W. F. Pihar & R. L. Irwin). Mahwah, NJ: Lawrence Erlbaum.

Bunting, E. (2000). *The memory string.* New York: Clarion Books.

Cairney, T. H., & Munsie, L. (1992). *Beyond tokenism: Parents as partners in literacy.* Victoria, Australia: Shortrun Books.

Clandinin, D. J. (1986). *Classroom practice: Teacher images in action.* Philadelphia: Falmer Press.

Clandinin, D. J., & Connelly, F. M. (1986). Rhythms in teaching: The narrative study of teachers' personal practical knowledge of classrooms. *Teaching & Teacher Education, 2*(4), 377–387.

Clandinin, D. J., & Connelly, F. M. (1995). *Teachers' professional knowledge landscapes.* New York: Teachers College Press.

Clandinin, D. J., & Connelly, F. M. (1996). Teachers' professional knowledge landscapes: Teacher stories—stories of teachers—school stories—stories of schools. *Educational Researcher, 25*(3), 24–30.

Connelly, F. M. & Clandinin, D. J. (1985). Personal practical knowledge and the modes of knowing: Relevance for teaching and learning. In E. Eisner (Ed.), *Learning and teaching the ways of knowing*. Chicago: University of Chicago Press.

Connelly, F. M., & Clandinin, D. J. (1988). *Teachers as curriculum planners: Narratives of experience*. New York: Teachers College Press.

Connelly, F. M., & Clandinin, D. J. (1999). *Shaping a professional identity: Stories of educational practice*. New York: Teachers College Press.

Connelly, F. M., & Clandinin, D. J. (2000). Narrative understandings of teacher knowledge. *Journal of Curriculum and Supervision, 15*(4), 315–331.

Engagement. (n.d.). In *Dictionary.com*. Retrieved on October 3, 2005, from http://dictionary.reference.com/search?q=engagement

Greene, M. (1995). *Releasing the imagination: Essays on education, the arts, and social change*. San Francisco: Jossey-Bass.

Harper, D. (2001). Engage. In *Online etymology dictionary*. Retrieved on October 3, 2005, from http://www.etymonline.com/index.php?search=engage&searchmode=none

Jeynes, W. H. (2005, May). A meta-analysis of the relation of parental involvement to urban elementary school student academic achievement. *Urban Education, 40*(3), 237–269.

Lightfoot, S. L. (1978). *Worlds apart: Relationships between families and schools*. New York: Basic Books.

McGilp, J., & Michael, M. (1994). *The home-school connection: Guidelines for working with parents*. Portsmouth, NH: Heinemann.

Pushor, D. (2001). *A storied photo album of parents' positioning and the landscape of schools*. Unpublished doctoral dissertation, University of Alberta, Edmonton, AB, Canada.

Pushor, D. (2007). Parent knowledge [Unpublished interim research text]. University of Saskatchewan, Saskatoon, Saskatchewan.

Pushor, D., & Murphy, B. (2004). Parent marginalization, marginalized parents: Creating a place for parents on the school landscape. *Alberta Journal of Educational Research, 50*(3), 221–235.

Pushor, D., & Ruitenberg, C. (with co-researchers from Princess Alexandra Community School). (2005, November). *Parent engagement and leadership*. Teaching and Learning Research Exchange, Project No. 134. Saskatoon, SK: Dr. Stirling McDowell Foundation for Research into Teaching.

Sykes, J. B. (Ed.). (1976). *The concise Oxford English dictionary* (6th ed.). London: Oxford University Press.

PART I

REPRESENTATIONS OF FAMILIES IN FORMAL AND INFORMAL CURRICULUM

CHAPTER 2

Disarticulating Parent Involvement in Latino-Impacted Schools in the Midwest

Gerardo R. López
Kent Stoelting

Over the past 25 years, there has been a demographic shift in this country, evidenced by the rapid increase in the number of Latinos in the general population (Hayes-Bautista, Hurtado, Valdez, & Hernández, 1992; Sosa, 1993; Valencia, 1991). This fact is supported by recent census figures (U.S. Census Bureau, 2008) indicating that cities and states across the nation are witnessing a dramatic change in their racial and ethnic composition, particularly in areas where there has been little previous Latino presence (Wortham, Murillo, & Hamann, 2002; Zúñiga & Hernández-León, 2005). This demographic shift, sometimes referred to as the "browning of America" (Aponte & Siles, 1994), has placed an enhanced demand on educational institutions to meet the needs of an increasingly diverse student population.

Inherent in this effort to meet the needs of Latino students is the quest to involve their families in their children's schooling specifically and in their education generally. This chapter provides an overview of both traditional representations of parent involvement and those that more appropriately characterize Latino parents.

AN OVERVIEW OF LATINO STUDENTS AND PARENT INVOLVEMENT

The recent influx of Latinos into nontraditional areas, such as the Midwest and Deep South, has presented public schools with the challenge of needing to adapt quickly in order to effectively serve the needs of the Latino community. Since most school districts in these areas have little knowledge of

19

or firsthand experience with this population, many of the adjustments and educational accommodations implemented have occurred at the surface level (e.g., hiring bilingual paraprofessionals, translating documents between home and school, and professional development or training in "cultural" competency). While these accommodations are tremendously important, they are just a first step in truly understanding Latino families, their background, and how to best accommodate them in the school and the community. Because most schools do little more after these initial accommodations have been introduced, many continue to struggle in their efforts to work with this community. Clearly, much more is needed in schools because these basic interventions largely ignore the rich "funds of knowledge" (González, Moll, & Amanti, 2005) and deeper level understanding that are the foundation of solid home-school-community relationships (Villenas, 2001).

Moreover, for most teachers and administrators, such accommodations have not occurred as rapidly or as comprehensively as they would like. This has resulted in increased stress and frustration as they attempt to work with this population on a daily basis (Suárez-Orozco & Suárez-Orozco, 2001). Adding to this stress are the increased demands placed on schools by the No Child Left Behind Act (NCLB, 2002) and its state-level accountability policies that are unforgiving in their push to demonstrate Annual Yearly Progress for all children (Meier, Kohn, Darling-Hammond, Sizer, & Woord, 2004; Sunderman & Orfield, 2006). Quite understandably, schools that are experiencing these demographic shifts encounter much difficulty at the classroom, building, and community levels.

To be certain, driving the concern of many educators and policy makers is the low educational attainment among Latino students (Crosnoe, 2006). Currently, 43% of the Latino population has less than a high-school diploma (Chapa & De La Rosa, 2004) and their educational futures do not look very promising. Thus, the continuous increase in the Latino population in the United States, coupled with their gross underperformance in school, urges everyone to recognize and address the dire educational circumstances of this particular group.

Fortunately, in this ever-changing context of educational remedies that aim to fix educational "problems" such as these, parental involvement has increasingly received widespread attention as a viable tool for educational reform (Henderson & Mapp, 2002). In fact, the promise of parental involvement is touted by educators, policy makers, and practitioners alike as a key mechanism for educational change and improvement, particularly in schools that enroll a large percentage of children of color (Delgado-Gaitan, 1992; Moles, 1993; Sipes, 1993).

Indeed, parent involvement holds many promises for educational reform: the promise to work collaboratively with those who have historically been marginalized from the larger educational conversation (Henderson, Marburger, & Ooms, 1986), the promise to work with parents as equal partners and decision makers in the educational process (Epstein, 2001), and the promise to transform schools into true learning organizations in which collaboration and partnership combine to increase productivity for all children (Henderson, 1987; Moles, 1993). In short, there is widespread agreement in the efficacy of parental involvement as an effective tool for school reform (Henderson & Mapp, 2002).

However, research also suggests that Latino parents are not "involved" at the same rate as their White, middle-class counterparts (López, 2001a). Therefore, if educators are to address the problem of student underachievement for this particular group, it is imperative that we begin to search for ways to get Latino parents involved in greater numbers. Nowhere is this effort more critical than in the midwestern states, where the impact of recent immigration is especially felt in the educational arena (Suárez-Orozco & Páez, 2002; Wortham, Murillo, & Hammon, 2002).

THE PROBLEM WITH INVOLVEMENT: DISARTICULATING[1] THE ROLE OF PARENTS FROM THEIR PARENTAL ROLE

The definition of *parent involvement* varies greatly depending upon the school setting and context. In terms of school-focused involvement, Broussard (2003) defines *traditional involvement* as parents helping schools reach specific goals (usually defined by the school administrators and teachers) that reflect the school's values and priorities. Parents, in other words, are "involved" when they work in a supporting role to advance the school's mission. The schools initiate the manner and types of involvement required of parents and prescribe the expected role that parents play or are expected to play in the daily life of school. These socially and institutionally constructed roles have been in effect for generations and have been faithfully executed by parents wanting their children to succeed. Because the institutional environment "sanctions" these organizational norms, they have become a normal and taken-for-granted fact of daily school functioning (López & Vázquez, 2006; Smrekar & Cohen-Vogel, 2001).

Based upon past practice, it has been determined by the schools that the vast majority of parents are generally supportive of these so-called traditional school-based practices and decision-making functions (Kreider, Caspe, Kennedy, & Weiss, 2007). For example, one of the main evaluation tools for parent involvement is a parent's physical presence at certain school-based functions, (i.e., open house, parent-teacher conferences, school meetings, and PTA/PTO). At these functions, teachers may converse with the parents for a specified period of time about the progress of their child, while the parents sit passively, albeit attentively, listening to the teacher (see, for example, Chapter 1 of this volume).

In effect, the structured times for parent-teacher interaction are brief, narrowly defined, and unidirectional. They may even be scripted in some instances. Typically, during such exchanges parents are informed about what the child needs to do in order to achieve in school, based upon the observations and demonstrations classroom performance of the child. While the scope and nature of this exchange may vary between elementary school and the upper-grade levels, the overarching discourse and unidirectionality of the exchange varies very little.

Teachers and school personnel place an important value in the efficacy of this particular exchange, largely recognizing and embracing it as an important signifier of involvement (Carvalho, 2001). In return, parents are perceived as caring more about their children's education when they are actively supporting and maintaining the school's focus, whether it is curricular or extracurricular. Parents not participating in school-sponsored activities may be viewed as not caring about or perhaps unsupportive of the school's efforts to educate the child (Goodwin & King, 2002).

Parental involvement can also take on a shared or collaborative focus. In this framework, involvement focuses on the whole family, providing connections with community agencies, a focus on the home and neighborhood setting, and an emphasis on the inherent strengths of families. Thus parent-school collaboration is centered on a culture of relationship building and reciprocity between the parents and the schools. In effect, the schools and parents work together to educate the whole child, and relationships are built over time through continuous dialogue between and among parents, teachers, and community members. Unfortunately, in most schools this particular approach has not yet taken place and there remains an unstated assumption about what involvement looks like and what we mean by the term *parental involvement*.

To this extent, Goodwin and King (2002) identify several misconceptions surrounding involvement, arguing that these misconceptions must be addressed when creating expectations for parental involvement:

1. Parents who don't visit the school don't care about their child's education.
2. Good parental involvement must look a certain way.
3. All parents respond to the same strategies.
4. Parents who are struggling financially cannot support the school.
5. All parents have the same goals for their children.

In effect, Goodwin and King suggest that there are many ways in which parents are or can be involved in their children's educational lives. Going farther, we argue that parents can be "involved" without necessarily doing or performing *any* additional functions. This understanding of involvement, however, tends to fall outside of conventional definitions and is rarely recognized or privileged in school settings (Carvalho, 2001; Valdes, 1996). In large part this is due to the fact that parents are expected to perform a particular role in schools, a role that is primarily determined by people other than parents themselves.

Parents' roles and perceptions provide a basis for how involvement and participation is framed in the larger social order (Hoover-Dempsey & Jones, 1997; Hoover-Dempsey & Sandler, 1995). When these roles are created for and by others, parents are viewed as "involved" only when they enact or perform a set of a priori roles and functions (López, 2001a). However, parental knowledge and awareness of this role are important, as well as whether the defined role conforms to the parents' own understanding and expectations of their involvement (Hoover-Dempsey et al., 2005).

Unfortunately, many parents resign themselves to the role assigned to them by the schools, largely because of the parents' unfamiliarity with the educational structure and the power imbalance engendered therein. In other words—parents, particularly from Latino and other underrepresented groups—may not believe that they have the knowledge, power, and insight to impact the system in ways that redefine their role within the school setting (López, 2001a). As a result, school-based understandings of parental involvement are often dictated by school norms, which ultimately define the roles and expectations for parents at the expense of parental insights and perceptions.

DISARTICULATING NONINVOLVEMENT FROM UNINVOLVEMENT: A DISCURSIVE PROBLEM

We maintain that the discourse surrounding parental involvement identifies involvement activity as finite, fixed, and performative moments that reify a set of predetermined home-school interactions. These actions include, but are not limited to, fund-raisers, booster clubs, PTA/PTO, back-to-school nights, volunteering in the classroom, attending school activities, participating in parent advisory councils, and membership in school governance councils (see also Epstein, 1990; Chavkin & Williams, 1993; Henry, 1996). They also include a host of other activities and actions that take place in the home, (e.g., reviewing homework, demonstrating "appropriate" parenting skills, and so on) that reinforce the culture of schooling outside the school (Sigel & Laosa, 1983). In short, to be "involved" is to enact or subscribe to a specific set of roles and rituals that signify appropriate involvement behavior. In this regard, the problem of noninvolvement is a discursive one, where certain interactions and forms of involvement are privileged over others (López, 2001a).

However, even the most novice scholars and practitioners would agree that there is a fundamental difference between noninvolvement in specific activities and uninvolvement in a child's educational life. Unfortunately, as sites of social and cultural reproduction, schools have naturalized and privileged certain involvement practices, while rendering other involvement forms invisible. As a result, certain parents are viewed as being "involved" while others are considered uninvolved altogether. Clearly, all parents and family members *are* involved in their children's educational lives to varying degrees, yet certain forms of involvement fall outside traditional or discursive understandings (Hidalgo, 1998; Valdes, 1996).

In these cases, families who fail to perform or enact certain functions may very well be highly involved, but their involvement may occur in ways that we fail to recognize within education's discourse. As such, we firmly believe that the more pressing "problem" surrounding involvement rests in an educational discourse that fails to explore and validate alternate conceptualizations of involvement.

Perhaps the most popular and widespread conceptualization of involvement has been promoted by Joyce Epstein (1989) who states that five major types of involvement should be present in every school.

> *Type 1. The basic obligations of parents.* This type of involvement refers to the responsibility of families for children's health and safety; parenting and child-rearing skills to prepare children for school; proper supervision, discipline, and guidance for children at each grade level; and the presence of positive home conditions that support school learning and behavior appropriate for each grade-level.
>
> *Type 2. The basic obligations of schools.* This type of involvement refers to communication from school to home about school programs and children's progress, including the form and frequency of these communications, such as memos, program and event notices, report cards, and upcoming parent-teacher conferences.
>
> *Type 3. Parent involvement at school.* This type of involvement refers to parent volunteers who assist teachers, administrators, and children in classrooms or in other areas of the school. It also refers to parents who come to support and watch student performances, sports, or other events.

Type 4. Parent involvement in learning activities at home. This type of involvement refers to parent-initiated, child-initiated requests for help, and particularly to ideas from the teacher to the parents for monitoring and assisting their children at home on learning activities that are coordinated with the children's classroom activities.

Type 5. Parent involvement in governance and advocacy. This type of involvement refers to parents in decision-making roles in PTO/PTA, advisory councils, or other committees or groups at the school, district, or state level. It also refers to parent and community activists in independent advocacy groups that monitor and work for school improvement. (p. 113)

While Epstein's conceptualization appears comprehensive at the surface, it really emerges from a particular discursive framework that insists the proper role of a parent is to assist the school in fulfilling its educative mission. It assumes that parents are welcomed at the school site, have the time and requisite skills to participate in school-based activities, and desire to provide a parallel home environment to the school that ensures the continuity of school-based learning (Carvalho, 2001). Moreover, this framework presupposes a certain universality surrounding the "basic obligations" of parents and teachers, while downplaying the fact that such obligations may be culturally defined or grounded.

For example, in a recent study López and Vázquez (2006) found that Latino parents held culturally distinct understandings of the teacher's role: They referred to themselves as the "first teachers" and to teachers as the "second parents." This study also found that Latino parents did not have different agendas or interests from teachers, nor did they view the home and the school domains as being separate. Rather, they understood the home and the school as being corresponding domains and viewed their roles as being intimately connected.

Such understandings of involvement are not widely circulated in mainstream literature and are rarely recognized in popular typologies. As such, they often go unnoticed in the broader parental involvement discourse. In this regard, these typologies disregard the ways in which marginalized parents negotiate the home-school terrain and fail to build on the cultural understandings of the home.

We know, for example, the importance of recognizing parents as the "first teacher," but what does it mean—theoretically, practically, and epistemologically—for teachers to serve as the "second parents" of children? These findings highlight the important ways in which culture mediates understandings of involvement, and the importance of recognizing and validating culturally specific understanding of involvement activity.

To Epstein's credit, she insists that her model is not intended to be pre-scriptive and that it does not signify a laundry list of activities for parents to do. Rather, she asserts that the categories in her typology are broad enough to engender a wide range of involvement activities at both the home and the school site (Epstein, 2001). We disagree. We believe her involvement typol-ogy is wrought with a priori understandings of involvement that range from very structured activities within the home (e.g., reading to children) to very specific activities within the school (e.g., PTA/PTO). Moreover, we believe that her typology also engenders culture- and class-specific renderings of involvement that not only privilege particular involvement acts but render marginalized parents as "uninvolved," when they fail to perform them.

When education becomes dependent on parental input, it not only runs the risk of perpetuating a potentially dangerous stereotype, it simultane-ously minimizes the educative function of the schools themselves. In other words, these typologies not only circulate a belief that school success rests in the homes of the children, they also proliferate a belief that schools play little to no role in contributing to student outcomes. Schools, in effect, are positioned as politically neutral sites stripped of their ideological and repro-ductive function. As a result, such typologies have the potential to blame parents for failing to get involved in schools, while effectively removing from schools the onus of contributing to student outcomes.

Epstein's framework, therefore, positions parents as the arbiters of edu-cational success and failure. In effect, parents are positioned as both the problem and the solution. Consequently, they must perform certain func-tions and regulate their behavior in order to effectively carry out the educa-tive mission of schools.

Yet parent involvement is rarely seen through this particular lens. In fact, most of the parental-involvement literature portrays schools as oper-ating in seemingly neutral ways: structuring opportunities for parents to get involved and expecting parents to carry out their end of the proverbial bargain in the home.

We contend that this normalcy itself communicates much about how schools view the role and function of parents. In other words, to be in-volved is to be subjected to these "social regularities" (Foucault, 1972) that engender the rules and roles of appropriate involvement behavior. As such, schools that subscribe to traditional definitions of involvement are actu-ally working from a particular ideological vantage point and structure to prescribe how parents are expected to interact with the school. Rarely are the parents' interests, needs, and preferences considered and rarely is this process viewed as anything but positive and neutral.

Perhaps this is why Hoover-Dempsey (Hoover-Dempsey & Jones, 1997) suggests that involvement should begin with the *parent's* understanding of what the term means. She argues that a parent's choice to become involved begins with the parent's conception of his or her own role in the educational process—a role that is shaped through past and present experiences in schools, demands placed on the parent, cultural norms and understandings, opportunities for involvement, and personal preferences. Hoover-Dempsey and Sandler (1995) suggest that the associations and groups to which parents belong also affect expectations about parental involvement (i.e., the higher the expectations of the group, the greater the involvement in the process or activity).

Moreover, the work by Hoover-Dempsey and Sandler finds that parents choose to become involved in those activities they believe will benefit the academic success and well-being of their child. In this regard Hoover-Dempsey separates the cognition of involvement from the actual involvement activity. As such, parents may perceive themselves as being highly involved in their child's educational life, but may not manifest those commitments in prespecified or sanctioned ways.

It is important to realize that each parent's concept of involvement is different. Therefore, parental involvement activity may be closely aligned to parental beliefs, and not necessarily to the beliefs and expectations set forth by the school. Indeed, involvement is a highly subjective construct; one that cannot be judged by expressed parental actions alone.

In addition, Hoover-Dempsey suggests that a parent's role construction is either: (a) parent-focused, (b) school-focused, or (c) partnership-focused. If a parent makes a parent-focused attribution, they subscribe to the belief that they, as parents, have primary responsibility for their children's educational outcomes. In like fashion, when parents make a school-focused attribution, they feel the school is primarily responsible for the child's educational outcome. Under the partnership-focused construct, parents believe that both the school and the parent working together are responsible for the child (Reed, Jones, Walker, & Hoover-Dempsey, 2000).

Under the parent-focused role construction, parents believe in the efficacy of their actions, and work with their children to create educational opportunities in both the home and the school. To reinforce and augment their actions, parents may create informal networks or alternative educational opportunities that are of value to the parents but may be missing from the traditional educational curriculum. In other words, parents act in accordance with their beliefs to impact and affect the educational experiences of their children. For example, the migrant parents in López's (2001b) study took their children to work with them, not because they needed the extra income, but to teach their children the value of hard work. These parents firmly believed that if their children were exposed to the harsh realities of migrancy at an early age, they would choose to study in order to avoid this lifestyle in the future. Similar examples of this parent-focused role construction can be found in the work of Delgado-Gaitan (1992) and Valdes (1996).

Under the school-focused role construction, parents believe that the school is ultimately responsible for their children's educational outcomes, and adopt a more laissez-faire approach to their interactions with schools. However, because of their absence or noninvolvement, parents may be viewed by teachers as being less involved in the child's education despite the fact that they may express their involvement through other means. Under this framework, parents believe that the school is the provider of academic knowledge while home is the provider of other types of nonacademic knowledge.

The third construct, partnership-focused perceptions, emphasize that the school and the parents work together to create educational experiences for the students. This third perspective suggests that it is important that the school and the parents communicate and understand the roles and expectations of both parties in order to maximize the resources for the child. A partnership-focused role is difficult to implement for many schools because of the amount of energy and time needed to sustain the process. In addition, both parties must be able to communicate their expectations to each other, as well as to the child who bridges these two worlds.

Needless to say, schools and parents are often at odds in terms of what constitutes a good education. For Spanish speakers, there is the added cultural construct of what it means to be "*bien educado*," which engenders much more than mere academic training and includes elements of "proper" upbringing characterized by comportment, demeanor, manners, and respect for others (Villenas, 2001). At the present time, a strong emphasis has been placed on student's demonstrated achievement on standardized measures regardless of ethnicity, socioeconomic status, or exceptionality. Because students and parents are anything but "standard," educators must increasingly look at the education of the child from within their respective home environment and learn from the funds of knowledge available in the home.

Nevertheless, school-based perceptions and preconceptions about culture and language may limit the possibilities and opportunities to truly learn from the home environment. Complicating matters is the fact that parents have varied expectations as to what they want from schools, as well as diverse understandings of their respective roles in school-related matters (Brilliant, 2001). Schools are beginning to realize that new and different approaches are necessary in order to move away from deficit-driven perceptions that position parents and families as uninvolved and uncaring.

MOVING TOWARD A MODEL OF BIDIRECTIONAL INVOLVEMENT

To begin the process, many schools are increasingly engaging in community walks and neighborhood tours in order to become aware of the social and cultural dynamics surrounding their school community (Garza, Reyes, &

Trueba, 2004). In addition, schools are moving into a more collaborative mode, where bidirectional communication is the foundation for increased dialogue, understanding, and partnership (Chadwick, 2004; Delgado-Gaitan, 1992, 2001, 2007).

With this evolving role of parental involvement come specialized interests and the hope of equal distribution of resources across all parent and student needs. The school's mission is becoming more focused, yet more diverse in meeting the needs of the school community. By redefining involvement, schools are becoming aware that they have a responsibility and a duty to serve all families, not just those families who fit into the school's traditional behavioral and organizational system. Indeed, schools are learning that parental values and perspectives can be valued and represented in the total mission of the school organization, and they can involve their communities and constituencies if they rethink and reconceptualize their understanding of involvement (Osterling & Garza, 2004).

In short, parent roles, role constructions, and parent-community input are essential when (re)designing and (re)developing effective parent involvement programs that meet the needs of multiple constituencies. School may not yet have the requisite knowledge or dispositions to implement the desired program and may be holding onto antiquated and outdated understandings of parent involvement. In this regard, professional development is essential and critical in providing a bridge for teachers and schools to work together in new and different ways.

DISARTICULATING PROFESSIONAL DEVELOPMENT: PARENT INVOLVEMENT AS A SCHOOL-BASED PROBLEM

The increased emphasis on students' academic performance has placed many schools in a perceived conundrum: How can schools create an efficient and expedient way of getting culturally and ethnically diverse parents involved in the school while simultaneously meeting high standards of achievement? There are no easy answers for addressing these issues separately; the answers lie in relationship building, which takes time but pays off in the long run.

In order to build relationships, schools must structure opportunities for firsthand interaction with parents and families—opportunities that are reciprocal, dialogic, and genuine, not prescribed, routine, and predictable. Instead of structured involvement opportunities at the school site, which are often ritualistic and scripted, schools need to create opportunities to get to know parents in less formal settings, without predetermined agendas but with a fresh perspective on home-school-community partnerships (González & Moll, 2002; Romo, 1999). Rather than subscribe to the notion of "school involvement" on the part of parents, schools should engage in professional development that emphasizes "home involvement" on the part of schools. Only then will schools and districts begin to realize that the problem of involvement is as much a school-based problem as it is a home-based one.

Unfortunately, getting to know parents and the broader community in this fashion is rarely viewed as a type of professional development. While some schools do engage in community walks or tours to expose teachers to a parent's lived reality, such attempts fail to couple these experiences with a cogent discussion surrounding home-school involvement, particularly involvement beliefs and practices that emerge from the school itself.

Instead, what often passes as professional development are activities and prescriptive programs designed to train teachers on best practices of how to effectively work and communicate with parents. Teachers, in effect, are given a toolbox of practical tips, techniques, and strategies that do very little to provide a cogent understanding and rearticulation of involvement. As a matter of fact, most professional development modules on parental involvement serve to reinforce traditional perceptions of involvement activity and thus fortify deficit assumptions of parental noninvolvement. In other words, instead of viewing parent noninvolvement as a symptom to be diagnosed, professional development modules often focus on strategies and tools to address the perceived causes of noninvolvement. As a result, teachers fail to interrogate their own deeply held assumptions about involvement, receive no firsthand knowledge about the children and families with whom they work, and reinforce deficit perceptions of parents.

Gibson (2002) states that most educators view Latino parents as "problems" that either need to be fixed or managed. He argues that many teachers believe that Latino parents are uneducated, don't have the knowledge or capacity to assist their children at home, and lack the desire to become involved in school matters (Gitlin, Buendia, Crosland, & Doumbia, 2003). Gibson suggests that such attributions might actually reflect the teacher's lack of preparedness or uncertainty in dealing with culturally and linguistically diverse populations. Therefore, if we are to make inroads into resolving the issue of Latino underperformance, it is imperative that teachers and schools make a critical examination and evaluation of their own assumptions and deeply held beliefs about Latino parents.

CONCLUSION: A PLEA FOR REARTICULATION

The influx of Latino families in the Midwest has presented schools with the challenge of quickly needing to adapt in order to serve the educational needs of these students and their families. Given the recency of this demographic shift, many midwestern schools have encountered difficulty when trying to assess the multifaceted needs of these newcomers, resulting in increased demands for professional development that capitalize on the unique linkages between the home and the school.

Often such professional development emphasizes the linguistic and cultural differences of Latino households, and identifies specific ways in which schools can become more "family-friendly" in order to overcome those barriers. The problem with this conceptualization, we argue, is that it fails to recognize the multiple ways in which families are *already* involved in the educational lives of their children and thus reifies deficit notions of Latino family functioning while promoting a false belief in the efficacy of schools to triumph over cultural differences.

The problem of involvement, therefore, rests in a limited understanding of what constitutes "involvement activity." These discursive understandings are then used to structure daily involvement opportunities, professional development for teachers, and reform strategies for schools. We believe that such efforts are dangerous, for they reproduce a very narrow conceptualization of involvement that effectively strips parents from their parental role, prescribes preferred roles for parents, and fosters a false belief in the efficacy of involvement. Moreover, it fosters the belief that student outcomes are dependent on parental participation and thus conveniently removes the onus of learning from schools themselves. In this regard, the uncritical embracement of parental involvement as a mechanism for educational change and school improvement ultimately serves to disarticulate the professional educator from the profession of education.

As a field, we need to ask ourselves what we really want from parents. In other words, when all is said and done, what kinds of actions and interventions do we want parents to make on behalf of their children? What does involvement boil down to? In answering those questions, we will not only reveal how we, as educators, view parents vis-à-vis the education of their children, but we will also reveal the kind of roles we want parents to have at both the school and in the home. But in answering those questions, we also need to be brutally honest with ourselves: Do we really want parents in classrooms and schools on a daily basis? Do we really want parents roaming the hallways, observing classrooms, and keeping a watchful eye on the teacher's every move? Do we really want parents who are advocates for their children, even if it means challenging and confronting teachers and school administrators?

Or do we want something else from parents? Parents who are "involved" on our terms, who engage in classrooms and schools in prespecified ways, who are nonconfrontational, and who do only what they need to do to support the educational function of the school? Perhaps we might be satisfied if parents performed specific acts at home (e.g., reviewing homework, creating a quiet place for the children to work, demonstrating "appropriate" parenting skills) that reinforce and parallel the culture of schooling (Sigel & Laosa, 1983).

Regardless of what we decide, we must recognize that there is an element of cultural reproduction involved, as well as a priori assumptions surrounding the role and function of parents in school-related matters. Only then can we begin to move away from these assumptions and start working with parents in fundamentally different ways: building on the funds of knowledge and cultural practices of the home and moving toward true bidirectionality by bringing schools into the home and involving them in the broader community.

Because we, as a field, have never taken the time to really think through what it is we want from parents, we've tended to support involvement practices that have been at work in schools for several decades. While we have made much progress in our understanding and articulation of involvement, most educators still tend to think of involvement in definite or finite ways.

Therefore, the key to involvement does not rest in rethinking our strategies for getting parents more involved, but in challenging ourselves first to rethink what we mean by involvement, and then to rethink strategies for how to work with parents in fundamentally different ways. The solution to the involvement problem cannot be found in professional development modules, in time-worn typologies, or in best practices that rehash what we believe involvement should look like. Rather, the solution rests in rethinking our most fundamental assumptions surrounding home-school-community partnerships.

Discussion Questions

1. What practical steps can schools take to move away from traditional notions of parental involvement?
2. What can schools do to reflect on their own taken-for-granted assumptions surrounding involvement?
3. What can parents do to collaborate with schools in order to build bridges of understanding between the home and school in ways that do not substantiate traditional assumptions surrounding parent involvement?
4. What is the role of researchers in helping educators improve home-school-community partnerships in light of the critique surrounding parent involvement?
5. What does professional development on parent involvement look like when one disarticulates it from its performative underpinnings?

NOTE

1. The term *disarticulate* means to disentangle or unravel, and within the context of this chapter it is used in urging readers to question what the term *parent involvement* means to different people in different contexts, in order to critically engage in a dialogue that redefines the parameters of parent involvement so that all families are included.

REFERENCES

Aponte, R., & Siles, M. (1994). *Latinos in the heartland: The browning of the Midwest* (JSRI Research Report No. 5). East Lansing, MI: Julian Samora Research Institute.

Brilliant, C. (2001). Parent involvement in education: Attitudes and activities of Spanish-speakers as affected by training. *Bilingual Research Journal, 25*(3), 252–274.

Broussard, C. (2003). Facilitating home-school partnerships for multiethnic families. *Children and Families, 25*(4), 211–223.

Carvalho, M. E. P. de. (2001). *Rethinking family-school relations: A critique of parent involvement in schooling.* Mahwah, NJ: Erlbaum.

Chadwick, K. (2004). *Improving schools through community engagement.* Thousand Oaks, CA: Corwin Press.

Chapa, J., & De La Rosa, B. (2004). Latino population growth, socioeconomic and demographic characteristics, and implications for educational attainment. *Education and Urban Society, 36*, 130–149.

Chavkin, N. F., & Williams, D. L. (1993). Minority parents and the elementary school: Attitudes and practices. In N. F. Chavkin (Ed.), *Families and schools in a pluralistic society* (pp. 73–83). Albany: State University of New York Press.

Crosnoe, R. (2006). *Mexican roots, American schools: Helping Mexican immigrant children succeed.* Stanford, CA: Stanford University Press.

Delgado-Gaitan, C. (1992). School matters in the Mexican-American home: Socializing children to education. *American Education Research Journal, 29*(3), 495–513.

Delgado-Gaitan, C. (2001). *The power of community: Mobilizing for family and community.* Boulder, CO: Rowman & Littlefield.

Delgado-Gaitan, C. (2007). Fostering Latino parent involvement in the schools: Practices and partnerships. In S. J. Paik & H. J. Walberg (Eds.), *Narrowing the achievement gap: Strategies for educating Latino, Black, and Asian students* (pp. 17–32). New York: Springer.

Epstein, J. L. (1989). Family structures and student motivation: A developmental perspective. In R. Ames & C. Ames (Eds.), *Research on motivation in education: Vol. 3. Goals and Cognitions* (pp. 260–295). Orlando, FL: Academic Press.

Epstein, J. L. (1990). School and family connections: Theory, research, and implications for integrating sociologies of education and family. In D. Unger & M. Sussman (Eds.), *Families in community settings: Interdisciplinary perspectives* (pp. 99–126). Binghamton, NY: Hayworth.

Epstein, J. L. (2001). *School, family, and community partnerships: Preparing educators and improving schools.* Boulder, CO: Westview Press.

Foucault, M. (1972). *The archaeology of knowledge* (A. M. Sheridan Smith, Trans.). New York: Pantheon Books.

Garza, E., Reyes, P., & Trueba, E. T. (2004). *Resiliency and success: Migrant children in the United States.* Boulder, CO: Paradigm.

Gibson, M. (2002). The new Latino diaspora and educational policy. In S. E. Wortham, E. G. Murillo & E. T. Hamann (Eds.), *Education in the new Latino diaspora: Policy and the politics of identity.* Westport, CT: Ablex.

Gitlin, A., Buendia, E., Crosland, K., & Doumbia, F. (2003). The production of margin and center: Welcoming–unwelcoming of immigrant students. *American Educational Research Journal, 40*(1), 91–122.

González, N., & Moll, L. C. (2002). Cruzando el puente: Building bridges to funds of knowledge. *Educational Policy, 16,* 623–641.

González, N., Moll, L. C., and Amanti, C. (Eds.). (2005). *Funds of knowledge: Theorizing practices in households and classrooms.* Mahwah, NJ: Erlbaum.

Goodwin, A., & King, S. H. (2002). *Culturally responsive parental involvement: Concrete understandings and basic strategies.* Hofstra University, NY: American Association of Colleges for Teacher Education.

Hayes-Bautista, D., Hurtado, A., Burciaga Valdez, R., & Hernández, A. (1992). *No longer a minority: Latinos and social policy in California.* Los Angeles: UCLA Chicano Studies Research Center.

Henderson, A. (1987). *The evidence continues to grow: Parent involvement improves student achievement.* Columbia, MD: National Committee for Citizens in Education.

Henderson, A. T., & Mapp, K. (2002). *A new wave of evidence: The impact of school, family, and community connections on student achievement.* Austin, TX: Southwest Educational Development Laboratory.

Henderson, A. T., Marburger, C. L., & Ooms, T. (1986). *Beyond the bake sale: An educator's guide to working with parents.* Columbia, MD: The National Committee for Citizens in Education.

Henry, M. (1996). *Parent-school collaboration: Feminist organizational structures and school leadership.* Albany: State University of New York Press.

Hidalgo, N. (1998). Toward a definition of a Latino family research paradigm. *International Journal of Qualitative Studies in Education, 11,* 103–120.

Hoover-Dempsey, K., & Jones, K. (1997, April). *Parental role construction and parental involvement in children's education.* Paper presented at the annual meeting of the American Educational Research Association, Chicago, IL. (ERIC Document Reproduction Service No. ED411054)

Hoover-Dempsey, K., & Sandler, H. (1995). Parental involvement in children's education: Why does it make a difference? *Teachers College Record, 97*(2), 310–331.

Hoover-Dempsey, K., Walker, J., Sandler, H., Whetsol, D., Green, C. Wilkins, A., & Closson, K. (2005). Why do parents become involved? Research findings and implications. *The Elementary School Journal, 106*(2), 105–130.

Kreider, H., Caspe, M., Kennedy, S., & Weiss, H. (2007). Family involvement in middle and high school students' education. (Family Involvement Makes a Difference Research Brief #3). Cambridge, MA: Harvard Family Research Project. Retrieved August 2, 2008, from http://www.hfrp.org/content/download/1340/48835/file/fi_adolescent.pdf

López, G. R. (2001a, April). *On whose terms? Understanding involvement through the eyes of migrant parents.* Paper presented at the annual meeting of the American Educational Research Association, Seattle, WA.

López, G. R. (2001b). The value of hard work: Lessons on parent involvement from an (im)migrant household. *Harvard Educational Review, 71*(3), 416–437.

López, G. R., & Vázquez, V. A. (2006). "They don't speak English": Interrogating (racist) ideologies and perceptions of school personnel in a midwestern state. *International Electronic Journal for Leadership in Learning, 10*(29). Retrieved May 26, 2009, from http://www.ucalgary.ca/iejll/vol10/vazquez.

Meier, D., Kohn, A., Darling-Hammond, L., Sizer, T. R., & Woord, G. (2004). *Many children left behind: How the No Child Left Behind Act is damaging our children and our schools.* Boston: Beacon Press.

Moles, O. C. (1993). Collaboration between schools and disadvantaged parents: Obstacles and openings. In N. F. Chavkin (Ed.), *Families and schools in a pluralistic society* (pp. 21–49). Albany: State University of New York Press.

No Child Left Behind Act of 2001 (NCLB). (2002). Pub. L. 107–110. Retrieved May 9, 2008, from http://www.ed.gov/policy/elsec/leg/esea02index.html

Osterling, J., & Garza, A. (2004). Strengthening Latino parental involvement: Forming community-based organizations/school partnership. *Journal of Research and Practice, 2*(1), 270–284.

Reed, R. P., Jones, K. P., Walker, J. M., & Hoover-Dempsey, K. (2000, April). *Parents' motivations for involvement in children's education: Testing a theoretical model.* Paper presented at the annual meeting of the American Educational Research Association, New Orleans, LA.

Romo, H. (1999). *Reaching out: Best practices for educating Mexican-origin children and youth.* Charleston, WV: ERIC Clearinghouse on Rural Education and Small Schools.

Sigel, I. E., & Laosa, L. M. (Eds.). (1983). *Changing families.* New York: Plenum Press.

Sipes, D. S. B. (1993). Cultural values and American-Indian families. In N. F. Chavkin (Ed.), *Families and schools in a pluralistic society* (pp. 157–174). Albany: State University of New York Press.

Smrekar, C., & Cohen-Vogel, L. (2001). The voices of parents: Rethinking the intersection of family and school. *Peabody Journal of Education, 76*(2), 75–100.

Sosa, A. (1993). *Thorough and fair: Creating routes to success for Mexican-American students.* Charleston, WV: ERIC Clearinghouse on Rural Education and Small Schools.

Suárez-Orozco, M., & Páez, M. M. (2002). *Latinos: Remaking America*. Berkeley: University of California Press.

Suárez-Orozco, C., & Suárez-Orozco, M. (2001). *Children of immigration*. Cambridge, MA: Harvard University Press.

Sunderman, G. L., & Orfield, G. (2006). Domesticating a revolution: No Child Left Behind and state administrative response. *Harvard Educational Review, 76*(4), 526–556.

U. S. Census Bureau. (2008). *The 2008 Statistical abstract of the United States*. Washington, DC: Author.

Valdes, G. (1996). *Con respeto: Bridging the distances between culturally diverse families and schools*. New York: Teachers College Press.

Valencia, R. R. (1991). *Chicano school failure and success: Research and policy agendas for the 1990's*. London: Falmer.

Villenas, S. (2001). Latina mothers and small-town racisms: Creating narratives of dignity and moral education in North Carolina. *Anthropology and Education Quarterly* 32(1), 3–28.

Wortham, S. E., Murillo, E. G., & Hamann, E. T. (Eds.). (2002). *Education in the new Latino diaspora: Policy and the politics of identity*. Westport, CT: Ablex.

Zúñiga, V., & Hernández-León, R. (Eds.) (2005). *New destinations: Mexican immigration in the United States*. New York: Russell Sage Foundation.

CHAPTER 3

Not the Real Thing: A History of Hollywood's TV Families

Shirley R. Steinberg

We need more families like the Waltons *than the Simpsons.*
—George W. Bush

Other than my own family, my earliest family memories are from television families. North American television viewers most probably could conjure up similar memories: those beginning with the bucolic 1950s families, continuing with the politicized families of the 1970s, and ending somewhere in the present with the hybrid postmodern depiction of small-screen families. I believe educators must be cognizant of the importance of the informal curriculum of media brought to school by our students. We must be critically aware of the blatant and insidious uses and effects of media in a hyperrealistic society. As educators we watch the media curriculum that pervades childhood and youth and understand that it would be impossible for young citizens to escape this curriculum. I believe that teachers and administrators are often unequipped and/or unwilling to address their students' embedded media curriculum. Students walk into schools with the expectation that they must shirk their knowledge (and often obsessions) of media to drink the weakened Kool-Aid of public-school curriculum. I believe that an essential part of listening to families in school must contain an understanding and literacy of the forms of families found in the media, consumed by both parents and teachers on a continual basis. Reading media is an act that can be performed either without consciousness or with a literate and informed worldview. I chose the latter as part of my right as a citizen in a media-obsessed world (Steinberg, 2007).

For the past 60 years, television has been the media weft within the fabric of American society. While some people may choose to not watch television, no one can deny the threads that unravel and pervade our language, our cultural capital, even our political worlds. Certainly, the common motif in both television comedy and drama has been family life. Coming from a healthy start in radio, faux families were the center of living room entertainment for the bulk of the twentieth century, with continued success in the twenty-first. It follows then that a discussion of television-family life cannot be left unaddressed within a television-based society. In this chapter, I discuss the history of television families and the dominant themes that emerge from a critical analysis of this history. I advocate for a critical media literacy for teachers, parents, and students in order to create an understanding of how televised stereotypes and family depictions serve to influence audiences and, indeed, serve to create difficult barriers between the understanding of family as a real cultural construct and as a form of small-screen simulacra.

In order to create a cohesive body of work, I discuss television families through the themes I detected in my research. Each is discussed chronologically as I attempt to articulate how the themes relate to an overall vision of the history of the television family.

SUBURBAN MIDDLE-CLASS FAMILIES: PAPA'S GOT THE SAME OLE BAG

There wouldn't be television families without television fathers. From the inception of television, the paterfamilias has been the nucleus of family comedy and drama. In 1952 *The Adventures of Ozzie and Harriet* premiered on ABC and aired for 14 years on prime time. Advertised as "America's favorite family," *Ozzie and Harriet* presented an audience-eye view of the Nelsons, a famous performing family. Ozzie, Harriet, David, and Ricky Nelson entered American homes each week with smiles, White angst, and picket-fence dilemmas. Ozzie Nelson, a well-known musician and man-about-entertainment, was the center of the family, a dopey dad, always engaged in family affairs, but never quite getting what was going on. Harriet Nelson, former singer turned pearl-laden TV mom, was the voice of rationality and sensibility, always dressed in, well, a dress; she had pressed tablecloths, sit-down dinners, and answers to all issues. David was the not-so-smart older brother, sort of plodding along, and a foil for Ricky's antics. Ricky, not surprisingly, was the impish, cute little brother who knew the answers to everything. America's family literally grew up on television, and viewers invested thousands of hours on the Nelson family.

Along with the Nelsons, the show had its cadre of zany neighbors, regular guys, moral-seeking plots, and great kids who came to great parties with the great Nelson parents making great hamburgers and drinking great soda pop. The Nelsons did not nag, nor did they try to control the kids. Parents discussed issues with the kids, and if either dad or son made a faux pas, resolutions came through humor and logic. Truly, the Nelsons were America's first family, the perfect family.

Closely following the success of the Nelsons, *Father Knows Best* premiered on CBS in 1954. Situating the Anderson family in a suburban neighborhood similar to the Nelsons', the show used similar plotlines centered on Mom and Dad Anderson and the children. The title misleads the audience with an ironic twist, as Dad didn't usually know best—Mom did. Bumbling though life with platitudes and bad advice, Robert Young as Dad manages to be saved continually by his wife's logical worldview, naturally accompanied by the requisite pearls, pressed tablecloths, and kitchen-sink sensibility.

During the runs of *Ozzie and Harriet* and *Father Knows Best,* actor/musician Danny Thomas starred in two shows: first, *The Danny Thomas Show* (1953–1957), and then *Make Room for Daddy* (1957–1964). Danny played Danny Williams, a comedian and nightclub entertainer who lived with his wife and two kids. Unlike most TV shows, however, this one had a bit of a twist when mom (played by Jean Hagen) left the show and the producers killed her off. After a season of dating different women in 1956, Danny finally married a widow with a little girl, and the show returned with a new title and a revamped Williams family. When Danny married his second wife, the ratings climbed to the top. It was apparent that audiences were not comfortable with a single dad. Danny's character was bumbling and often in trouble, and as one might expect, the formulaic sensible mom saved many a day in the 11 years of the show.

Generations of viewers will be familiar with *The Dick Van Dyke Show,* which did not begin as a "family" comedy, but still maintained similar family patterns. CBS aired this successful comedy from 1961–1966. Few can forget the bumbling Rob Petrie, played by Van Dyke, and his sensible, worrying wife, Laura, played by Mary Tyler Moore. While the family was childless for the first seasons, Rob and Laura reinscribed the traditional TV-family roles as bumbling dad and logical, sane mom. When they did become parents, the roles magnified and the Petries became an important television institution.

While the first Hollywood family shows were comedies, they were followed by hour-long family dramas, which were patterned upon their humorous counterparts. ABC's *Family* was a suburban drama, which aired from 1976–1980; a midseason replacement, the show quickly became popu-

lar for viewers of all ages. In a departure from silly, stupid dads and deceit, the story lines tackled sincere problems and challenges confronted by
a suburban, middle-class family in Pasadena. Still very White and without
money problems, the show was critically acclaimed, winning many dramatic awards. The Lawrence family consisted of dad Doug (James Broderick),
mom Kate (Sada Thompson), and three children. Mom Kate remained the
stalwart voice of sensibility through her older daughter's divorce, son Wil-
lie's gay best friend, and daughter Buddy's experiences with the homophobic
behavior of her school (firing her lesbian teacher). As matriarch, Kate exhibited a strong leadership role in the family construction, companioned by
Doug. *Family* created coparenting roles in Doug and Kate, roles which have
seldom been replicated in network television.

Building on *Family*'s success, ABC followed with Dick Van Patten in
Eight is Enough (1977–1981). Van Patten's character, dad Tom, was modeled after newspaper columnist Tom Braden, who had eight children. In fact,
the popularity of a book by the same name had encouraged ABC to create
the show. Capitalizing on the overwhelming idea of large families, the family of 10 lived in an ample suburban home in Sacramento. Lacking any type
of social statement, the show featured the tried-and-true motifs of earlier
family television: a goofy but loving dad, a sensible mom, and antic-ridden
kids. The show's topics were safe and lacked the grit of *Family*'s plots.

NBC entered the family arena with blockbuster *Family Ties* from 1982 to
1989. For the first time, roles traditionally assigned to parents were usurped
by the kids. The Keaton family, while White, middle-class, and certainly
suburban, consisted of former hippie parents dealing with kids who were
far more conservative than they were. Michael J. Fox, in his groundbreaking role as Alex Keaton, became the ultimate smart-ass son to his bumbling
peacenik parents. The ability to laugh at the upside-down political system
gave the audience comic relief from the post-Nixon debacle to the comfort-
ing Reagan years. Often acerbic, *Family Ties* challenged the notion that the
kids were the ones who needed reining in.

Suburbanly urban, *The Cosby Show* burst onto the television family
scene in 1984 and ran on NBC until 1992. Reproducing suburban comfort,
Brooklyn's Huxtables have been critiqued largely as a body-of-work high-
lighting the first upscale Black family on network television. While ostensi-
bly set in Brooklyn, the lack of urban challenges was apparent throughout
the show. The luxurious brownstone could have been Anywhere, USA, but
Cliff and Clare Huxtable and brood took family to a new level. Balancing
medicine as an OB-GYN, Cliff seldom seemed to work, and Clare's law
practice also seemed to run itself. Having inordinate amounts of time to
interact in their kids' lives, both parents had a propensity for inserting their
opinions at every instant. Again, dad was bumbling, comic, and silly, and

mom, as the voice of reason and sanity seemed to have the final say. The show revolved around Cliff, who did little more than act as a comic foil for the family.

Underplaying the obvious—that the Huxtables were indeed Black—*The Cosby Show* chose to address race only in a peripheral sense—race was more about Martin Luther King Day or reggae music than about any challenges that Black families might face. Indeed, Sut Jhally and Justin Lewis (1992) indicate that the show had little to do with race and class, but perpetuated the concept that anyone can make it in America, if they try. In the attempt to be a "normal family," the Huxtables created a mythical family unit, not only unbelievable for a Black family, but for any American family. Their lack of concern for finances, the ease of the parental vocations, and the compliance of all the children created an unreal family depiction. Considered a comedy, the humor lacked originality, and Cliff was the continual nucleus of any laughs. Apparently the least comic of all television family comedies, *The Cosby Show* ironically starred one of the most famous comedians of the century, Bill Cosby.

The mid-1980s into the 1990s produced a series of middle-to-upper-class suburban comedies. ABC's *Growing Pains* (1985–1992) contained the archetypical family themes: befuddled Dr. Jason Seaver (Alan Thicke), psychiatrist dad who works at home; Maggie Malone, mom-with-her-maiden-name, a newspaper reporter; brainy Carol; smart-ass little Ben; and always-in-trouble Mike. This family comedy reran the typical household dilemmas; the most interesting note was that dad took care of the kids because mom worked out of the house. On the heels of the successful *Growing Pains,* ABC launched *Mr. Belvedere* (1985–1990). Like earlier comedies with a butler, caretaker, and maids, the Owens household contained the expected antics of a family of three children with professional parents. Mr. Belvedere, the butler, kept track of the days in his personal diary. Occasionally, the show did address social issues, and highlighted episodes dealt with a student's HIV status and the boundaries of touching between adults and children.

In 1989 ABC introduced TV's second middle-class Black family show, *Family Matters*. Situated in Chicago, but devoid of urban trappings, the show focused on dad Carl Winslow, wife Harriet, and three children: Eddie, the rebellious one; Laura, the smart one; and little Judy. Viewers will probably remember *Family Matters* best because of Steve Urkel, the ultimate next-door neighbor. Carl was well-meaning, awkward, and pompous; Mom was sensible—you know the drill.

One of the longest running family dramas aired from 1996 to 2007: *7th Heaven*. Another suburban-family show—this time located in Glen Oak, California—*7th Heaven* was a nonreligious yet overtly Christian show. The series followed a Protestant minister, his wife, their seven children, a lovable dog, a happy home, and a wholesome community. When the show began, Reverend Eric Camden (Stephen Collins) and his wife, Annie (Catherine Hicks), had five children of varying ages: The oldest two children, Matt and Mary, were high school students; Simon and Lucy were in junior high; and the youngest, Ruthie, was just beginning school. During the third season, as the older children moved on in life, the show's producers decided to add twin babies to the Camden family, Sam and David. The fact that the family was Protestant is rarely stated in the show but was inscribed on every scene.

Just as most other Christian-based shows shy away from the majority of controversial topics, so did *7th Heaven*. The most heated issues were alcoholism (preacher's sister) and premarital sex (preacher's daughter); however, topics like homosexuality and abortion were never mentioned. Each week the Camden family endured "typical" American problems of everyday life: not having a date to the homecoming dance, knee surgery, a mean teacher, not getting the perfect job, and so on. Everything turns out well in the end and family solidarity remained intact. *7th Heaven* was a wholesome television show that never failed to warm the heart. It portrayed the *average* (White, middle-class, Christian) family as the *perfect* family. In fact, the show was so wholesome that even the villains were somewhat benevolent.

The American TV family shows definitely spoke to 40 years of viewers seeking a validation of similar lives. Their popularity lay in their ability to make the regular just that, regular, on TV; the common, common on TV; the zany, just a bit more zany, on TV; the dad really stupid; the mom really sensible; and to contain elements like a smart-ass kid (usually a boy), a brainy kid (usually a girl), and a lovable but inconsequential baby or two. Formulaic television families rarely deviated from the normal or ordinary, and appealed to the American audience who craved a laugh from its own insular point of view. However, these mainstream families rarely tackled issues that troubled the minds of millions of viewers; it was working-class TV families that broke that ground.

POOR AND WORKING-CLASS FAMILIES: LAUGHTER IS LOUDER WHEN YOU'RE BROKE

Blue-collar work has always been a theme of American television. Early radio dramas often dealt with poor and/or immigrant families. In 1955 television history was made when CBS launched *The Honeymooners*. Not a family comedy in the traditional sense, it is included in this study because it established the repeating themes and motifs that have been recreated for over half a century in television families. Jackie Gleason's Ralph Kramden was a loud, simple, bus driver who felt he was worth more, but certainly didn't prove it in intellect or ingenuity. Alice (Audrey Meadows) played the long-suffering, sensible wife to Ralph's chaos. These roles would be replicated in scores of television families to follow. Two years later ABC launched *The Real McCoys* (1957–1963), a multigenerational family from the mountains of West Virginia, who had moved to be dirt farmers in California. Grandpa McCoy was played by the eternal grandfather, Walter Brennan, and well-known actor Richard Crenna got his start as grandson, Luke. The show was different from family shows of the time, as the grandfather was apparently widowed, and Luke eventually also became a widower. Luke had a young sister, Hassie, and a little brother, Little Luke. Southern and folksy in nature, the show was an "aw shucks," often moralistic depiction of dignified poor people and their struggles.

Working-class television took the reins of programming with plant worker Archie Bunker's debut in 1971 in *All in the Family*. CBS hit the jackpot by casting Carroll O'Connor as the stubborn, bigoted, ignorant, and right-wing father, tempered by his wife Edith or "Dingbat" (Jean Stapleton), who was dense, chaotic, and confused. Daughter Gloria (Sally Struthers) and son-in-law, Michael or "Meathead," lived with the Bunkers in a tiny, humble home somewhere in Queens. Nothing was sacred to Archie's rants: his sarcasm, his anger, and his indignation at being poor and working class. With *All in the Family*, television families became politically involved and needled American-family sensibilities. Viewers quickly identified with members of the family, and even the most conservative of heart felt uncomfortable being cast as Archie. Creator Norman Lear successfully jabbed at the nation's innermost thoughts.

Spinning off from *All in the Family* in 1975 was *The Jeffersons*. Archie Bunker had had one problem with next-door neighbors George and Louise (Weezy) Jefferson—they were Black. But Archie became even more outraged when the Jefferson family struck it rich and found themselves "movin' on up, to the Eastside, to a deee-luxe apartment in the sky." Again a working-class television family brought politics, ethics, morals, and essential issues to the prime-time screen via Norman Lear. The Lear television family was harsh, severe, critical, and angry, but the anger was directed to "the Man," to the feds, to the corporation, to the power brokers. Television was beginning to make a social difference with these programs, and the family was the site of the sea changes.

Another Black family moved into CBS territory from 1974 to 1979, right into the projects of Chicago. *Good Times,* spun from the sitcom *Maude,* takes place in the cramped, low-cost-housing apartment of the Evans family. Mom Florida Evans (Esther Rolle), a maid, and husband, James, had three kids: James Jr. or "JJ" (Jimmie Walker), Thelma, and Michael. Florida was level-headed, the hearth of the family; Thelma was, well, the girl; JJ was the loud-mouthed comic; and Michael—you guessed it—was the genius with all the answers, the smart-ass. James was a hardworking man who couldn't always hold a job. His anger at this position in life was obvious, and as in Norman Lear's other family sitcoms, he is conscious of race and class—a departure from the lack of consciousness of race and class in the middle-class television families. Even though *Good Times* is not unique in the stereotypes of family comedies, it is edgy and distinctly Black, poor, and working-class. Norman Lear redefined *family* on television, and even though there have been attempts to revive the suburban middle- and upper-class families, few have been as successful as Lear's three CBS families, which are still quoted and remembered more than 30 years later.

The American television family hadn't gotten edgy enough, however, until *Roseanne* debuted on ABC in 1988 and lasted nine Olympian seasons. Created by comedian Roseanne Barr, the show centered on the Connor family: parents Dan and Roseanne, good-girl daughter Becky, smart-ass and bored daughter Darlene, and little DJ; the Connors also had a new baby boy in the eighth season. While the previous three working-class shows certainly tackled social issues, *Roseanne* often dealt with personal problems, challenges, and tragedy. The Connors didn't have "a profession"; during the 9-year run of the show, both Dan and Roseanne changed jobs or were unemployed at different points. Dialogue in *Roseanne* often articulated what American families "probably" said in real life. Roseanne constantly reinforced the difficulty of raising children and used sarcasm to delineate her frustration: "I'm grouchy because I hate kids—and, I'm not your real mom." Dan was a strong but silent husband, loving and supportive, yet occasionally whipped by Roseanne. Roseanne's demeanor (both on the show and in reality) has often been discussed as low-class, trailer-trashy, and disgusting. As a loud woman, Roseanne appeared crass and loose-lipped: "You screw up, and I'll kill you." *Roseanne* followed the first "hard" female role created by Bea Arthur in Norman Lear's *Maude*. These so-called harsh women were the post-feminist-movement moms who had to scratch and scrape to make a difference. Often depicted as frightened, the kids scurried upon hearing a matriarchal command, and even banded together with dad in order to avoid mom's ire. Television families do not depict a father with these traits—only mom is fair game in TV land.

FAMILY FROM THE KID'S POINT OF VIEW: YOUNGER IS ALWAYS SMARTER

One type of television family existed in spite of social class. While many of the aforementioned shows contained a smart-ass kid, one who reflects the absurdity of parental voice, some TV-family shows were created around the omniscient voice of a kid. In 1957 Beaver Cleaver's ABC television family became iconic as the quintessential American unit in *Leave It to Beaver*. Airing six seasons, the show dealt with the adventures of Theodore "Beaver," parents Ward and June, and brother Wally. The Cleavers lived in a ubiquitous suburban two-story house, June wore ironed full skirts and pearls, Ward carried a briefcase to and from work each day, and the boys got into scraps. Wally, although the elder son, was none too bright, and Beaver's point of view drove the show. Plots were naive and life was never difficult. For over 60 years, American families have been compared to the Cleavers.

Evidently, the viewing audience didn't clamor often for a kid's point of view. It was not until 1988 that ABC premiered *The Wonder Years*, which ran for 6 years. The plot was set 20 years in the past, thus covering 1968–1973 in content. The series dealt with historical events and political and social concerns of the time. Kevin (Fred Savage) was the focus of the show, which dealt with his growing-up challenges. An older Kevin (voice of Daniel Stern) narrated the show in retrospect and discussed his own feelings of what happened at the time, and how he learned from it. This reflective narrative voice allowed viewers to watch a kid and listen to his future voice. In 1993, *Boy Meets World* became another ABC kid-narrated show, lasting for 7 years. Cory Matthews observed his young life and loving family—learning lessons and growing as the show continued the sweetness of life as narrated by the kid. Less sweet was ABC's short-lived but critically acclaimed *My So-Called Life*. Narrated by Angela (Claire Danes), viewers were treated to the frustrated soundings of a teenage girl. Dealing with serious issues, the show may have been a bit too cutting-edge, and a female as narrator/protagonist didn't seem to sustain the studio's interest.

FOX Television created its memorable family with *Malcolm in the Middle* in 2000, which aired for almost 7 years. Hal and Lois were saddled with four boys in a tiny home in Nowhere, USA. Malcolm (Frankie Muniz) was the narrator, who spoke directly to the audience and contained a smug awareness of both the television medium and his position within the family as middle kid. Hal (Bryan Cranston) was stereotypical as the tripping, stupid dad, tolerant and dull. Taking cues from *Roseanne*, Lois (Jane Kaczmarek) was a screeching, annoying, crazed mother who was the source of all fear and loathing in the family. The boys rarely exhibited love, and the working-class family was "stuck" within a Walmartized existence. The show ended with two more boys added to the family, and genius Malcolm won every struggle to the bitter end. Caricatured as a homely Cruella DeVille, Lois was the continual loser, while Hal only thought he was.

Television families from the kid's point of view brought a fresh outlook on the concept of family. Taking the "one smart/smart-ass kid" prototype and turning him/her into the voice of the family somehow made viewers feel part of the plot. It was interesting how few shows managed to be successful with that model. Class wasn't a denominator in that equation, merely the voice of the kid, often in direct conflict with audience expectations.

MOTHERLESS FAMILIES:
LIFE WITHOUT MOM IS ALWAYS FUN

As evident in the discussion of television families so far, parents figure greatly in the construction of the American family. Until the mid-1960s, television families kept to the mom and dad model. The only times a parent became single was when an actor left the show, and the network had to quickly replace the lost spouse. Ratings were clearly higher with two-parent families. In the mid-1960s, shows featuring families sans mom were created. Common themes pervaded most of these shows: The families were middle or upper class homes and money was never an issue; the father (or faux father) was professional, fun, loving, and always had time for the kids; there was a sidekick quasi dad to take up the slack (grandpa, uncle, brother, butler); the mother was dead and quite forgotten; and, it was apparent that a family didn't need a mom to be successful.

In 1960 ABC created *My Three Sons,* a sitcom about a zany widowed engineer, Steve Douglas (Fred MacMurray), who was raising his three boys with their maternal grandfather. The show moved to CBS in 1965 where it lasted 7 more years, and after Grandpa left, his brother Charley came to take up the slack. Plots were benign, but the show became one of the most popular shows in television history, second only to *The Adventures of Ozzie and Harriet* as the longest-running family show.

In 1966 CBS created *Family Affair,* which ran for 7 years. In this comedy an uncle raises his brother's three children with the assistance of Mr. French, the butler. Smart and agreeable 15-year-old Cissy and adorable twins Jody and Buffy ran Mr. French ragged; but he, in turn, ran a tight ship. Devoid of social issues or personal trauma, *Family Affair* continued America's television romance with motherless families.

The Courtship of Eddie's Father was ABC's addition to the motherless family genre in 1969. Starring Bill Bixby as a single father and widower in Los Angeles, the show focused on Eddie's desire to match up his dad with a new wife. The house was run by Mrs. Livingston, and Eddie and dad Tom spent 3 years of warm audience sighs with poignant dad and son bonding. It was apparent in the late 1960s that a dad with kids and no mom made for great TV. Like Disney families, television began to instill a romanticized family who flourished in love, comfort, and male bonding without nary a matriarch in sight. And like Bambi, Aladdin, Cinderella, Snow White, and Ariel, TV-family kids found mom easy to forget.

It was not only the biological dad who made a good father. NBC's *Different Strokes* (1978–1985) blended orphaned Black kids from the hood with single, rich, bumbling dad, Mr. Drummond (Conrad Bain) in Manhattan. When Mr. Drummond's housekeeper died, she left her two boys, Arnold and Willis (Gary Coleman and Todd Bridges) to Mr. Drummond to adopt. Along with his bright daughter, Kimberly (Dana Plato), smart-ass Arnold and slow-but-steady Willis laugh and play through a life wrought with chauffeurs, Mrs. Garrett, and more money than imaginable. Unlike *The Cosby Show, Different Strokes* did not shy away from a discussion of race, but was eager to engage in a consciousness of urban racism and the difficulties of multiracial families.

For 8 years, beginning in 1987, ABC aired *Full House,* which featured widowed dad Danny, his best friend, and his brother raising Danny's three daughters. Re-creating the previous dead-mom/happy-dad shows, the three men fumbled their way through idyllic child raising. NBC joined the widowed bandwagon in 1987 with *My Two Dads.* The show opened with mom dying and custody of daughter Nicole being awarded to the two men (Paul Reiser and Greg Evigan) who had long vied for mom's love. The sitcom dealt with the awkward issue of the two rivals raising a teenage daughter. Paternity was not considered in any meaningful way, and the show never resolved who Nicole's father was. Heartwarming and loving, *My Two Dads* was engagingly forgettable.

In 1993 CBS determined that while a single, widowed dad was romantic, a female opposite (in every way) made for good TV. Reviving the notion of nagging, classless women—and doing nothing to counter the anti-Semitic stereotypes that have plagued Jewish people for years—*The Nanny* featured Fran Drescher as loud, tacky, and outrageous Fran Fine. The Jewish nanny from Queens fell in love with her upper-crust British employer, winning the hearts of the butler, the kids, and eventually Mr. Sheffield himself. Again, the motherless television family exhibited the delirious happiness and self-actualized selves which did amazingly well given the circumstances of a mother's death creating the plot.

Two-and-a-Half Men is a current CBS show that premiered in 2003. A surprising hit, the motherless plot has a twist: Uncle Charlie (Charlie Sheen) is invaded by his newly separated brother, Alan, and young Jake. Upscale and successful, Charlie has to realign his life to accommodate the double-dad approach to child raising. This is one of the first family shows that articulate separation and divorce as the raison d'être for the lack of a mom on the scene.

Motherless families are big bucks in Hollywood. From the early death of Bambi's mother in the forest, audiences seem to be sucked into a romanticized view of life without a mom. The TV family sitcoms that highlight the "happy without mom" discourse can add to an already alienated view and opinion of the importance of a mother to a child. Ironically, and sadly, the alternative is not the case in dadless television families.

SINGLE MOTHERS: LIFE WITHOUT A DAD IS ALWAYS HARD

Hollywood quickly found that moms without dads didn't sell like dads without moms. Somehow the romantic notion of a single mother didn't fixate viewers, and few television families lasted with this configuration. It took television quite a while to trust a woman to raise her own family. NBC's *Julia* was a groundbreaking attempt to address the new Women's Liberation Movement in 1968 and ran until 1971. Diahann Carroll was Julia, a nurse who was widowed when her pilot husband was killed in Vietnam. While *Julia* was the first show to cast a Black woman as a lead character (and not a maid) on television, race was not addressed actively in the show. The series was quiet and dignified, and lacked any interest in social causes and politics. The relationship of Julia and her son was endearing, and Julia had two love interests, but the family unit consisted of Julia, her White boss, Dr. Chegley (Lloyd Nolan), and her son. Chegley was the voice of reason and benevolent patriarchy.

Probably the most memorable dadless family in American TV history is the sitcom, *One Day at a Time,* developed by Norman Lear and airing on CBS from 1975 to 1984. Divorced Ann Romano (Bonnie Franklin) moved to Indianapolis with her two daughters to prove that she could make it on her own. Julie was the 17-year-old smart-ass and Barbara was the 15-year-old level-headed baby sister. Courted by different beaus, Ann refused to give up her self-worth to a man, yet dealt continually with building superintendant Snyder, a greasy, pain-in-the-ass guy who installed himself as quasi dad. The show dealt with significant female issues and covered new areas related to second-wave feminism. Divorce and separation were addressed, and the difficulties of being a female head-of-household were clear. Certainly not idyllic, it is astonishing that Lear's female-driven comedy-drama lasted for 9 years.

Quickly following the success of *One Day at a Time,* ABC launched *Who's the Boss?* in 1984 as a counterpoint to CBS's successful show. Advertising executive Angela Bower (Judith Light) hires widower Tony Micelli (Tony Danza) to be a nanny-housekeeper for herself, son Jonathan, and mother Mona. Reversing the traditional role as breadwinner, Angela is competent and clever in her work. Tony is an attractive man, and has many girlfriends over the years. Throughout the run of the show, there is an obvious attraction between Angela and Tony, and eventually they do consummate

the relationship. The show created a discourse surrounding ethnic stereotypes, with macho Italian Tony (a former pro-baseball player) situated in a
traditionally female role, and does cover some more weighty social issues. It
is one of the few dadless shows which does not show financial angst on the
part of the single mother.

Probably one of the more unusual television family units was created
by CBS in *Kate & Allie* in 1984. Originally a midseason replacement, the
show was a surprising hit with the combined family of Kate (Susan Saint
James) and daughter Emma, and Allie (Jane Curtin) and two children, Jerry
and Chip. Both women were divorced and dated frequently. Kate and Allie
were successful in their careers and not desperate to remarry. This was the
one dadless show in which there was no frustration with single motherhood,
finances were intact, and children were relatively happy. The show lasted 6
years and ended when a newly married Allie had Kate move in with her (Allie's husband traveled a lot). Evidently family-loving America was uncomfortable with the radical decision to create such a nontraditional unit.

BLENDED FAMILIES: IT'S ALWAYS EASY ON TV

In a country with a high divorce rate, one would expect that divorce would
not make viewing audiences uncomfortable; however, divorce is not a common theme among family television shows. Excuses to blend families has
been successful, and much like the romantic notion of a momless family,
blended families have occasionally titillated viewers. ABC's *The Brady Bunch*
(1969–1974), is the hands-down winner of blended television families. The
success of the show seemed directly connected with the rising divorce rates
in the United States in the mid-1960s. However, Mike Brady—the dad with
three boys—is not divorced, but widowed, and Carol Brady—the mom with
three girls—well, we never really find out what happened to her former
husband. The vacuous show dealt with issues like getting braces, lost dogs,
and spoiled dinners, never addressing anything social or political, and the
Bradys all personified the ease of suburban middle-class life. Even Alice—
the ever-present housekeeper—was middle-class, and one never questioned
her class or value within the family unit.

Step by Step was first an ABC show in 1991, but moved to CBS and stayed
until 1998. Imitating the three-to-three pattern set by the Bradys, divorced
Frank Lambert and his three kids marry widowed Carol Foster, who also has
three children. The show deals with the adjustments of a blended family and
does not shy away from the apparent "stepness" of each family member. A
bit more compelling than *The Brady Bunch,* the plots were still simplistic, and

the show forgettable. Both shows made shorts use of the blended motif, and television families were more successful with other formulas.

HISTORICAL FAMILIES: THE GOOD OLD DAYS THAT NEVER HAPPENED

No discussion of television families would be complete without a mention of the good old days of historical families. How can our media history forget the "aw gee, good night, John-Boy" hours of *The Waltons* up on Virginia's Walton Mountain? CBS's multigenerational family show began in 1972 and lasted 8 years, until Hollywood was virtually buried in the thick molasses of family humility, morals, and church-going values. John and Olivia Walton were hard workers who ran a sawmill during the depression. Americans were able to grow up with *The Waltons,* just as previous generations did with Ozzie and Harriet. The show encompassed the values that would eventually elect Ronald Reagan president: back-to-the-basics, one-room-schoolhouse, patriotic values that Americans of the 1970s and 1980s seemed to crave. The show dealt with human issues, illness, war deaths, light comedy, and tragedy. *The Waltons* became the mythical history of the American family.

In 1974 NBC followed the CBS lead to romanticize the mythical past in *Little House on the Prairie,* with the Ingalls family: Charles, Caroline, and four daughters. Building a log home with no funds, hardworking family man Charles Ingalls (Michael Landon) wore his overalls with pride as he moralized the American values of church and country to his girls and wife. Little humor was discovered in this all-American drama that lasted 10 years. Following the series of books by Laura Ingalls Wilder closely, the show dealt with the difficulties of settling the new land in the westward expansion.

ANIMATED FAMILIES: HYPERSTEREOTYPES IN HYPERCOLOR

I end this chapter with the most colorful group of American television families: the animated cartoon comedies. Just as Disney Ducks Huey, Dewey, and Louie follow the military and political changes in the United States in comics, cartoon families parallel human family television shows from the 1960s. Modeled after *The Honeymooners,* ABC's *The Flintstones* (1960–1966) was the first working-class Stone Age family. Stupid father, nurturing and frustrated mother, and overly involved neighbors followed archetypical characters as they wound in and out of deceit and dilemma.

But the big payoff came in 1989, when FOX Television introduced *The Simpsons*, which has become the longest running television series in history. Matt Groening's characters magnify the traits discussed within television families in color and in parody. Dull, Duff-Beer-drinking dad Homer and sensible, worried mom Marge lovingly plod through working-class life with prodigy daughter Lisa, smart-ass son Bart, and pacifier-sucking baby Maggie. No political, social, religious, or sacred issues have been ignored in this parody of American life. Groening makes a comment on the American family with vision, yet with love. It is still a vibrant memory to recall the pulpit warnings about the possible effects that Bart Simpson could have on children, and public outrage was great. I recall picking up a Bart doll in the store for my son Ian, and a neighbor passed me in the aisle and instructed me about the influence Bart would have on my innocent boy. Americans were intrigued by, but frightened of, the Simpson family. Other cartoon families have emerged, but it is hard to imagine that anything will surpass this 2-decade television family and its impact and redefinition of the American family. *The Simpsons* have become the family barometer of television viewers. That which cannot be said is said, and Homer, Marge, and the kids get away with it.

THANKS FOR WATCHING

Our television families have become our families. Nostalgically our own, we have adopted the different family units and plots. How do we make sense of these depictions and how they affect the consciousness of teachers, parents, and students? In 1984 the video recorder became a household appliance, followed by various incarnations; we are now able to watch one of the plethora of channels that feature reruns of the shows discussed in this essay. The families we grew up with have found a new home with subsequent generations. In a society filled with divorce, troubled by financial woes, afraid of adjusting to "alternate lifestyles," and emancipated minors, how do we make sense of what a family *really* is? It would be impossible to imagine that viewers are not affected by the thousands of hours they absorb from television. A media-literate society is able to understand that the plots, themes, and stereotypes can be viewed for entertainment, but cannot be used to model or negate reality. Unfortunately, the themes first introduced by radio and television have perpetuated negative themes that reinforce already damaging stereotypes. Bumbling dads, stern mothers, smart-ass kids make great TV, but what does that say about real families? Why is it that television audiences crave stories with dead moms? Why do families succeed with ease when mom is gone? Why is it more difficult when there is no dad? Who are these families with butlers and housekeepers? Why are most plots of family comedies grounded in white lies and simple deceit? How is it that the only stable families on TV are God-fearing, hardworking, and continually pulling themselves up by their bootstraps? Is there a place for the postmodern mediated family in real life? Why do we not see television families (other than the Simpsons) watch TV?

Engaging our students and children in a discussion about the reality and nonreality of television families creates a healthy dialogue about the hidden curriculum that media creates in today's mind. It is impossible to escape the references, the images, and the concepts presented by television families, but it is not impossible to engage in an informed dialogue, which addresses the fictionalized depictions of families that don't exist.

Discussion Questions

1. In what way do TV families create a patriarchial context?
2. How does race, class, and gender intersect in television families?
3. Find out viewing patterns in the last 5 decades for television-family shows. Have they changed? What are the demographics of the viewers?
4. Do you feel that television creates a context in which viewers draw conclusions about North American families?

REFERENCES

Jhally, S., & Lewis, J. (1992). *Enlightened racism: The Cosby Show, audiences, and the myth of the American dream.* Boulder, CO: Westview Press.

Steinberg, S. (2007). Reading media critically. In D. Macedo & S. Steinberg (Eds.), *Media literacy: A reader* (pp. 299–315). New York: Peter Lang.

CHAPTER 4

Messages Protagonists Send Us: Families in Young Adult Literature

Tamara P. Lindsey
Linda T. Parsons

It's funny how when you watch people from a long distance, it all seems voiceless. It's like watching a silent movie. You guess what people say. You watch their mouths move and imagine the sounds of their feet hitting the ground. You wonder what they're talking about and, even more so, what they might be thinking.

—Markus Zusak, *I Am the Messenger* (p. 67)

Zusak provides us with a striking image not only for people-watching, but for reading as well. Our journeys through books are often like watching life as it unfolds before us. We cannot actually see mouths move, but in our mind's eye we do. With our imagination we hear feet hit the ground, and we are always caught in the act of wondering what the characters are thinking, what is happening that is not on the page in front of us, what is happening that has not yet been revealed, and what is happening as we relate our own lives to those of the characters. We are continually sending our own messages to the text as we place ourselves alongside the people we watch in life and in books. But what happens if we never see ourselves and those we love in texts? What if the life stories revealed in them leave us disconnected from many of the lived experiences of our own existence? These are the questions that motivated us to examine how different kinds of families are represented in the leading adolescent books of our time.

In this chapter, we study the messages contained in adolescent literature to see if a rich variety of family compositions and interactions are represented or if our young people are merely exposed to texts that maintain the status quo about conventional family structures, lifting those portraits up as the way a life should be lived. We know that in 2006 there were 510,000 children in foster care, another 129,000 waiting for adoption as a result of the termination of parental rights, and 51,000 children adopted domestically (U.S. Children's Bureau, 2008). With just these few statistics we can see that there are hundreds of thousands of children experiencing "extreme circumstances [in which] family systems fail" (Marks, 2008, p. 82), who are forced into drastic, life-changing family configurations.

Many different kinds of families are represented in our schools, and these family types have been present since colonial times (Marsh, 2008), yet they have continued to be marginalized in the messages we send about our children and their families. There has always been and always will be a need to use books as mirrors and windows—books that reflect and validate children's personal experiences as well as books that open onto worlds unlike their own (Bishop, 1990). Our chapter explores the messages embedded in the leading adolescent literature. We question whether the reading of these books allows us and our children to "craft narratives that will create, sustain, and support a variety of family forms" (Marsh, 2008, p. 118) or if, instead, it will continue to limit our understanding about ourselves and others.

EXPLORING OUR METHODOLOGY

I want to tell them, but I realize that all I do is deliver the message. I don't decipher it or make sense of it for them. They need to do that themselves.
—Markus Zusak, *I Am the Messenger* (p. 177)

As teachers of teachers and avid readers of children's books, we acknowledge that children receive explicit and implicit messages from the books they read. As we thought about listening to families in school contexts, we began to wonder what children would implicitly learn about families in the course of hearing books read aloud, reading in literature circles, and reading independently for pleasure. For this specific analysis, we chose to focus on the award-winning and honors list books for three highly regarded children's book awards: the Coretta Scott King Award, the Newbery Medal, and the Michael L. Printz Award. Our reason for choosing this set of books was twofold. First, we believe that teachers often incorporate these lauded books in their classrooms, and librarians are likely to purchase them for school libraries (Bucher & Manning, 2006; Galda & Graves, 2007). The second reason was more practical: We needed a structure for deciding how to include and exclude books. Focusing on award-winning books from the years 2005 through 2007 gave us an objective way to limit the set of books to a viable number.

Our data were generated through deliberate readings and purposeful content analyses of the books that enabled us to "characterize and compare documents" (Manning & Cullum-Swan, 1994, p. 464). We approached the reading with three a priori questions: (1) What family structures are represented? (2) What is the main character's experience of family? and (3) What messages about family are conveyed in the book? We took extensive notes on each book in response to these questions and verified our personal perceptions through discussion and deliberation. We both read 25 of the 34 books to increase the validity of our responses.

According to Schwandt (1997), *content analysis* means "comparing, contrasting, and categorizing a corpus of data" (p. 21). As we began this process, we were faced with a series of additional questions and decisions. First, we wondered if different messages would be conveyed depending upon book award or genre. We decided to view the set as a whole and not disaggregate for award or genre, believing that keeping the set intact would more closely reflect the variety of books children read and listen to in classrooms. Next, the question of protagonist and secondary characters arose. Although we recognize the significance of secondary characters and the messages they impart, we found it necessary to focus only on the protagonist in each book in order to limit the data to a manageable size. It is important to note that two titles have two protagonists: Ishmael and Sam in *Dark Sons* (Grimes, 2005) and Sarah and Emma in *Day of Tears* (Lester, 2005). Finally, we had to decide how to deal with the collections of short stories. Defining overarching messages for the entire collection seemed to diminish the power of the individual stories and to deny their importance in the lives of adolescent readers (Bucher & Manning, 2006), so we chose to treat each story as an individual entity. Short stories are identified with quotations marks, novels with italics, throughout this chapter.

In the next phase of analysis, we made iterative passes through our notes looking for patterns in the characters' experiences and in the messages conveyed. We tried to bring "order, structure, and meaning to the mass of collected data" (Marshall & Rossman, 1989, p. 111) by keeping careful track of our process. We identified thematic patterns that eventually became messages about families that were merged, collapsed, or separated as we gradually moved to more consistent and verifiable themes. At this point, different aspects of each theme became categories. Short (1995) explains that "the key to content analysis is the development of specific criteria for interpretation" (p. 21). We repeatedly refined our definitions of the themes and the categories as we considered examples and negative cases therein. We realized that even within categories there were still nuanced differences that needed to be noted. Thus we further divided some categories into topics.

We recognize that our analysis reflects our personal subjectivities and transactions with these texts. When we began this process, we had no idea of the profound effect these characters and the messages they conveyed would have on us. We are reminded of a comment by novelist Donald Ray Pollock: "I really wouldn't see how it worked until I got closer to it" (quoted by Simon, 2008). Immersing ourselves in these books and in the lives of these characters made this analysis possible. It is our sincere hope that those who read this chapter and the books discussed in it will identify messages that lie "in the same general 'truth space'" (Miles & Huberman, 1984, p. 22) as the messages we have identified.

These books convey several messages about families: they can be separated and created; they offer security, support the child's welfare, and cultivate a legacy. In the remainder of this chapter, we examine each of these messages separately. We open each section with a quotation from Zusak's (2005) novel, *I Am the Messenger*, which itself employs, as a narrative device, intriguing messages in its examination of personal relationships. The protagonist, Ed, notes that "Somewhere along the line, I feel like somehow I introduced myself. To myself. And here I am" (p. 306). Once we did the deep readings of these books, we both felt the characters were reintroduced to us and Zusak's words guide us as we introduce them to our readers.

MESSAGE 1: FAMILIES CAN BE SEPARATED

I want to stay here in this moment, and never go to other places; where we don't know what to say or what to do.
                                                    —Markus Zusak, *I Am the Messenger* (p. 155)

Families are fragile. Our analysis revealed that families can be physically separated through divorce, abandonment, hostility, and death. We identified three topics within the category of hostility: acts of war, slavery, and bigotry. Also, although it is not a physical separation, we found that the represented families were often divided by resentments. Table 4.1 shows the ways in which family members were separated in all the stories that conveyed this message.

Families can be separated by divorce. There are three strong exemplars for this category. In *The Higher Power of Lucky* (Patron, 2006) Lucky's father divorced her mother because he did not want children. Lucky knows that parents "can decide they don't even want you" (p. 80). In *The Road to Paris* (Grimes, 2006), Paris's father also did not want her: "Apparently he couldn't be seen walking down the street with a child whose skin was so much darker than his own. He'd wince every time she called him Daddy in public" (p. 9). In *Dark Sons* (Grimes, 2005) Sam resents his mother for his parents' divorce, yet she lovingly comes to his aid as she encourages him to encounter his father, rip "off [his] bulletproof vest" (p. 183) of defensiveness and reestablish the close bond they once had.

The second category of separation is abandonment. In *The Road to Paris* (Grimes, 2006) Paris not only experiences divorce, but she also suffers because her mother deserts her. In "The House of the Many" (Lanagan, 2005) a son abandons his mother, who then becomes the sole caretaker for his sibling with profound physical challenges. In "A Letter to My Daughter" (Flake, 2004), a father writes a letter of apology to his daughter, first admitting that he has been a horrible husband and father and then encouraging her to love herself enough to "stay whole" (p. 218), be strong, and expect to be treated well.

The topics of acts of war, slavery, and bigotry comprise the category of hostility. In *Hitler Youth* (Bartoletti, 2005) we see Jewish families forcibly separated in concentration camps, and the families of many Hitler youth killed in bombing raids. In *Day of Tears* (Lester, 2005), we see family members literally torn from the arms of those they love as they are sold into slavery. *The Legend of Buddy Bush* (Moses, 2004) offers us a look at the kind of bigotry that sends Black men to prison for crimes allegedly committed against White women, leaving behind those who love them.

There are many examples of death in these books. In *Penny from Heaven* (Holm, 2006) death is the main theme as the protagonist, Penny, tries desperately to unearth the clouded story surrounding her father's death. In *I Am the Messenger* (Zusak, 2005), Ed laments his father's death throughout the book, worrying that this kind and gentle man was always treated with less respect than he deserved. *Surrender* (Hartnett, 2006) offers us a chilling look at a son who accidentally murders his older brother, but then intentionally does the same to his parents.

Adults and children are often estranged by resentments that arise from living together. The four topics we established within this category were the need for more attention from parents, the responsibility of caring for siblings, overprotection, and—the most tragic one—abuse. The need for parental attention is witnessed in "Rite of Spring" (Lanagan, 2005). In this mythic tale, Young Girl braves the winter mountain to bring forth spring. Once she returns, she expects to be greeted with praise, but she does not even receive a greeting. In *Al Capone Does My Shirts* (Choldenko, 2004), Moose is expected to act on a daily basis as caretaker for Natalie, his sister with special needs. He resents his parents for making him do so and for the great amount of time they focus solely on Nat. Although he loves Nat, he is ashamed of how she behaves and tells us, "The last thing I want is to meet new kids when Natalie's around" (p. 11). In "Jacob's Rules," D'Little is always complaining that his mother is way too much in his business. *Surrender* (Hartnett, 2006) reveals that Gabriel is physically and emotionally abused, and he admits he was never touched as a young child except to be beaten with his father's belt.

TABLE 4.1. Families Can Be Separated

Title	Divorce	Abandon-ment	Hostility	Death	Resent-ments
Airborn				X	
Al Capone Does My Shirts					X
Astonishing Life of Octavian Nothing			X	X	X
Black Juice: "Earthly Uses"					X
Black Juice: "House of the Many"		X			
Black Juice: "Rite of Spring"					X
Black Juice: "Yowlinin"				X	
Book Thief		X	X		
Chanda's Secret				X	X
Copper Sun			X	X	
Criss Cross					X
Dark Sons	X	X	X		X
Day of Tears	X		X		X
Hattie Big Sky				X	
The Higher Power of Lucky	X			X	
Hitler Youth			X		
How I Live Now			X	X	X
I Am the Messenger				X	X
John Lennon	X	X			X
Kira-Kira					X
Legend of Buddy Bush			X		

TABLE 4.1. Continued

Title	Divorce	Abandon-ment	Hostility	Death	Resent-ments
Lizzy Bright and the Buckminster Boy				X	X
Penny from Heaven				X	X
Princess Academy				X	
Road to Paris	X	X			
Rules					X
Show Way			X		
Surrender				X	X
Voice that Challenged a Nation: Marian Anderson . . .				X	
Who Am I? "Hunting for Boys"					X
Who Am I? "Letter to My Daughter"		X			
Who Am I? "Jacob's Rules"					X
Who Am I? "Not a Boy"					X
Wreath for Emmett Till			X	X	

MESSAGE 2: FAMILIES ARE CREATED

His answer is written there in black ink. It says, "Of course you're real—like
any thought or any story. It's real when you're in it."
                                    —Markus Zusak, *I Am the Messenger* (p. 354)

Just as families can be separated, they can be created. Some re-forma-
tions of family are purposeful while others evolve naturally. Some are entered into willingly, and others are forced upon its members. In these books,
as shown in Table 4.2, we observed families being created as foster families,
as guardianships, by forming bonds that develop into chosen families, or
through the integration of stepparents. In exploring this message, we looked
beyond the initial creation of a traditional family, recognizing that these
families, too, are created.

Only two books in this set portray children in foster care, and they
come to their foster families under very different circumstances. *The Road
to Paris* (Grimes, 2006) shows that Paris is no stranger to the foster system.
After escaping from a foster home in which she was beaten and locked in
a closet, she is placed with the Lincolns with whom she experiences acceptance, love, and security as a full-fledged member of their family. She feels
divided loyalties, however, because of her biological mother and brother.
Paris says, "I wish there were two of me. . . . That way, both of us could
have the family we want" (p. 13). In *The Book Thief* (Zusak, 2006), Liesel
comes to her foster family as a result of war. Her foster mother, Rosa Huberman, initially abuses her verbally and physically; but from the moment
her foster dad coaxes her out of the car, Hans Huberman loves her uncon-
ditionally. Hans comforts her night after night when she is awakened by
terrible nightmares, and her stay with them becomes a time of bonding as
he teaches her to read.

Some families are created through the assignment of guardianships. and
exemplify this. In the *Higher Power of Lucky* (Patron, 2006) Brigitte is the
quintessential guardian. When this former girlfriend of Lucky's father heard
that Lucky's mother had died, she rushes from France to Hard Pan, California, to assume this position. Although Lucky fears that Brigitte is planning
to return to France, she experiences love and security with her. Lucky tells
us that Brigitte's hugs make her "heart fill up with molecules of hope and
pump them all through her veins" (p. 81). Similarly, the title character in
John Lennon (Partridge, 2005) was taken in by his Aunt Mimi and Uncle
George, who provided a stable and loving environment. On the other hand,
in *Hattie Big Sky* (Larson, 2006) Hattie was passed from one inhospitable
relative to the next staying until they no longer needed the extra hands to
help out and began to resent the extra mouth to feed.

TABLE 4.2. Families Are Created

Title	Foster Families	Guardians	Chosen Families	Step-parents
Astonishing Life of Octavian Nothing		X		
Black Juice: "House of the Many"				X
Black Juice: "Sweet Pippit"			X	
Book Thief	X		X	
Chanda's Secret			X	X
Copper Sun			X	
Dark Sons				X
Day of Tears			X	
Hattie Big Sky		X	X	
Higher Power of Lucky		X		
How I Live Now			X	X
I Am the Messenger			X	
John Lennon		X		
Legend of Buddy Bush		X		
Penny from Heaven				X
Road to Paris	X			
Whittington			X	

Chosen families is another family structure created in these books. In three stories chosen families are created to meet physical and psychological needs. In *Hattie Big Sky* (Larson, 2006) Hattie is isolated on a homestead in Montana, and the Muellers become her chosen family. They teach her skills that enable her to survive on the homestead and provide the human contact she desperately needs. Bonds are solidified when she serves as midwife to Perilee Mueller. Similarly, the family created by Amiri, Polly, and Tidbit in *Copper Sun* (Draper, 2006) also springs from great need and ensures survival. Together, they escape from servitude on a plantation and flee to a refuge in Florida, providing strength and support to one another. In "Sweet Pippit" (Lanagan, 2005) we see a chosen family of a different kind. After their keeper, Pippit, is jailed, a group of elephants sets off to rescue him. After breaking him out of prison, they find a place to live, sing songs of strength to each other, and care for one another.

The integration of stepparents into a family is also explored in these books. In *Penny from Heaven* (Holm, 2006) Penny is purposefully hateful toward the milkman, Mr. Mulligan, when she realizes he may become her stepfather. Yet he treats her with such respect and kindness that he eventually wins her over. After his marriage to her mother, he tells her she can call him whatever she wants to, and she muses, "Maybe someday I'll call him Dad, but not yet. We have plenty of time. He's not going anywhere" (p. 247). In *Chanda's Secret* (Stratton, 2004) Chanda's initial experience with a stepfather is far different from Penny's because Chanda is sexually molested by him. Life with her second stepfather, however, is happy and safe. After his death, she regrets not calling him Papa and hopes that he knew she loved him. Finally, in *How I Live Now* (Rosoff, 2004) Daisy refuses to find any redeeming qualities in her stepmother whom she calls Davina the Diabolical. Davina was not overtly cruel to Daisy; however, neither was she ever a warm and nurturing parent figure. She frequently made snide remarks about Daisy to her husband, and often did so within earshot of her stepdaughter.

MESSAGE 3: FAMILIES OFFER SECURITY

Her fingertips are made of love.
—Markus Zusak, *I Am the Messenger* (p. 56)

Many of the families in these books were a source of security for the protagonists. We encountered families that were dysfunctional and destructive, but these are discussed in other sections of this chapter. In this section, we look at the families that offered security through support, communicating a strong sense of love, instilling hope, offering protection (defending, hovering, providing opportunity), or creating bonds through working together. Table 4.3 details the ways families in the individual books offered security.

The families in these books offer different types of support to the protagonists. In *Rules* (Lord, 2006) Catherine initially feels neglected by her parents. Her father works extra hours so that her mother can work part-time from home and care for Catherine's brother who is autistic. However, when her mother provides much-needed art supplies and her father comes through for her when she needs it most, she realizes that she can count on them for the support she needs. Support of a very different kind is provided by the parents in *Remember: The Journey to School Integration* (Morrison, 2004). The parents in this book "sue school boards that required their children to travel to schools miles away from white ones closer to their homes" (unpaged). Finally, support offered in an extreme circumstance is shown in "Singing My Sister Down" (Lanagan, 2005). This short story takes place in an unknown location at an unknown time. Ikki is being executed for killing her husband in a fit of rage. This government-sanctioned punishment takes the form of death by slowly drowning in a tar pit. Ikki's mother and brothers stay near her, feeding her rich food, soothing her with stories, music, and words of comfort, and washing her scorching body until "it was surely gone, was just a nose or just a mouth with the breath crushed out of it, just an eye seeing nothing" (p. 18).

Some families communicated an extraordinarily strong sense of love to the protagonists. In *Penny from Heaven* (Holm, 2006) Penny lives with her mother and maternal grandparents and spends Sundays with her deceased father's large Italian family. Her Italian grandmother, Nonny, and her aunts and uncles shower her with love through the sharing of family stories, ethnic foods, and gifts. Similarly, in *The Voice that Challenged a Nation: Marian Anderson and the Struggle for Equal Rights* (Freedman, 2004), Marian Anderson was loved both by her immediate family and also by the extended family of her church community. The loving support from this faith community inspired her to change the lyrics of "America" to "Of thee *we* sing" (p. 68) instead of *I*. Finally, in *The Book Thief* (Zusak, 2006), there are myriad ways that Hans shows Liesel she is loved. He teaches her to read, tells her stories about his life, plays the accordion for her, and trusts her to work alongside him to protect a Jewish man they are hiding in their basement.

Many of the protagonists gain a sense of hope due in large part to their families, but that hope takes different forms. In "The Ugly One" (Flake, 2004), Asia has a skin disorder that hideously disfigures her face, and she is often the brunt of cruel taunts. Asia wants to be "invisible—to curl up like a dot at the end of a sentence and disappear" (p. 51), yet her grandmother assures her that someday she will become beautiful as the ugly duckling did. Hope of a different kind is represented in *Copper Sun* (Draper, 2006) as Amiri, Polly, and Tidbit realize their dream of freedom from slavery. In *Show Way* (Woodson, 2005), many kinds of hope are exemplified: the hope of freedom, the hope of racial equality, and the hope born of opportunity.

Families protect their children in a variety of ways and for different reasons. We identified three types of protection: defending, hovering, and providing opportunity. In *The Higher Power of Lucky* (Patron, 2006) Brigitte is willing to fend off anyone who would harm Lucky. Brigitte tells her, "You know if anyone ever hurt you I would rip their heart out" (p. 132), and Lucky knows that she would. Katie's mother in *Kira-Kira* (Kadohata, 2004) hovers and overprotects her. Katie comments, "Our mother didn't like us to run or play or climb, because it was dangerous. She didn't like us to walk

TABLE 4.3. Families Offer Security

Title	Support	Strong Sense of Love	Hope	Protection	Working Together
Al Capone Does My Shirts				X	
An Abundance of Katherines	X				
Astonishing Life of Octavian Nothing				X	
Black Juice: Earthly Uses	X				
Black Juice: House of the Many		X			
Black Juice: Perpetual Light		X			
Black Juice: Singing My Sister Down	X				
Black Juice: Wooden Bride		X			
Book Thief	X	X		X	X
Chanda's Secret				X	
Copper Sun		X	X	X	X
Criss Cross	X				
Dark Sons	X	X		X	
Day of Tears	X		X		X
Hattie Big Sky			X	X	
Higher Power of Lucky		X	X	X	
John Lennon	X		X		
Kira-Kira		X		X	
Legend of Buddy Bush		X	X	X	X
Looking for Alaska	X				
Maritcha	X			X	
Penny from Heaven		X		X	
Princess Academy		X		X	X

TABLE 4.3. Continued

Title	Support	Strong Sense of Love	Hope	Protection	Working Together
Remember: The Journey to School Integration	X				
Road to Paris		X	X	X	
Rules	X				
Show Way		X	X		X
Voice that Challenged a Nation: Marian Anderson		X			
Whittington					X
Who Am I? Don't Be Disrespecting Me	X			X	
Who Am I? Girl, Didn't I Say I Don't Write Letters?	X			X	
Who Am I? Hunting for Boys				X	
Who Am I? Letter to My Daughter				X	
Who Am I? Not a Boy	X				
Who Am I? Ugly One	X		X	X	
Wreath for Emmett Till	X				

in the middle of our empty street, because you never know" (p. 17). Protection came in the form of opportunity in *Hattie Big Sky* (Larson, 2006). Her mother died 2 years after her father and left Hattie $400. When she inherited her uncle's Montana homestead, this money allowed her to take advantage of the opportunity to homestead the land. This level of independence proved to be a form of protection for Hattie.

Working side-by-side with other members of the family afforded a level of intimacy and promoted feelings of competence that fostered security for the protagonists in several books. In *The Book Thief* (Zusak, 2006), Liesel often accompanied Hans to work as a house painter. He told her stories, played the accordion after lunch, and showed her how he mixed the paint. "It was well and good to share bread and music, but it was nice for Liesel to know that he was also more than capable in his occupation. Competence was attractive" (p. 356). In *Copper Sun* (Draper, 2006), before Amiri's village was annihilated by slave traders, she loved doing daily tasks with her mother. The familiarity of the tasks and the rhythm they achieved together led to a feeling of security. Similarly, in *The Legend of Buddy Bush* (Moses, 2004), Pattie Mae works side by side in the garden with her grandmother where they pick strawberries and pull weeds for hours on end. After chores Pattie Mae is usually rewarded with a slice of orange candy, her grandmother's "way of saying 'I love you'" (p. 51).

MESSAGE 4: FAMILIES SUPPORT THE CHILD'S WELFARE

If I'm ever going to be okay, I'll have to earn it.
—Markus Zusak, *I Am the Messenger* (p. 270)

Good parents do what they think is best for their children's welfare. We found that the adults demonstrated this care by giving advice, imparting expectations, establishing rules, or serving as role models. The manner in which parents offered their support was not always well received by their children. And some of these examples illustrate that the parents' motivations were not always positive. Table 4.4 shows the ways families in the books we studied support the child's welfare.

Giving advice seems to come with the territory of parenthood. The German children in *Hitler Youth* (Bartoletti, 2004) are determined to reject their parents' views about the Nazi Party. One father tells his son that there is, "no glory nor heroism in war and battle . . . only madness, desperation, fright, and unbelievable brutality" (p. 30). In *A Wreath for Emmett Till* (Nelson, 2005) Emmett's mother realizes how young and brash he is. Before she sends him to his grandmother's house in the South, she advises him to be subservient in his dealings with White folks. Tragically, his visit there leads to his brutal beating and lynching. On a much lighter note, the father and mother in "Not a Boy" (Flake, 2004) furnish all kinds of advice to their 15-year-old son who is going on his first date. They've bought a bouquet for him to present to this young girl. The son is mortified by his parents' old-fashioned notions, but is pleasantly surprised at the positive response he receives from the girl's family.

Expectations can often be imparted much more harshly than by merely offering advice. In *Rules* (Lord, 2006), Catherine's parents merely want to fill all of her time. But two of the narratives in this category, deal with unreasonable expectations from parents. In *Lizzy Bright and the Buckminster Boy* (Schmidt, 2004) Turner Buckminster's father controls every move he makes. Added to that is the weight of being the preacher's kid. Turner laments, "I am not my own, . . . but belong body and soul to every parishioner in Phippsburg who might have a word to say about me to my father" (p. 42). There is a similar tone in the story "Hunting for Boys" (Flake, 2004), in which five young teenage girls decide to rebel against their families and church teachings by sneaking out in search of boys. Although they know "God's gonna punish us for going after boys" (p. 171), they ignore their religious training and place themselves in harm's way.

Closely aligned to setting expectations is establishing rules that regulate family life. In *Rules* (Lord, 2006), one of the many ways in which Catherine cares for her brother who is mentally challenged is by creating lists of rules for him to follow. She keeps them in her sketchbook and tells us, "I keep all the rules I'm teaching David so if my some-day-he'll-wake-up-regular-brother wish doesn't ever come true, at least he'll know how the world works, and I won't have to keep explaining things" (p. 9). In *Penny from Heaven* (Holm, 2006) Penny's mother is so overprotective that she will not allow her daughter to swim in the local pool for fear that Penny might contract polio. Penny feels suffocated by the restrictions set down by her mother. The final example, *Surrender* (Hartnett, 2006), is the most extreme. In response to the many rules and subsequent forms of violence his parents inflict upon him, Gabriel says, "I tried to build a wall of good behavior behind which Vernon and [I] might hide. I could never make the wall strong enough; it was forever toppling and leaving us exposed" (p. 152). This quote reveals how unreasonable regulatory behavior can be when it serves to demean and punish children.

Several books offer interesting examples of parents who serve as positive role models for their families. In *Airborn* (Oppel, 2004), Matt's interest in becoming captain of an airship is sparked as a young boy when his father teaches him about the constellations and is himself on the crew of an airship. In *The Legend of Buddy Bush* (Moses, 2004), Pattie Mae adores her

TABLE 4.4. Families Support the Child's Welfare

Title	Giving Advice	Imparting Expectations	Establishing Rules	Serving as Role Models
Airborn				X
Al Capone Does My Shirts		X		X
An Abundance of Katherines		X		
Astonishing Life of Octavian Nothing		X	X	
Black Juice: House of the Many			X	
Black Juice: Rite of Spring		X		
Book Thief				X
Chanda's Secret		X		
Copper Sun				X
Criss Cross			X	
Dark Sons	X			X
Day of Tears		X		
Hitler Youth	X			
How I Live Now		X		
I Am the Messenger		X		
John Lennon		X		
Kira-Kira		X	X	X
Legend of Buddy Bush			X	X
Lizzy Bright and the Buckminster Boy		X		
Looking for Alaska	X			
Maritcha				X
Penny from Heaven			X	

TABLE 4.4. Continued

Title	Giving Advice	Imparting Expectations	Establishing Rules	Serving as Role Models
Princess Academy				X
Remember: The Journey to School Integration				X
Rules		X	X	
Surrender		X	X	
Who Am I? Don't Be Disrespecting Me	X			
Who Am I? Girl, Didn't I Say I Don't Write Letters?	X			X
Who Am I? Hunting for Boys			X	
Who Am I? I Know a Stupid Boy When I See One			X	
Who Am I? Jacob's Rules	X			
Who Am I? Letter to My Daughter	X			
Who Am I? Not a Boy	X			
Who Am I? So I Ain't No Good Girl		X		X
Who Am I? Wanted: A Thug			X	
A Wreath for Emmett Till	X			

grandfather, not only because of his demonstrative love for her, but also because of all the knowledge he shares. Although he is mostly illiterate, he is a wise man who has built many things on the family property "with his bare hands" (p. 39). In *Kira-Kira* (Kadohata, 2004) Katie's father proves to be a brave man when he admits a wrongdoing to his superior and then loses his job. He actually takes Katie with him when he makes amends, telling her in the aftermath that although the outcome was certainly not what he had wished, it was still the right thing to do.

MESSAGE 5: FAMILIES CULTIVATE A LEGACY

I also fear that nothing really ends at the end. Things just keep going as long as memory can wield its ax, always finding a soft part in your mind to cut through and enter.
—Markus Zusak, *I Am the Messenger* (pp. 267–268)

The reproductive function of families extends beyond bringing new life into the world. It includes the perpetuation of beliefs, ways of being, and emotional maturation. We interpreted these acts as cultivating a legacy. In these books, families do this in several ways. They promote moral codes, tell cultural stories, share family history, keep secrets, and expect children to rise to the occasion and assume responsibilities. Table 4.5 shows how families cultivate a legacy in the individual books.

Specific moral codes are promoted within families. Although this is a strong aspect of creating a legacy in several books, the moral code is specific to the situation and culture. In *Maritcha: A Nineteenth-Century American Girl* (Bolden, 2005), Maritcha's parents were involved in various humanitarian causes including the Underground Railroad and conveyed these values to their children. When Maritcha was denied entrance in the Girl's Department of Providence High School, her parents took the case all the way to the state legislature. This sent a strong message to Maritcha about what was morally right. In *Chanda's Secret* (Stratton, 2004), Chanda lives in the midst of the AIDS epidemic in Africa. People in her family and in the community prefer to deny that AIDS exists because they equate it with immorality. The silences that surround AIDS are literally life-threatening. In "Hunting for Boys" (Flake, 2004) the families convey a strong moral message that young girls should love Jesus rather than boys and pray rather than have fun, so the girls rebel and end up in a disastrous situation.

Families also create a legacy by maintaining cultural traditions through stories. Some protagonists resist this enculturation while others seek out these stories. In *American Born Chinese* (Yang, 2006), Jin's mother tells him old Chinese parables to teach morals and pass along their heritage.

He considers these stories outdated and irrelevant. In *The Astonishing Life of Octavian Nothing, Traitor to the Nation* (Anderson, 2006), however, when Octavian was little, he implored his mother to tell him stories about when she was a princess, and she would "tell him softly of [her] homeland" (p. 30). *Show Way* (Woodson, 2005) features the traditions of jumping the broom and later of marching for equality and justice as part of the cultural stories.

Many protagonists yearn to know more about themselves and about their family history, and family stories are integral in several stories. In *How I Live Now* (Rosoff, 2004) Daisy's mother died giving birth to her, and Daisy's father refuses to talk about her. Daisy is desperate to know simple, boring things about her mother. When she goes to stay with her aunt and cousins in England, Aunt Penn tells her stories about her mother that satisfy her desperate need for connection. In *The Book Thief* (Zusak, 2006), the stories Hans tells Liesel increase Liesel's feelings of devotion and belonging. Sometimes family stories can serve not only to document fact, but to create it. In *Criss Cross* (Perkins, 2005) Debbie "usually sounded pretty good in her mother's stories, though not quite like herself. The stories themselves were that way, too; more entertaining than what really happened" (p. 169). Debbie's mother shares family stories to create a heroic spin to ordinary family tales.

A legacy of secrets and silence is created by some families. These secrets deny members the right to know and drive wedges between members of a family. At times, secrets serve to conceal something the family does not want known. In *Penny from Heaven* (Holm, 2006) Penny wants to know what caused the rift between her mother's and her father's families. The families do not immediately reconcile once the secret is revealed, but a tentative step is made in that direction. Silence, rather than secrets, is the issue in *Lizzy Bright and the Buckminster Boy* (Schmidt, 2004): Many things are left unsaid as the Buckminsters' plates are "pass[ed] around a silent table" (p. 116). Silence is also a feature of *Princess Academy* (Hale, 2005). Miri is plagued by feelings of inadequacy because her father will not allow her to work alongside him in the linder mines. Finally, a wise woman in the village, Doter, tells her that her mother did not die giving birth to her but instead died as the result of an accident at the mine. She says, "Your pa is a house with shutters closed" (p. 176). Once the truth is revealed, her father breaks his silence.

Finally, families create a legacy when their children assume responsibilities. The nature of these responsibilities falls into two categories: assuming a parenting role and being of service to others. In *Al Capone Does My Shirts* (Choldenko, 2004), Moose is expected to play a significant role in the care of his autistic sister. Sometimes the protagonists provide a service to those around them In *Princess Academy* (Hale, 2005) Miri learns about commerce and advises the people of her village leading to increased profits

TABLE 4.5. Families Cultivate a Legacy

Title	Promoting Moral Codes	Telling Cultural Stories	Sharing Family History	Keeping Secrets	Children Assuming Responsibility
Airborn			X		X
Al Capone Does My Shirts				X	X
American Born Chinese		X			
An Abundance of Katherines					X
Astonishing Life of Octavian Nothing		X	X	X	X
Black Juice: Earthly Uses					X
Black Juice: Perpetual Light		X			
Black Juice: Rite of Spring		X			X
Black Juice: Sweet Pippit			X		
Black Juice: Wooden Bride		X			
Book Thief	X		X	X	X
Chanda's Secret	X		X	X	X
Copper Sun		X	X		X
Criss Cross			X	X	
Day of Tears	X				
Hattie Big Sky			X		
Hitler Youth	X			X	X
How I Live Now			X	X	X
I Am the Messenger					X
John Lennon	X				
Kira-Kira	X				X

TABLE 4.5. Continued

Title	Pro-moting Moral Codes	Telling Cultural Stories	Sharing Family History	Keeping Secrets	Children Assuming Responsiility
Legend of Buddy Bush	X		X		X
Lizzy Bright and the Buckminster Boy	X			X	
Looking for Alaska				X	
Maritcha	X		X		
Penny from Heaven			X	X	
Princess Academy				X	X
Remember: The Journey to School Integration	X				X
Rules					X
Show Way		X	X		
Surrender				X	
Whittington			X		
Who Am I? Don't Be Disrespecting Me	X				
Who Am I? Girl, Didn't I Say I Don't Write No Letters?	X				
Who Am I? Hunting for Boys	X				
Who Am I? I Know a Stupid Boy When I See One	X				
Who Am I? Mookie in Love	X		X		

on the sale of linder. In *I Am the Messenger* (Zusak, 2005) Ed Kennedy touches and changes individual lives as he follows the clues on playing cards delivered to him. Ed develops a sense of familial care and responsibility to the people for whom he becomes the messenger. Like other characters who assume responsibility, feelings of competency lead to a heightened sense of identity and pride in a job well done. Ed says, "and I laugh again, feeling every bit like a true messenger" (p. 53).

CONCLUSIONS

. . . but there are other messages to deliver.
—Markus Zusak, *I Am the Messenger* (p. 61)

Despite the fact that we've identified these multiple messages about families, there are, as Ed reminds us, many messages still to be delivered. Many portrayals of family were not mere idealized versions of the nuclear family. Instead, they described genuine dilemmas faced by children and the adults with whom they live. However, we did not see many of the dilemmas dealing with the complicated and heartbreaking issues that surround families who are unable to stay together. Often, the dissolution of family structures are the result of alcoholism, drug abuse, parents without jobs, families living without permanent housing, and mental illness—human conditions that affect many people across all socioeconomic levels of our society. If these issues are crucial to families and their well-being, then this begs the question of why these concerns are not reflected in more of the award-winning books.

Moreover, we also noted a lack of people of color representing protagonists and their families. None were Middle Eastern, Native American, or Latino, and only two were Asian. In addition, not one single gay or lesbian person was represented even as a minor character in any of the books and stories. Likewise, adopted children and their families were never mentioned. If it were not for the Coretta Scott King Award, there would be few African American families highlighted in these adolescent texts. In the Michael L. Printz Award, characters of color were at least present, even though the numbers were low. We are sorry to report that, for the years we studied, the Newbery Medal focused almost exclusively on books featuring White children and their families. As Colabucci and Conley (2008) tell us, "Neglecting these stories further perpetuates the dominance of the White, middle-class experience in children's literature" (p. 158). If diversity of individuals and their families and cultures are not revealed in our award-winning books, then the messages we educators send when we use them with children are exclusionary rather than invitational to all children in our classroom communities.

We know that these books are part of the curriculum in our schools, yet if they fail to feature children and families of color or children and families dealing with difficult issues, then these significant topics become what Turner-Vorbeck (2008) tells us are part of the "null curriculum" in schools. She describes this kind of curriculum as the "lack of inclusion in the explicit curriculum of diverse forms of family, either through materials or through lessons themselves" (p. 181). Rieger (2008) discusses the many ways she is intentional about welcoming all children into her elementary classroom and notes that "it is their stories about their changing lives and experiences that will hold us together and drive the curriculum" (p. 70). So if, like Rieger, we want to respond to the messages that children send us, then we need shared texts to open up the invitational process—books that children read with one another that offer them complex views of life to consider, critique, and discuss.

Future research should expand the text set to include additional years of text analysis, as well as the inclusion of a wider range of awards. The Pura Belpré would increase the representation of cultural diversity, the Geisel would include messages sent for very young children, and the Schneider Family Book Award would represent books which honor children with disabilities. It is also important to draw from awards like the Notable Books for a Global Society to include an international perspective and the Jane Adams Book Award for books that focus on social consciousness. The Stonewall Book Awards honors gay/lesbian/bisexual/transgender themes and the Amelia Bloomer List celebrates books that extend the boundaries of what it means to be a woman or a girl. All of these awards and their listings can be found on the Internet.

We make these additional recommendations not only for extending future research, but also for professionals who select books for young learners. If we want our children to receive texts rich in a variety of messages about family, then we must ensure that they share these books in an environment designed to provide a safe space in which to examine them through a critical lens. Smith (2003) reminds us that "reading is the greatest technology ever devised for bringing people together" (p. 86). As we bring learners of all ages together, then it would appear that an exclusive reliance on the most notable books would not always be wise, especially if we want to explore a variety of books illustrating examples of all kinds of viable family structures.

In the final pages of *I Am the Messenger*, Ed realizes that all people are capable of becoming more than they ever thought that they could be. He tells us, "I'm not the messenger at all. I'm the message" (p. 357). As educators, when we place adolescent literature in the hands of young people, we not only offer them the messages held within their pages, but we also become the message when we make the choices of books for them—choices of books that can be used to highlight possibility and promise for the protagonists and their families, choices of books that offer dilemmas to be explored with a critical eye, and choices of books that broaden everyone's perspectives of acceptable and honorable ways of living and being in family.

Discussion Questions

1. Which messages about family are the most important to you on a personal level? Which messages do you think are the most important from a cultural standpoint?
2. How can the messages help teachers and parents create more effective literacy experiences with young adults that could expand their notions of viable family formations?
3. How might these texts be utilized to inform readers' notions of normativity as it relates to characterizations of family?
4. Which of the five topics concerning families addressed in this chapter would be the most difficult to serve as discussion topics among and between adults and adolescents? Why? Which would be the easiest ones? Why?

YOUNG ADULT BOOKS CITED

Anderson, M. T. (2006). *The astonishing life of Octavian nothing, traitor to the nation. Vol. 1: The pox party.* Cambridge, MA: Candlewick Press.

Armstrong, A. (2005). *Whittington.* New York: Yearling.

Bartoletti, S. C. (2005). *Hitler youth: Growing up in Hitler's shadow.* New York: Scholastic.

Bolden, T. (2005). *Maritcha: A nineteenth-century American girl.* New York: Abrams Books for Young Readers.

Choldenko, G. (2004). *Al Capone does my shirts.* New York: Putnam.

Draper, S. M. (2006). *Copper sun.* New York: Atheneum Books for Young Readers.

Flake, S. G. (2004). *Who am I without him?* New York: Hyperion Paperbacks for Children.

Freedman, R. (2004). *The voice that challenged a nation: Marian Anderson and the struggle for equal rights.* New York: Clarion.

Green, J. (2005). *Looking for Alaska.* New York: Dutton.

Green, J. (2006). *An abundance of Katherines.* New York: Dutton Books.

Grimes, N. (2005). *Dark sons.* New York: Hyperion Paperbacks.

Grimes, N. (2006). *The road to Paris.* New York: Putnam.

Hale, S. (2005). *Princess academy.* New York: Bloomsbury.

Hartnett, S. (2006). *Surrender.* Cambridge, MA: Candlewick Press.

Holm, J. L. (2006). *Penny from heaven.* New York: Random House.

Kadohata, C. (2004). *Kira—Kira*. New York: Atheneum Books for Young Readers.
Lanagan, M. (2005). *Black juice*. New York: Harper Collins/EOS.
Larson, K. (2006). *Hattie big sky*. New York: Delacorte Press.
Lester, J. (2005). *Day of tears*. New York: Jump at the Sun, Hyperion Books for Children.
Lord, C. (2006). *Rules*. New York: Scholastic Press.
Morrison, T. (2004). *Remember: The journey to school integration*. Boston: Houghton Mifflin.
Moses, S. P. (2004). *The legend of Buddy Bush*. New York: Margaret K. McElderry Books.
Nelson, M. (2005). *A wreath for Emmett Till*. Boston: Houghton Mifflin.
Nelson, M. (2004) *Fortune's bones: A manumission requiem*. Ashville, NC: Front Street.
Oppel, K. (2004). *Airborn*. New York: HarperCollins.
Patron, S. (2006). *The higher power of Lucky*. New York: Atheneum Books for Young Readers.
Partridge, E. (2005). *John Lennon: All I want is the truth*. New York: Viking.
Perkins, L. R. (2005). *Criss cross*. New York: Greenwillow Books.
Rosoff, M. (2004). *How I live now*. New York: Wendy Lamb Books.
Schmidt, G. D. (2004). *Lizzy Bright and the Buckminster boy*. New York: Clarion.
Stratton, A. (2004). *Chanda's secret*. Toronto: Annick Press.
Woodson, J. (2005). *Show way*. New York: G. P. Putnam's Sons.
Yang, G. L. (2006). *American born Chinese*. New York: First Second.
Zusak, M. (2005). *I am the messenger*. New York: Alfred A. Knopf.
Zusak, Markus. (2006). *The book thief*. New York: Alfred A. Knopf.

REFERENCES

Bishop, R. S. (1990). Mirrors, windows, and sliding glass doors. *Perspectives, 6,* ix–xi.
Bucher, K., & Manning, M. L. (2006). *Young adult literature: Exploration, evaluation, and appreciation*. Upper Saddle River, NJ: Pearson.
Colabucci, L., & Conley, M. (2008). What makes a family? Representations of adoption in children's literature. In T. Turner-Vorbeck & M. M. Marsh (Eds.), *Other kinds of families: Embracing diversity in schools* (pp. 103–120). New York: Teachers College Press.
Galda, L., & Graves, M. F. (2007). *Reading and responding in the middle grades: Approaches for all classrooms*. Boston: Pearson.
Manning, P., & Cullum-Swan, B. (1994). Narrative, content, and semiotic analysis. In N. Denzin & Y. Lincoln (Eds.), *Handbook of qualitative research* (pp. 463–478). Thousand Oaks, CA: Sage Publications.
Marks, I. (2008). Wards of wisdom: Foster youth on a path toward postsecondary education. In T. Turner-Vorbeck & M. M. Marsh (Eds.), *Other kinds of families: Embracing diversity in schools* (pp. 81–99). New York: Teachers College Press.

Marsh, M. M. (2008). Evolving images: Crafting family lives in colonial Pennsylvania. In T. Turner-Vorbeck & M. M. Marsh (Eds.), *Other kinds of families: Embracing diversity in schools* (pp. 103–120). New York: Teachers College Press.

Marshall, C., & Rossman, G. (1989). *Designing qualitative research.* Newbury, CA: Sage Publications.

Miles, B. M., & Huberman, A. M. (1984). Drawing valid meaning from qualitative data: Toward a shared craft. *Educational Researcher, 12,* 20–30.

Rieger, L. (2008). A welcoming tone in the classroom: Developing the potential of diverse students and their families. In T. Turner-Vorbeck & M. M. Marsh (Eds.), *Other kinds of families: Embracing diversity in schools* (pp. 81–99). New York: Teachers College Press.

Schwandt, T. (1997). *Qualitative inquiry: A dictionary of terms.* Thousand Oaks, CA: Sage.

Short, K. (Ed.). (1995). *Research and professional resources in children's literature.* Chicago: International Reading Association.

Simon, S. (Host.) (2008, April 12). *Knockemstiff* writer pulls no punches. [Interview with Donald Ray Pollock]. In *Weekend Edition—Saturday.* Washington, DC: National Public Radio.

Smith, F. (2003). *Unspeakable acts, unnatural practices: Flaws and fallacies in "scientific" reading instruction.* Portsmouth, NH: Heinemann.

Turner-Vorbeck, T. (2008). From textbooks to the teachers' lounge: The many curricula of family in schools. In T. Turner-Vorbeck & M. M. Marsh (Eds.), *Other kinds of families: Embracing diversity in schools* (pp. 103–120). New York: Teachers College Press.

U.S. Children's Bureau (2008). *Trends in foster care and adoption—FY 2002–FY 2007.* Retrieved April 18, 2008, from http://www.acf.hhs.gov/programs/cb/statsresearch/afcars/trends.htm

Literature Conversations for Inquiring Into the Influence of Family Stories on Teacher Identities

Janice Huber
Deborah Graham
Anne Murray Orr
Nathalie Reid

> *Stories have to be told or they die, and when they die, we can't remember who we are or why we're here*
> —Sue Monk Kidd, *The Secret Life of Bees* (p. 107)

This quotation speaks to us of the intricate connections between stories and identities, that is, stories as a way of understanding who we are and who we are becoming (Vinz, 1997). Between 2004 and 2007 our group of four teachers and teacher educators from diverse backgrounds engaged in literature conversations as a way to understand our becoming, our shifting, our evolving—always necessarily incomplete (Miller, 1998)—teacher identities.

Our thinking about teacher identity draws on Connelly and Clandinin's (1999) narrative conceptualization of "stories to live by" as a way to understand the connections among teachers' "knowledge, context, and identity" (p. 4). Inquiring into our identities in this narrative way meant that as we read and reread the transcripts of our literature conversations we were inevitably attending to relationships between the knowledge we storied as teachers, shaped through experiences with people and in situations across times and places. Our transcripts documented multiple insights about the potential of literature conversations as spaces to help us more fully under-

79

stand our stories to live by. Also documented were our awakenings to possible shifts in our stories to live by. What surprised us, however, and subsequently shaped the focus of this chapter, was the vital place of literature conversations in uncovering the shaping influence of family stories on our stories to live by.

TWO DIFFERENT KINDS OF STORIES: FAMILY STORIES AND STORIES OF FAMILIES

Our literature conversations led us into dialogues about the many different experiences we had as teachers, experiences we often storied as shaping, or shaped by, feelings of tension. Attending to them gradually shaped our awareness of the layers of, and frequent conflict between, "family stories" and "stories of families" (Clandinin et al., 2006) shaping our stories to live by. *Family stories* are those lived and told experiences shaped by and shared across generations in families. In Anne's rural Canadian family, for example, there is a family story about the importance of education as a way to escape the hardships of subsistence farming. This family story, known by Anne and each of her siblings, is a story that has shaped the unfolding of each of their lives.

In contrast, *stories of families* are composed around dominant cultural, institutional, and social narratives; they are stories often experienced or told to individuals or families when they are seen by members outside of the family to be living in ways that conflict with dominant narratives. For example, a common North American story of family is that a family is composed of two parents—one mom and one dad—along with one or more children who are the biological offspring of the parents. However, as Laidlaw (2006) has shown, "a growing number of North American families . . . do not quite fit [with this normative narrative shaped by] the historical categories and assumptions applied to the notion of 'family'" (p. 2).

Stories of families take on a "sacred" quality because they are deeply knotted into the fabric of cultures, societies, and institutions, and as a result are often unquestioned (Crites, 1971). Stories of families can frequently shape family stories and, subsequently, the stories lived by family members. Teachers compose their lives within particular families and carry these experiences into their work where, as they live on school and university landscapes alongside children, youth, families, other teachers, and administrators, they work in the midst of their own and others' family stories and culturally, institutionally, and socially influenced stories of families. Yet little research has focused on ways teachers' stories to live by are shaped in relation with family stories and stories of family. In this chapter we foreground the complexities and possibilities shaped in the meeting of these diverse and at times conflicting stories in our evolving stories to live by.

THE IMPORTANCE OF UNDERSTANDING
THE INTERWOVEN LIVES OF TEACHERS AND FAMILIES

The growing literature on the resonances and dissonances that children and families experience in schools shows that when children and youth experience dissonance between their family lives—and the stories their families nurture, recount, and live out—and the stories of "good" or "right" families that often inform many aspects of their experiences in schools, the impact can become profoundly miseducative (Dewey, 1938). Children and youth caught in these conflicting narratives can experience feelings of shame about their cultures, differences, familial contexts, languages, and parents—feelings that can reshape their stories to live by with plotlines of estrangement from school and, in some cases, from family members, contexts, and relationships (Chamoiseau, 1997; Chan, 2006; Clandinin et al., 2006; Fine, 1987; Mickelson, 2000; Rodriguez, 1982; Smyth & Hattam, 2004; Steeves, 2006; Turner-Vorbeck & Marsh, 2008). Dissonance experienced in conflicting family stories and stories of families can have lifelong reverberations. In many families of Aboriginal ancestry in Canada, the damaging impact of residential schools has shaped "intergenerational reverberations" (Young, 2005) as the loss of culture and language continues to impact the lives and the identities of the current generation of Aboriginal children and youth.

A SKETCH OF OUR NARRATIVE INQUIRY

As we first came to know one another as women in a Faculty of Education in eastern Canada, we shared stories of our previous teaching and research experiences with children, youth, families, and teachers. In this way we realized we shared the growing sense of urgency raised by others for increased respect for the diversity of children, youth, and families as they negotiate classroom and school contexts (Clandinin et al., 2006; Ladson-Billings, 2001; Pushor & Murphy, 2004; Tompkins, 1998). Tacitly, we understood that this kind of school reform necessarily begins as children, youth, teachers, and administrators, through inquiry into their storied lives and landscapes (Clandinin & Connelly, 1995), can discover more about who they are and who they are becoming in relation with one another (Clandinin & Connelly, 1998a, 1998b).

Another commonality across our experiences was a belief in the transformative nature of engagements with literature (Calkins & Harwayne, 1990; Coles, 1989, 2004; Florio-Ruane, 2001), such as Galda (1998) discusses:

> Aesthetic reading makes possible a transformational experience whenever a reader picks up a book. Whether looking at mirrors of ourselves or through windows into the lives of others, our experience during aesthetic reading affords us the opportunity to reconstruct ourselves, to understand living better. This is the transforming power of engagements with story. (p. 4)

As part of our narrative inquiry we read, wrote about, and discussed five books and one film: *The Secret Life of Bees* (Kidd, 2002), *The Girl with the Brown Crayon* (Paley, 1997), *Big Fish* [motion picture] (Burton & Zanuck, 2003), *Invisible Shadows: A Black Woman's Life in Nova Scotia* (Thomas, 2002), *The Curious Incident of the Dog in the Night-Time* (Haddon, 2004), and *The DaVinci Code* (Brown, 2004). As we became aware of the presence of family stories and stories of families across our literature conversations, we became drawn toward writing "Where I'm From" poems which Christensen (2001) describes as initiating spaces where youths' families, homes, and neighborhoods become more central in classroom curriculum making. Christensen explains that the power of these poems is shaped through the opportunities they create in school for youth to evoke memories and to recall details of their lives.

As we subsequently inquired into our "Where I'm From" poems, at times experiencing dissonance between our family stories and one another's family stories, and between our family stories and the stories of families portrayed in the books and film, we came to two realizations: The first realization was how little we understood the familial entanglements in our stories to live by. Our second realization was how little we had attended to family stories and stories of families in our becoming as teachers. It seemed important to us that if schools and universities are to become more inclusive of family diversity, spaces for teachers to inquire into these familial entanglements were vital. In the next section we show some of our inquiry into our familial entanglements, the ways in which family stories and stories of families shape our stories to live by.

TRACING FAMILIAL ENTANGLEMENTS
IN OUR STORIES TO LIVE BY

On a summer evening in early June 2007 we came together to explore the family stories portrayed in the texts and film alongside those we called forward in our responses, both our individual responses to the texts and film, and as we listened to one another's stories in our literature conversations. Although our earlier literature conversations brought us together for just a few hours in an afternoon or evening, this time, we decided to rent a cabin over a weekend. Some time after we had all arrived, standing together on the porch, soaking in the beauty around us—the peaceful, shimmering lake, the smell of new green grass, and the warmth of the summer evening—we became more contemplative. Encouraged by the trust established between us, we began, one after another, reading aloud our "Where I'm From" poems. Long into the night we talked, cried, and laughed.

The next morning we awoke to another beautiful day. After breakfast we continued to talk about our poems and the entanglements of family stories and stories of families shaping our stories to live by. The evening before, as the stories living between the lines of our poems were shared, we commented to one another about feeling as though we were coming to deeper understandings of our own, as well as each other's, stories to live by.

In our conversation in the morning we also talked about vulnerabilities we felt in telling our family stories. At that time we felt that these feelings were at least in part shaped by our knowing of ways that family stories do not always fit neatly within or alongside dominant stories of families. This conversation about the vulnerabilities we experienced in sharing our poems stayed with us, eventually shaping our decision to write word images composed of only a few lines from each of our poems. *Word images* are interim research texts developed by weaving together fragments of lived and told stories that emerge across field texts (Clandinin et al., 2006).

In the following section, we share our word images and our inquiry into them, inquiry attentive to family stories and stories of families.

Anne's Tracings

Four younger sisters
A farmhouse on the hill
Hay to be made and brought in
Memories of Ireland
Memories of family, kept alive

In this word image drawn from my poem, my relationships with family members are central. Growing up on a small farm in Nova Scotia, my sisters and I played together and worked together every day. The relationships that grew between us are complex and, like the roots of the huge maple tree in the front yard, run deep and intertwine through each of our stories to live by. An important part of my youth was a ritual in which my father's family would engage my sisters and me (especially me, the oldest) maybe once every month or two. My grandmother and uncle (who both lived with us) liked to recite the family lineage, traced back to our ancestors of seven generations before me in Ireland. It was very important to them to know this oral history, to repeat it often, and to pass it along. There were details like the sad story of how my grandfather's father died when he was young, and grandfather had to be the "man of the house." My father took us to the graveyard where we could see the headstones of each of the Murrays with their birth and death dates. It was important not to lose this information; it was part of who we were. So relationships and family stories were not only carried forward but also traced back in time, all the way back to Ireland.

When we responded to the texts and film in our literature group, the thread of family relationships often stood out for me, perhaps in part because of my father's family stories and my awareness of their fragility. For example, when we read *The Curious Incident of the Dog in the Night-Time* (Haddon, 2004), this story of Christopher, a young man with autism, made me think about my young nephew, Jonathan, who also carries this label and its challenges. Jonathan was 7 at the time we discussed this book; reading about Christopher was like looking ahead down one of several possible paths Jonathan might move along as he grows into a teen. This book brought me face-to-face with the realization that life may not be easy in the coming years for Jonathan, or for his parents, my sister and her husband, just as Christopher and his parents had great difficulties that arose because of Christopher's needs and actions. It also made me aware of my own frustration with the fact that I cannot "fix" things this time for my younger sister. As the oldest of five sisters, I composed a story for myself as the one who takes care of everyone, who keeps things going smoothly. In reality, however, I cannot do this for Jonathan and my family, and it is a source of angst for me. When we talked about the book in our group, I became aware of how differently others responded to it, and yet their responses, too, were all about relationships, with children in their classrooms, parents, families, and friends. As a teacher educator, I began to realize the importance of spaces to inquire into family stories, spaces that might be shaped by literature conversations such as ours.

Nathalie's Tracings

From appearances are everything
To knowing you can do anything

I am from "you toucha my sista, I breaka you face"

I am from "the albums" that silently record

The history of my vibrant life
In the neat, handwritten captions of my mother

I am from our stories that anchor us
And situate us in particular places at particular times

I am from fearful, sunglassed goodbyes
And converting a doubter
Into a Defender

The central focus of the film *Big Fish* (Burton & Zanuck, 2003) is the relationship between a father, Ed Bloom, and a son, Will Bloom. Ed and Will have differing perspectives on truth. Will perceives there to be a lack of trust, a lack of truth, a lack of valuation, a lack of reality in his and Ed's relationship, all resulting from Ed's propensity to tell "stories" and not "the facts" of his life. This divide between fact and story first seems insurmountable in their relationship.

As I viewed *Big Fish* I was drawn into the differing perspectives held by Will and Ed and within my family, which I show below by weaving threads from the movie with my word image:

I am from "the albums" that silently record
The history of my vibrant life
In the neat, handwritten captions of my mother
         I've told you a thousand facts, Will.

I am from our stories that anchor us
         That's what I [we] do, I tell stories!

And situate us in particular places at particular times
         A man tells his stories so many times
          that he becomes the stories.
I am from fearful, sunglassed goodbyes
         They live on after him.
And converting a doubter
Into a Defender
         And in that way, he becomes immortal.

Big Fish made me think about the power of stories and the central place they hold in my family stories. I often attribute my family's propensity for storytelling to the fact that we moved often because my father was in the military. While other people have stories of "family homes" or "kindergarten friends," we have multiple stories of place, of home, and of people. To remember the multiplicity of these experiences we have had to tell and retell stories of them. However, the more I think about it, I think we share our stories for the pure enjoyment of them. We often sit around with cups of coffee and tell the "remember when's . . . " or "when we were in Germany . . . " stories. These stories situate us, they ground us.

My master's thesis (Millar, 2007) involved working with texts like *Big Fish* and the potential of these texts for shaping conversations about death. My family story was that we did not talk about death, which lived easily alongside the story of school that says we should not talk about death at school. My fear of death and conversations about death subconsciously and powerfully underlined my first years of teaching. It dictated which literature I chose in the classroom, and it dictated how I taught what I chose. For example, *Hamlet* is a thorough psychological examination of death, perfectly suited to deep and rich conversations. During my first few years of teaching, however, because of my family story, I stayed away from this aspect of the play, and instead discussed existentialism. For years, I missed an invaluable opportunity. Our research conversations around *Big Fish* opened my eyes to the power of my early family experiences in shaping my stories to live by as a teacher and as a person. Through our inquiry process I learned there is importance in telling and retelling stories when it comes to family. Family stories, some happy and some difficult, are central to who I am as a teacher and, by extension, to who I am as a person. They are the threads that weave across continents, across time, and through all of my relationships.

Debbie's Tracings

> I am from my grandfather's rhubarb patch
> Of being curled up in a big bed with my two sisters
> From West Street and Rose Street
> And Ste. Christine where Eugene and Rose lived

As I attempt to uncover what the above lines from my poem mean for me, the underlying stories, memories, and emotions attached to each, I am struck by the power of these words and their significance in my life. Relationships are formed in distinct places and moments in time. Like Lily Owen in *The Secret Life of Bees* (Kidd, 2002) who spent 14 years in Sylvan, South Carolina, before finding her way to Tiburon, I too hold memories of the places in which I lived. Each place has attached to it the faces of those with whom I lived and learned. Throughout *The Secret Life of Bees,* Lily recounts her life in Sylvan and living with T. Ray on their peach farm. Readers witness her struggle, living with a father who was so overcome with his own pain that he inflicted more on his daughter. Both had experienced deep loss, T. Ray the loss of his wife, and Lily the loss of her mother.

I made many personal connections with this amazing book. Memories of living in places like "West Street" and "Rose Street" flooded my mind and took me back to my own reminiscences of a difficult childhood, being raised for a time by a father who was overcome with his own pain and attempting to come to terms with the absence of my own mother at an early age. For Lily, life was a challenge as well. Along with physical abuse, like having to kneel in grits, she also experienced a degree of mental abuse—not being permitted to read and being told that "college for girls was a waste of money" (p. 15).

While these experiences were difficult for Lily, she held onto the memory of her mother, who died as a result of a gun accident when Lily was only 4. Lily held a vague memory of being the one who pulled the trigger on that fatal day. After this experience she carried a void inside her, trying to hold onto any memory she could—the color of her mother's hair, the smell of her perfume. Through all of this, Lily found spaces of refuge too; observing the coming and going of bees, and lying on the grass outside. Spaces of refuge for me were found in places like my grandfather's rhubarb patch; I have a memory of standing in his garden at age 4 and asking the question, "What makes the rhubarb grow?" I felt to some degree a sense of connection to my grandfather. I loved the sound of his British accent and the big old-fashioned peppermints he gave me as a child, the kind that seemed to fill up your whole mouth. My father called him "Father," which I always found interesting. I remember his beautiful garden and his prize roses. As children, when my siblings and I went to visit him in the autumn with our parents, we would gather all the leaves together on West Street and jump in them. My grandfather's history was amazing to me. He came to Canada from England at the age of 17, and worked for a farmer. Eventually he married the farmer's daughter and raised five children, of whom my father was the youngest.

I also hold memories of cherished times spent with my sisters. As children we were inseparable; we even slept together in our very early years in a big double bed. At that time we lived out in the country—on the Twelfth Line. At night we would lie awake and stare out the window at the sky. Even then it seemed we were trying to figure things out. I still recall one conversation—wondering if all the stars were really people who had died.

Lily did not have any brothers or sisters, but she did have an African American nanny, Rosaleen, who "loved her beyond reason" (p. 11). She also had August, who loved Lily just as she had loved her mother Deborah. Sometimes family ties are formed regardless of blood connections.

The power of writing my poem was, for me, immeasurable. It brought to the surface stories that have been dormant for some time. These stories, although they lay dormant, have remained a part of me, shaping me as a teacher and teacher educator, helping me to see the world and those in it in different ways.

Janice's Tracings

I am from learning that people need one another
From a community contoured by intergenerational fear and mistrust of peo-
*   ple and practices not the same*
I am from stories told and retold at a large and worn kitchen table
From found and chosen family I cannot live without

Life in my family and first community was complex, yet I am often hesitant to share these experiences. As I read and we first discussed *The Girl With the Brown Crayon* (1997), Paley's stories of the ways Reeny, her mother, and her grandmother taught Paley about the complexities Reeny experienced in composing her identity as a child of African American ancestry in a school not always awake to her racial differences and history, drew me strongly backward in time and place to similar awakenings I experienced alongside children and families in elementary classrooms. I was called toward memories of Corina, a girl in a multiage Year 3/4 classroom with an insatiable passion for literature, for stories revealing complex lives that, like her own, included experiences of parental separation, of composing a biracial identity, and of moving between multiple home places.

Yet, as I later read the transcripts of our literature conversation when we discussed this book, I began to see that my deeply felt connections with Paley's storied moments of lives in the making could also be traced further back in my life. In this tracing I was drawn toward experiences I knew first as a child and that figure largely as I recall the "shapes of [my] childhood" (Greene, 1995, p. 74). My remembered experiences include the following:

—memories of the fur, mostly worn off, of the stuffed tiger my
youngest brother carried everywhere in the first days and months
of his life with my family. He was 4 and I was 7 when we first met.
He arrived, having lived more than 3½ years in foster care, carrying
two plastic shopping bags containing a few cloth diapers, two pairs
of flannel pajamas, and his much-loved tiger.
—memories of my dad's eyes filling with tears slowly running down
his face, when I, in the midst of his telling stories of his life as a
young boy, asked him to tell us about his dad's death. He was 15
years old when his dad died in a train accident. My dad was probably in his 40s at the time of my question.
—memories of the first summer Darcy arrived, a 16-year-old boy
with long hair, tattered jeans, and cigarettes. He lived with my fam-

ily because his parents worried he'd become involved in drugs if he stayed in the city. As summers with Darcy passed and he continued to return, first with the woman he loved and soon with one, then two, then three, then four beautiful children, he became a person in my chosen family.

—memories of my excitement, when my mom filled birthday cakes with money sterilized through boiling and my brothers, sister, and I could hardly wait to learn whose piece was the richest.

—memories, especially during my years in junior and senior high school, of my parents often asking me to stay at the kitchen table after supper to explain why the principal called about my behavior.

—memories of the countless times elbows rubbed as many people squeezed in alongside each other to eat after a long day of working with cattle. Even though there were mostly adults around the table at these times, I still knew I could join in the conversation.

My memories of living through these experiences are contoured by celebration, tears, anger, joy, messiness, laughter, questions, and uncertainty; moments when lives spilled forward, over, into, and against one another; resonances and dissonances lingering in the often indelible threads weaving—over days, months, years, a lifetime—into the understandings, the identities, made and remade. In those meetings of lives I formed relationships with people who both do and do not share my ancestral lines yet each person is someone I name as "family."

As I think forward from my childhood experiences and across the stories shared in Paley's (1997) book alongside my memories of life with children and families in elementary classrooms, I realize that the experiential thread connecting each of these landscapes, is, as Bateson (2004) described, the possibility of spaces and relationships where life stories that include "lots of surprises and choices, of interruptions and disappointments" (p. 68) can be told. In seeking to understand the reverberations I feel between my family stories, my teacher stories, and Paley's stories, I am awakening to ways in which, in my early family life, I came to know something of the frayed, messy nature of lives. It is knowledge I can only hope to live as well with my daughter, and with teachers in teacher education classrooms.

IMAGINING POSSIBILITIES FOR RESPECTING DIVERSE FAMILY STORIES

Similar to how our literature conversations unfolded, our tracings in the previous section of some of our family stories shaped an additional inquiry space. This space became filled with our imaginings of the possibilities of respecting diverse family stories in school and university classrooms. As a way to show some of these imaginings we read and responded in writing to each other's earlier tracings. We then wove this response into the following word image:

Dominant stories of families can shape

stories of normalcy
of one size fits all
at school   at home

What does it mean: to not fit?
What does it mean: sibling sameness?
What does it mean: family?

How do our stories to live by become entangled
with dominant stories of family,
stories of fairy-tale and happily-ever-after landscapes,
with potential to silence differing, shifting stories?

How does behavior
become expected?
How do positions
become shaped?

How might we make spaces
for knowing
for speaking
for being vulnerable
for inviting into classrooms . . .
. . . our intergenerational stories reverberating within us
of roots
tangled and deep
supporting
underlying complexities in lives unfolding?

Might this begin . . .
. . . by honoring, awakening, surfacing, voicing,
making spaces
for
vital stories
of composing lives
as people, as families
always in the midst?

Composing this word image called us to think hard about the resonances, dissonances, and vulnerabilities we each felt in sharing our family stories. As we thought about each of these aspects, together and alone, we realized how common it is across our experiences to say little or nothing about where we are from. In this recognition we awakened to how our silencing was often linked with our knowing that the people, places, and situations that shape our family stories were often quite different from the smooth, happily-ever-after narratives surrounding us. For example, as a child, youth, and eventually a teacher, Nathalie learned that to talk about death, a family story, a family reality given that her dad was in the Canadian Armed Forces, did not fit with the stories of family that were shaping not only her family, but the schools and universities she attended. It was (and is) a family story kept silent by the dominant cultural and social narratives in Canada, narratives that may only begin to shift for the current generation of Canadian children and youth as they, unlike their parents and grandparents, may find spaces to restory silences around death and dying, spaces that might begin to open in schools and teacher education programs.

As our family stories illustrate, who we each are and who we each are becoming, as teachers, teacher educators, parents, friends, family members, community members, and so on, are indelibly shaped by these familial and social experiences. Sharing some of our family stories with one another supported us to attend to experiences that were foundational in the stories we live by as teachers. Our sharing also drew us toward questions about the deep connections among teachers' and teacher educators' stories to live by, family stories, and dominant stories of family that shape the institutions where we work. For example, we asked ourselves two important questions:

1. How might we, as teachers and teacher educators, inquire into our family stories in such a way that we are better able to attend to the diverse and sometimes tension-filled family stories of children, youth, and adults as we meet them in school and university settings?
2. How might our curriculum making in schools and universities shape respectful spaces where the possibilities for inquiring into the shaping influence of family stories in teachers', children's, youths', and family members' stories are valued?

Through this process we were awakened to new ways of living in the future as we interact with children and families in schools and with pre- and in-service teachers. By staying attentive—with children, youth, families, teachers, administrators, and teacher educators—to questions such as these, there is, we believe, much hope of challenging the hegemony shaped by dominant stories of family.

Thinking back across our narrative inquiry shows us that the spaces in schools and universities that our questions seek to open up will not happen without the vulnerability we experienced in writing this chapter. As we meet children, youth, and families in schools and as we meet teachers in universities, rather than handing out worksheets to be completed or detailed course outlines, we realize we will need, instead, to make spaces with them for telling and inquiring into stories of who we are—stories about the people, places, relationships, and experiences we carry—the people, places, relationships, and experiences that shape who we are and who we are becoming. And, as we meet children, youth, families, and teachers who, like us, keep silent about the people, places, relationships, and experiences they are from, we might wonder, quietly and out loud, if their silences have anything to do with the differences they see, hear, and feel between their families and the stories of families that seep into what is (or is not) made visible, said, or attended to in school and university classrooms.

Discussion Questions

1. Think about a family story that stands out for you from your childhood or youth. As you reflect on your family stories and the family stories of children and youth with whom you've worked, what resonances and/or dissonances do you remember experiencing in the meeting of these stories?
2. How has this meeting of family stories shaped your relationships with the young people you have worked with? How has your practice changed as a result?
3. How has knowing family stories increased your awareness of the importance of social justice in ways that make a difference for children and families inside of schools? Outside of schools?
4. What books/films/other media might you suggest for conversations of the kind in which Nathalie, Debbie, Anne, and Janice engaged around family stories? Why?
5. What are some additional collaborative ways you create or might create spaces for respectful attention to family stories in your classroom? In your school?

ACKNOWLEDGMENTS

We would like to acknowledge the funding we received from the University Council of Research, St. Francis Xavier University, which supported our inquiry: *Teaching and the Cultural Imagination: Inquiring into the Shaping and Reshaping of Teachers' Stories to Live By Through Engagements with Literature.* We also want to acknowledge our appreciation of Marilyn Huber who gave important response to our chapter.

REFERENCES

Bateson, M. C. (2004). *Willing to learn: Passages of personal discovery.* Hanover, NH: Steerforth Press.

Brown, D. (2004). *The DaVinci Code.* New York: Doubleday.

Burton, T. (Director), & Zanuck, R. (Producer). (2003). *Big fish* [motion picture]. United States: Columbia Pictures.

Calkins, L., & Harwayne, S. (1990). *Living between the lines.* Toronto: Pearson.

Chamoiseau, P. (1997). *School days* (L. Coverdale, Trans). Lincoln: University of Nebraska Press.

Chan, E. (2006). Teacher experience of culture in curriculum. *Journal of Curriculum Studies, 38*(2), 161–176.

Christensen, L. (2001). Where I'm from: Inviting students' lives into the classroom. In B. Bigelow, B. Harvey, S. Karp, & L. Miller (Eds.), *Rethinking Our Classrooms, Vol. 2, Technology for equity and justice* (pp. 6–10). Milwaukee, WI: Rethinking Schools.

Clandinin, D. J., & Connelly, F. M. (1995). *Teachers' professional knowledge landscapes.* New York: Teachers College Press.

Clandinin, D. J., & Connelly, F. M. (1998a). Asking questions about telling stories. In C. Kridel (Ed.), *Writing educational biography: Explorations in qualitative research* (pp. 202–209). New York: Garland.

Clandinin, D. J., & Connelly, F. M. (1998b). Stories to live by: Narrative understandings of school reform. *Curriculum Inquiry, 28,* 149–164.

Clandinin, D. J., Huber, J., Huber, M., Murphy, S., Orr, A. M., Pearce, M., & Steeves, P. (2006). *Composing diverse identities: Narrative inquiries into the interwoven lives of children and teachers.* London: Routledge Falmer.

Coles, R. (1989). *The call of stories: Teaching and the moral imagination.* Boston: Houghton Mifflin.

Coles, R. (2004). *Teaching stories: An anthology on the power of learning and literature.* New York: Modern Library.

Connelly, F. M., & Clandinin, D. J. (1999). *Shaping a professional identity: Stories of educational practice.* New York: Teachers College Press.

Crites, S. (1971). The narrative quality of experience. *Journal of the American Academy of Religion, 39*(3), 291–311.

Dewey, J. (1938). *Experience and education.* New York: Collier Books.

Fine, M. (1987). Silencing in public schools. *Language Arts, 64*(2), 157–174.

Florio-Ruane, S. (2001). *Teacher education and the cultural imagination: Autobiography, conversation, and narrative.* Mahwah, NJ: Erlbaum.

Galda, L. (1998). Mirrors and windows: Reading as transformation. In T. Raphael & K. Au, (Eds.), *Literature-based instruction: Reshaping the curriculum*. Norwood, MA: Christopher-Gordon.

Greene, M. (1995). *Releasing the imagination: Essays on education, the arts, and social change*. San Francisco: Jossey-Bass.

Haddon, M. (2004). *The curious incident of the dog in the night-time*. Toronto: Anchor Canada.

Kidd, S. M. (2002). *The secret life of bees*. New York: Viking Press.

Ladson-Billings, G. (2001). *Crossing over to Canaan: The journey of new teachers in diverse classrooms*. San Francisco: Jossey-Bass.

Laidlaw, L. (2006, April). *Found: A narrative of family, diversity, and schooling*. Paper presented at the annual meeting of the American Educational Research Association, San Francisco, CA.

Mickelson, J.-R. (2000). *Our sons are labeled behavior disordered: Here are the stories of our lives*. Troy, New York: Educators International Press.

Millar, N. (2007). *Fish tales: A hermeneutic narrative exploration of the multi-layered texture of death*. Unpublished master's thesis, St. Francis Xavier University, Antigonish, NS, Canada.

Miller, J. L. (1998). Autobiography and the necessary incompleteness of teachers' stories. In W. Ayers & J. Miller (Eds.), *A light in dark times: Maxine Greene and the unfinished conversation*. New York: Teachers College Press.

Paley, V. G. (1997). *The girl with the brown crayon*. Cambridge, MA: Harvard University Press.

Pushor, D., & Murphy, B. (2004). Parent marginalization, marginalized parents: Creating a place for parents on the school landscape. *Alberta Journal of Educational Research, 50*(3), 221–235.

Rodriguez, R. (1982). *Hunger of memory: The education of Richard Rodriguez: An autobiography*. New York: Bantam.

Smyth, J., & Hattam, R. (with Cannon, J., Edwards, J., Wilson, N., & Wurst, S.). (2004). *Dropping out, drifting off, being excluded: Becoming somebody without school*. New York: Peter Lang.

Steeves, P. (2006). Sliding doors—Opening our world. *Equity & Excellence in Education, 39*(2), 105–114.

Thomas, V. (2002). *Invisible shadows: A Black woman's life in Nova Scotia*. Halifax: Nimbus.

Tompkins, J. (1998). *Teaching in a cold and windy place: Change in an Inuit school*. Toronto: University of Toronto Press.

Turner-Vorbeck, T., & Marsh, M. M. (2008). *Other kinds of families: Embracing diversity in schools*. New York: Teachers College Press.

Vinz, R. (1997). Capturing a moving form: "Becoming" as teachers. *English Education, 29*(2), 137–146.

Young, M. (2005). *Pimatisiwin: Walking in a good way: A narrative inquiry into language as identity*. Winnipeg, MB: Pemmican.

CHAPTER 6

A Tale of Two Adoptive Families

Monica Miller Marsh
Tammy Turner-Vorbeck

Children are forced to face their differences in a variety of ways. Many children have been openly teased about their difference in the classroom—with a teacher present at the time. A simple but poignant example of this occurred in Tammy's family when a worksheet designed by the teacher to gather information about new students in the class was completed by her youngest child, Kristen, in the third grade. The worksheet was taken out of her hands by a classmate and read aloud. Sarah was very happy to report to the class that their new classmate was an adopted child. Instead of addressing this issue with the class, the teacher elected to offer a simple reprimand to Sarah and let it go at that. The subsequent recess conversation that ensued went something like this:

> *Sarah:* I can tell you're adopted.
> *Kristen:* How?
> *Sarah:* You don't look like your Mom at all so I knew you must be adopted.

Not so bad, you might be thinking; not all biological children physically resemble their parents. But it didn't end there.

> *Sarah:* Do you know why you were adopted? Nobody wanted you so you *had* to be adopted.

Ouch! This sort of classroom interaction is clearly a painful experience for a child. It is also frustrating and difficult for a parent to learn that such devastating dialogue might take place, unchallenged, in the school. This marginalization of children from "other kinds of families" begs the question: How can classrooms become more inclusive and accepting environments for children from differing family structures just as we know they

95

should be sensitive to the gender, racial, cultural, and language differences in students? One of the logical places to begin to answer this question is with the curriculum selected and employed in the classroom.

This chapter draws upon the powerful narratives of foster and adopted children and their stories of exclusion in school curriculum and classroom settings. In sharing these highly personal narratives, we hope to provide the reader with unique insights into the lived experiences of students from different forms of family and to understand what went wrong in the educational system to allow these children to become outsiders of the curriculum. We discuss several points of awareness that school personnel such as teachers, administrators, and counselors, as well as curriculum developers and marketers, can attend to in order to avoid abatement of students. We examine specific examples of curriculum that did not work for these children and offer improvements upon those examples to yield inclusive treatment of foster and adoptive families in multiple forms of school curriculum.

A STORY FROM MONICA'S FAMILY

A couple of years ago the mother of one of our daughter's friends left the following message on our family's answering machine:

> I just wanted to call and tell you that there is a great new movie out, *Meet the Robinsons*. Your kids are going to love it—it is your family story!

It was hard to imagine what a movie depicting our family story would look like. We are continually attempting to craft a coherent narrative of family with our adopted children. Our two sons and a daughter are a sibling-group that we adopted from Poland 6 years ago. At the time of adoption they were 5, 4, and 2 years old. As with many children who have been adopted, little historical information came with them. They, of course, have some memories of their life before the adoption, but things are not always clear and they have many questions that we are not able to help them answer.

Meet the Robinsons (McKim & Anderson, 2007) is a 3-D movie so it was already on our list of movies to see; there is something about objects flying off the screen and appearing to land in your lap that makes 3-D movies especially appealing to our family. We had no idea that there was an adoption theme threaded through the movie, but, once we heard, my husband and I thought this might just be an added bonus.

From the moment we entered the theater, we were on the lookout for reflections of ourselves projected by the images that moved across the screen.

Yet, it doesn't take the viewing of a movie or the words of a friend to motivate any of us to look for various images of ourselves in others. As Bakhtin (1920/1990) explains, each of us is "constantly and intently on the watch for reflections of our own life on the plane of other people's consciousnesses, and moreover, not just reflections of particular moments of our life, but even reflections of the whole of it" (p. 16). The other people to whom Bakhtin refers include all the individuals with whom we come into actual contact as well as those in texts such as movies, books, songs, and video games. It is through our interaction with the stories embodied in others that we piece together our own identities.

For those of you who haven't seen *Meet the Robinsons*, it is a computer-animated Disney movie that focuses on the story of a 12-year-old boy named Lewis, who, as an infant, was left on the doorstep of an orphanage by his birth mother. Early in the movie we learn that he has had 124 failed adoption interviews and has given up hope of finding an adoptive family. Lewis, an inventor, makes a time machine for the school science fair with hopes that it can take him back to the past so that he is able to find his birth mother. Instead of going back to the past, he ends up being thrust into the future when Wilbur Robinson, a 13-year-old from the year 2037 appears at the science fair. Wilbur takes Lewis on a wild ride into the future as he works to save Lewis from an evil man in a bowler hat who has stolen Lewis's time machine. While in the future, Lewis meets his adopted family. He sees that this group, whose mantra is "from failure you learn, keep moving forward," welcomes his unconventional ideas that often lead to failed inventions and accepts him for who he is. He is also able to speak with himself as an adult who has become a successful inventor and comes to the realization that his time machine, does, indeed work. Yet, when he is faced with the opportunity to meet his birth mother, he gives up his dream, recognizing that he will change the future if they meet. He no longer wants to go back in time because he likes the adoptive family that he sees in his future.

It was at the moment in the movie when Lewis gave up the opportunity to meet his birth mother that my older son, who was 10 years old at the time, turned to me in disgust and said, "I hate this movie! I *hate* it!" This typically mild-mannered child was ready to leave the theater before the movie had ended. Later, we asked our older son to share with us more of his thoughts about the movie:

> I hated it because the mother had a baby and she left the baby at the orphanage; she didn't even kiss him good-bye. Lewis didn't like her because she left him alone and he was really mad at her. He should have talked to her and said hello. Maybe they could have lived together. He could have said to the Robinsons that his *real* mother

was there now—and that he was going to live with her and she was
going to take care of him.

Our older son wanted to change the outcome of Lewis's life completely.
While he expressed anger at Lewis's birth mother for leaving him at the
orphanage, he also expressed anger at Lewis for not wanting to meet her.
Ultimately, he wanted them to be reunited as a family and he wanted Lewis's
birth mother to care for him.

Our younger son, who was 9 years old at the time, did not have such a
negative response toward the movie, but he too, was very unsatisfied with
Lewis's choice:

> I didn't like it. Why didn't he talk to her? He could have said hello
> and just seen if she was a good person . . . you know if she was
> kind and caring. He would not have to live with her.

Our younger son wanted assurance that Lewis's birth mother was a com-
passionate person, that she gave Lewis up for adoption because it was the
best thing for him. Knowing that this was the case would have been enough
for Lewis to stop wondering about his birth mother and live his life with
the Robinsons.

Our daughter, who had just turned 7, thought it was a great movie. The
adoption theme didn't seem to matter to her one way or another. When we
asked her how she felt about Lewis not taking the opportunity to meet his
birth mom, she said, "Oh, I liked when the Robinsons met Lewis but my
favorite part was watching those singing frogs." Our daughter, who loves
animals and often talks of becoming a veterinarian, wondered if you really
could teach frogs to sing and talked about how she might experiment with
that in the future.

HOW STORIES IMPACT OUR IDENTITIES

What did our friend, who is also an adoptive mother and an elementary
school teacher, mean when she said this was our family story? That we are
wacky like the Robinsons and that our children feel so content with us that
they wouldn't make the choice to live with, or get to know, their birth family? We are kind of wacky, so that part did fit. But, if she was talking about
the part where our children were so content that they could just forget about
the past, obviously, this wasn't the case based on the comments made by
both of our sons. My husband and I, like our sons, found very little in the

movie that we felt mirrored our perceptions of our role as parents or our image of family. For each of us there appeared to be a mismatch between what Bakhtin refers to as the "I-for-myself,"—how myself looks and feels in my own consciousness—and the "I-for-others"—how myself appears to those outside my own consciousness (Morson & Emerson, 1990, p. 180). I was still contemplating all of this the day after we had seen the movie when one of the prospective teachers with whom I was working at the time walked into our social studies methods class and said:

> I saw the best movie this weekend: *Meet the Robinsons*. You have to see this movie—your family will love it! And it completely relates to what we have been talking about in social studies about the inclusion of all family types. I have already thought about how I can plan some lessons and activities around the movie for my class. It just shows how you don't have to have a birth family to be happy. Once this kid found a family who loved him just as he was, he was perfectly happy, he could forget all about the past. . . .

She must have read the look on my face because she abruptly stopped talking and said, "Uh-oh, what have I said?" I proceeded to share with her the comments that our children had made about the movie and some of the discussion that my husband and I had been having about our children's reactions. To want to go back in time, to want to know and make sense of the past and its relationship to the present is a strong desire in our sons, and, I can imagine in many children who have had disrupted family stories. The problem with the *story of family* (see Chapter 5 of this volume) that *Meet the Robinsons* promotes is that it trivializes the notion of an adoptive family and suggests that once the child who is adopted is placed in a safe, accepting family environment there are no more struggles on the part of the child—that the child is able to just make the choice to turn his or her back on the past and keep moving forward. It presumes that all historical family narratives are severed once the child is integrated into a new family and that a completely new identity emerges. But if we think about identities as collections of stories or narratives about persons (Sfard & Prusak, 2005), those stories of the past are always a part of the entire collection of who we are. The telling and sharing of stories is what "makes us able to cope with new situations in terms of our past experience and gives us tools to plan for the future" (p. 16). Yet we continually see the stories of children who have been adopted or are in foster care obscured within informal curricula, such as movies, magazines, and books, as well as in formal curricula presented in schools.

Pretending to Be Normal

An example of the same type of message being promoted through the formal curricula happened right around the time we were discussing *Meet the Robinsons*. Our daughter's first-grade religion education class was going to talk about how physical characteristics are passed down through families. She was asked to make a chart on which she was to include her parents' physical characteristics, as well as those of her paternal and maternal grandparents. I shared with the teacher that our daughter was adopted and that we didn't have that specific information. The teacher, who was also an adoptive parent, asked us to complete the assignment by "imagining" with our daughter what a pretend birth mother and father might look like, in other words, fabricate a story about the past so that our child could complete the required assignment. The message here is that the story is so unimportant that we can make it up. As Lindsey (in press) tells us, we have to be careful that "our everyday storytellings of schooling are not mistakes—mistaken representations and misperceptions . . . mistaken beliefs in stories which are no more than fairy tales" (p. 2). In essence this teacher asked our daughter to create a fairy tale about her past. As educators we support the crafting of fairy tales when we ask students to provide personal information that is uncomfortable to share or that they simply do not have.

Personal Narratives and Identity with Family

When asking our children to share their thoughts in order to provide our readers with a deeper and highly personal insight into the lived experiences of children, we were surprised at their candor and willingness to express their frequent frustration over the repeated ignorance of their teachers to their individual situations. The following are the narratives of Tammy's three adopted children (now 25, 24, and 16), who all have distinct memories of the anguish imparted by the curricular assignments they received throughout their school years.

Justin's Narrative

I remember when we had to do a huge project over our family history. We had to write about our favorite Christmas present as a child and our happiest time as a young child. My early childhood was not a happy time for me and presents were few and far between. It was hard because I didn't want to be different and I didn't want people feeling sorry for me or making fun of me. It wasn't really the teacher's fault. She probably didn't think that a lot of kids have different backgrounds than her.

Cassie's Narrative

Elementary School—Family Portraits—We would have to draw/
color the members of our family. That was difficult because being
in a foster home at the time, the number of people in the household
changed regularly.
Middle School—Family Trees—During history classes we were
asked to explore our family's heritage. I personally used my adopted
family's background, but it did make me wonder what my biological background was.
High School—Biology—In high school biology we learned about
genetics. Where did your hair/eye color come from? Are you prone
to any genetic health disorders? I wasn't able to answer those questions because I had no idea what the answers were.

These types of activities that obscure our children's stories happen within
the formal curricula all too often. While on the surface these activities may
seem benign and actually appear to shield children from family histories
that may be painful, they send messages to children that this part of their
life no longer exists. Madeline Grumet (1988) has written extensively about
the relationship between family life and curriculum. She says,

> For many of us the family is the place of feeling. There sound and touch compete
> with sight. Sensual, engaged, caring, it appears to offer us a first nature much
> richer than the culture of the public world, and we fall to the task of describing
> it with earnest effort. Because the family is the first nature for all of us, because
> its politic is threaded through our bodies, separating ourselves from our assump-
> tions about our mother, our father, our own children, our spouse, is like separat-
> ing ourselves from breath, hunger, and from sleep. (pp. 63–64)

Grumet's message is that we can't separate ourselves from our family
stories. It is in the realm of family that feeling and emotions are learned
and become a part of one's lived experiences. These early experiences shape
the way we view the world and our relationship to others and our selves.
Grumet asks us to consider the family stories that surround the child as we
create curriculum so that we are able to "diminish the distance between
the private and public poles of our experience" (p. 65). This is especially
true for children who have been adopted or are in foster care whose early
years include stories of loss. Many of these children are working to fill in
the missing pieces in their family stories and to understand their emotions
and responses to particular situations while at the same moment they are
simultaneously trying to integrate themselves into new and different family
narratives. Tammy's younger daughter, now 15, illustrates this well in her
own words.

Kristen's Narrative

In class every year for the last 9 years of my school life, every teacher has given us a worksheet asking our names and personal stuff. There have always been some questions that were difficult for me to answer. For example, they asked, "What inspired your parents to give you the name you have?" or "Were you named after a family member?" They also asked related questions such as, "Where did your family come from? Were they immigrants?" There's really nothing threatening in these questions themselves. In fact, it can seem kind of fun to find out about all of this stuff. But for a lot of us, these kinds of questions really get to us. Some kids don't have parents or they may be adopted, like me. I was adopted when I was younger. I love my family and there's no problem now for me, but when these questions pop up on these worksheets, it kind of hurts me. I don't know who I was named after or what country my ancestors are from.

As another example, in biology class we got a genetics worksheet that asked which physical traits you were given by your parents. I had no clue how to do that worksheet and I got upset by it. I could not compare my looks to my parents'; they're different. In seventh grade, we had to bring in baby pictures. I only have two and those pictures were taken at the foster home I lived in before I was adopted. I got really jealous of the other kids in my class because they had *loads* of them. I've gone home every year deciding to put my nickname on those worksheets and then I can explain why I was given the nickname I have.

These kinds of things that teachers make us do are really unfair. I don't like to raise my hand in class and ask, "What about the adopted kids? How do we answer this?" year after year after year. The other kids just stare and a sadness came over me, not knowing anything about my biological family. It is a terrible feeling and I believe teachers should think about all of the kids in foster homes, adopted kids, and kids without parents. There isn't just one kind of family and teachers should rethink these worksheets. I love my family and I am not mad that I was adopted; I just wish those worksheets and assignments would be well thought-out by teachers.

Negotiating Perceptions

Bakhtin (1920/1990) explains the process of self-formation as being both individual and social through the use of the categories mentioned earlier: I-for-myself and I-for-others. For Bakhtin, the category of I-for-myself, the inner self, is shaped from the outside in through the narratives with which we come into contact as we interact with others. Since we are constantly interacting with others, the I-for-myself is open and always in a state of flux.

While the I-for-myself is the way I perceive myself, the I-for-others is my perception of how others see me. For Bakhtin (1990), identity formation is a complex process that involves incorporating other people's evaluations of us into the way we think and feel about who we are. This is the collective work of individual identity formation. Morson and Emerson (1990) explain, *"I-for-myself* is never identical with, but always learning from the image of *I-for-others"* (p. 191). This type of sense making, this attempt to integrate perceptions of *I-for-myself* and *I-for-others* is exactly what our children are trying to negotiate as they interact with their peers, teachers, and family members.

Upon careful examination, it is clear that these examples of formal and informal curricula present very limited narratives for the crafting of identities for children who have been adopted or in foster care. Of course we all want our children to be happy and to keep moving toward their future dreams and desires. And we are not advocating that teachers ask families to share the private and painful stories of the past. But, simply ignoring that those stories exist or asking children and families to rewrite a brighter, happier past denies children a part of their identity. What we are advocating is the creation of curriculum that "becomes tentative and provisional, a temporary and negotiated settlement between the lives we are capable of living and the ones we have (Grumet, 1988, p. xiii). In other words, curriculum making should be done carefully, sensitively, and in collaboration with students and families. Developing and implementing curricula that are sensitive to the lived experiences of all children and their families is about providing activities that include multiple story lines in which teachers present strong, positive family images of the I-for-others from which children can draw as they are in the process of crafting an I-for-myself.

In the following section we scrutinize some of the lessons and activities that have been presented in the elementary and secondary curricula in schools that our children have attended. We then specify ways that multiple story lines could be integrated into each activity so that teachers "create a field of open potential" (Morson & Emerson, 1990, p. 191) for the identity formation of all children.

RETHINKING EXAMPLES FROM THE SCHOOL CURRICULUM

We would like to focus on a couple of the most common and most troublesome activities we have identified and which were named by our children.

There are countless variations on these activities and more activities that we do not have time to detail here, but these are a good place to begin.

Origin of Names Activities

Where did you get your name?
Why did your parents give you the name you have?
Were you named after an ancestor?

There are some creative ways to tackle this assignment, mainly by not limiting it to first names. When Monica's daughter brought home this assignment in the first grade, she could not complete it because she did not know how she had gotten her first name. Monica asked the teacher if they could change the assignment so that she could write about her middle name, which Monica and her husband did choose, naming her "Joyce" after both maternal and paternal grandmothers. The shift in the assignment actually made it quite interesting and informative for their daughter to complete, though that would not necessarily be the case for many children. Similarly, when Tammy's younger daughter brought home this standard issue assignment, she brainstormed with her adoptive parents about how she might honestly complete the assignment. They came up with the idea that she write about her nickname, which was given to her after adoption, and as in Monica's family's case, the assignment turned out to be a fun and productive one.

Historical Photography Activities

Bring in your baby pictures.

The narratives written by Tammy's children above illustrate the discomfort that springs forth from this assignment for so many children who have no physical records of their early childhoods due to neglect, displacement, sealed court records, and so on. In Monica's family, two of their children have been asked to bring in baby pictures to display on the school bulletin board for a "guess who?" type of activity to show growth and change. Having no baby pictures is a constant source of stress for her children, as it is for so many. The earliest pictures they have of their older son are from when he was 4 years old, a fact known only by the date on the back of the photograph. He has no memory of where he was or who he was with when the photograph was taken. At first glance, this may not seem like a major issue, but it becomes an issue when the rest of the class begins to discuss the experiences captured in the photographs and he cannot join in those conversations. In this case, the adoptive parents communicated with the teacher and the next year, the assignment was changed in time for their younger son and his class to be free to choose any picture of themselves they wanted to share with the group.

In Tammy's family this had been an issue, as illustrated by her children's narratives, for each of her three children, documenting the popularity and prevalence of this type of curricular assignment. A nice alternative to this assignment of historical family documentation was provided by one of Kristen's high school (world history) teachers this year. Her assignment for the class was an inclusive one from the very beginning. The title of the assignment was Impact of History and stated, "You are going to be a historical researcher with your family." The steps in the assignment were as follows: (1) Make a list of events that took place the year you were born (ask your family or check Google). (2) Find out what your parents/family members were doing when they were your age. (3) In a paragraph explain how any of the items in the first two questions may have had some impact on your life and/or development. Of course, photographs could be a part of the assignment but the shift is clearly away from restrictive or exclusive depictions of an ideal childhood, so common with the "Bring in your baby pictures" assignments.

CONCLUSION

These are just a couple of our recommendations for reconceptualizing activities that are problematic for many children and their families. Embedded within each of these revised activities are multiple story lines that carry limitless images of the I-for-others from which children can draw as they are in the process of crafting an I-for-myself. If we as adults truly believe that all children have the potential to craft strong, positive self-identities, then we must reach out to the members of the diverse families present in our classrooms and communities and integrate them into our curricula. It is our responsibility to provide opportunities for every child to become an insider of the curriculum and to view their family story as one possible representation in a boundless text.

Discussion Questions

1. Can you describe a time when you have unintentionally asked a child to craft a "fairy tale" about a personal aspect of his or her life?

2. What are some of the multiple story lines of the I-for-others that children can draw from as they are in the process of crafting an I-for-myself?
3. What is a teacher's general responsibility to an adopted child in the classroom? In terms of curriculum? In terms of identity formation?

REFERENCES

Bakhtin, M. M. (1990). Author and hero in aesthetic activity. In M. Holquist & V. Liapunov (Eds.) (V. Liapunov, Trans.), *Art and answerability: Early philosophical essays by M. M. Bakhtin* (pp. 4–25). Austin: University of Texas Press. (Original work written ca. 1920)

Grumet, M. R. (1988). *Bitter milk: Women and teaching*. Amherst: The University of Massachusetts Press.

Lindsey, T. P. (in press). Classroom stories of Katrina. *Teachers and Teaching: Theory and Practice*.

McKim, D. (Producer), & Anderson, S. (Director). (2007). *Meet the Robinsons* [motion picture]. United States: Buena Vista Pictures.

Morson, G., & Emerson, C. (1990). *Mikhail Bakhtin: Creation of a prosaics*. Stanford, CA: Stanford University Press.

Sfard, A., & Prusak, A. (2005). Telling identities: In search of an analytic tool for investigating learning as a culturally shaped activity. *Educational Researcher*, *34*(4), 14–22.

PART II

FAMILY-SCHOOL COLLABORATIONS

"I Always Feel They Don't Know Anything About Us": Diverse Families Talk About Their Relations with School

Elizabeth Graue
Margaret Hawkins

> *I think this is kind of going against the grain, but I really like the fact that I didn't know anything about any of my students. I didn't want to hear that they had disciplinary issues. I just liked coming in on a fresh clean slate. I feel like I'm going to be with them probably as much if not more than their parents are going to be with them and that I spend time with them in a different environment, a more academic environment, which the parents might not see them in. In asking a few of my moms, for example, what their child likes to learn about or how their child learns best, I'm sure they could go on and on and on, but that wouldn't necessarily be accurate. And I feel like if I put that question out there, and I don't teach the way that they said works best for their child, that just gives them ammunition.*
> —Erin Newton, Grade 1–2 Teacher, Forward Elementary School

This comment, made by a participant in a group of K–3 teachers focusing on improving home-school relations, represents for us a dominant perspective on the value of family input into schooling. For many educators, home knowledge is a form of bias, something that muddies the professional expertise that can be applied in a classroom. From this perspective, relationships with parents are best limited to one-way flows of information, with parents needing to understand the practices of the school and teachers' assessments of their children, so that they can provide homework (and maybe disciplinary) support at home. Listening to information parents have to offer is seen at best as a waste of time, and at worst as a form of pressure that must be actively resisted.

The comment has within it a number of assumptions. First, teaching is best when it is approached "on a clean slate," unburdened by other knowledge that might not be as accurate as the teacher's. Second, a teacher is with children for more hours per day than a parent so they will have more reliable conceptions of a child's need. [In reality, children spend just 20% of their time in school (Miller, 2003).] Third, it portrays parent-teacher relationships metaphorically as a battle, and one would never want to give the enemy "ammunition."

We find this attitude to be problematic. We compare it to teaching without assessing (you wouldn't want to be swayed by the knowledge that your students have) and antithetical to a view of parent-teacher relationships as partnerships formed to support the education of children. In this chapter we hope to reimagine how schools might connect with home by examining what a small group of parents told us about their relationships with school. We listen to them talk about what they think schools know about their families, what they would like the schools to know, and then we explore how this knowledge might help shape their relationships.

PARENT-INFORMATION FORMS
AS WINDOWS ON THE CHILD AND HOME

Most schools require parents to fill out a parent-information form. This provides a first window into a child's home. What does that window allow us to see? In some schools it is just the facts: names, addresses, pertinent contact information. This type of form allows schools to contact family members with questions (Emily says she is going to LaShonte's after school; is that true?) or to address problems (Joaquin is in the nurse's office, when can you come pick him up?).

In other schools it provides a character sketch of a child, asking parents to describe their child for school personnel. This approach assumes that parents have valuable knowledge about their children that might impact the schooling experience. At the institutional level this information can be used to balance classrooms or cluster children with particular needs. At the classroom level it provides advance information for teachers so that they can interpret a child's actions in relation to historical knowledge. An example of this kind of form is provided in Figure 7.1.

FIGURE 7.1. Family Information Form Focused on the Child

Forward Elementary Parent-Information Form—Kindergarten

Child's full name_____Birthdate_____Boy____Girl____

Name (or nickname) child will use at school_____

Child's address_____Phone number_____

Parents' name(s)_____

Names/ages of brothers or sisters_____

Does your child have any speech difficulties?_____

Does your child have any allergies or other health problems?_____

Does your child have any particular fears?_____

Does your child have special interests?_____

What responsibilities does your child have at home?_____

What form of discipline do you use at home?_____

How well do you feel your child learns new things?_____

Please write "Y" for yes or "N" for no for each of the following characterizations:

___is shy   ___is aggressive (bites, hits, kicks)

___has temper tantrums   ___is well behaved

___cries easily   ___sometimes wets during the day

___makes friends easily   ___has trouble making friends

___likes quiet activities   ___likes to move around frequently

___is moody   ___cannot sit still

___is artistic   ___is musical   ___is athletic

What are your expectations for the kindergarten program? What specific things
would you like to see happen this year?_____

_____

_____

_____

_____

In still other schools, it opens a conversation between partners in the educational process, seeking information about the context of home but also asking what might be learned to enrich the relationship. There are three keys to making this type of sharing relevant: (1) Be clear about who has access to the information; (2) be committed to doing something that will benefit families; and (3) provide culturally relevant language translation (in some cases that will mean translation of the form; in others it will require resources for oral translations).

Similarly, many schools have beginning-of-the-year parent conferences. Some teachers use this time to outline curricular and behavioral expectations. Others use it as a time to begin making connections with families and learning about them. One such example is Montford Elementary's Hopes and Dreams conferences, where parents are asked to describe their hopes for their children and those hopes are documented as input for the child's educational program.

We argue that to fully support children's learning, home-school relationships must have a two-way flow of information, so that parents are kept apprised of school and classroom events, curricular and instructional practices, and their children's performance; and teachers are privy to family needs, interests, histories, and events. Further, teachers must know how to incorporate knowledge of families into their instruction in ways that connect children to learning. Although it might appear that schools are much too busy to cultivate a relationship with the many parents they serve, we argue that it is vital: Reorienting home-school interaction from parent-involvement to home-school relationship is exactly what needs to happen.

To make the case, we analyze discussions with 13 parents from diverse backgrounds who shared with us their perceptions of what schools know about their families and their hopes for what schools would know. We explore their goals for their children, their experiences with school personnel, and their conceptions of their roles as parents. The conversations constitute data from a study we conducted on one diverse school community, interviewing African American, Hmong, Latino, and White parents (representative of the school population) of fourth-grade children. Methodologically, the sample represents research-participant identity issues. Graue interviewed parents of her son's friends, White middle-class professionals who shared her neighborhood. Hawkins interviewed African American, Hmong, and Latino parents with whom she shared no community affiliation. Representing families from five neighborhoods that came together for integration purposes in an elementary school community, these conversations illustrate the strengths that parents bring to school, the complexity and narrowness of mainstream views about "good parenting," and the degree to which many schools miss opportunities to connect with families.

What Parents Think the School Knows About Their Families

In our conversations with parents we explored how they get information about school and how they communicate information to educators. We got some fascinating responses when we asked families what they thought the school knew about them. On the hopeful end of the continuum, many parents thought the school had general information about their families: family members, housing arrangements, language needs. For example, Lauren, a White, middle-class, divorced mother, was worried that her son might be teased because of her marital status. She made a point of letting the school know that her son spent time with both his mom and his dad in different houses:

> They have us write those profiles and I write about our situation with him having two houses and that it's amicable and that he seems fine with it so that the teacher knows what is going on with it. I think it's important just in case there was going to be some bullying involved. I don't know if kids pick on each other about things like whether their parents are split up.

Lauren worked to normalize what she felt was an atypical living pattern by making sure that teachers understood how her son spent his time. Denise, a White, middle-class, married mother of two, focused on her household census and their family disposition toward learning:

> I think they know who Don [dad] is, they know who I am, they know who Bart [brother] is, so they know Alicia's [focus child] family. That's important. I think they know that we're involved and committed to our kids' learning. I think that's what they need to know.

This sentiment of knowing general things was echoed by Ramon, a Latino, working-class father of three:

> I don't believe that they know a lot . . . just the members of the family maybe, the progress of the kids . . . or possibly the participation we have as parents in the school . . . after that I don't think they know much! Well, maybe they know a little bit of the culture of Mexico, but as a community I speak generally about the country of Mexico . . . but not details of family . . . maybe just general knowledge.

Knowing the members and marital status of the family, something usually found on most parent-information forms, is one element of school knowledge. But both Denise and Ramon alluded to another element of school knowledge—they thought the school saw them as "involved." This is a form of knowledge that a number of parents have: it reflects positively on the family, and on the child, when school staff perceive that parents are "involved" in their children's schooling. When families are involved, the teacher shares the burden of educating the student. The meaning of *involvement* is seemingly unitary but is in fact diverse and culturally determined. It is framed by the goals that families have for their children, their views of their roles as parents, the opportunities set by the school for involvement by the limits and affordances of work and home life, and perceived skills and resources, such as language (Hanafin & Lynch, 2002).

While "involved" was a label that many of the parents used and valued positively, others talked about other inferences the school might make about their home context. Amy, a White, middle-class, married mom of two, wryly noted that school personnel probably thought she wasn't married:

> I suspect that since they never see Parker [children's dad] at conferences and I don't wear a wedding ring, they suspect I'm a single mom. And that may tag me. I suspect that everybody gets tagged. That tag implies something less than a fully intact family. Or whatever the correct language is. And when Anna was having so much trouble behaving herself at school, that was one of the first questions that would come up: "Is there a father involved?"

The notion of "tagging" also came up in our discussion with Sally, who described a chain of inference that educators used to place families in categories:

> They know the kid has a lunch every day and doesn't eat hot lunch very often, and isn't in a bracket that he's buying breakfast. He's not in an after-school program. Those are little indicators of economic status. Economic status is an indicator, I think, of class. Which is an indicator of how involved the parents are—I don't say that in a negative way. I just think it's true. You know, it's a middle-class value.

Both Amy and Sally recognized that knowledge is not neutral—that it exists within an interpretive framework that individuals and institutions use to make sense. Schools (not families) label some children as "at-risk." Indicators used in assigning such a label are, in fact, living in poverty, coming from a single-parent household, speaking a language other than English as a first language, or having a summer birthday. "Being involved" or "being a single-mom" or "not being in an after-school program" are, indeed, all indicators of something; they are part of an invisible school code. What they indicate is complex and has value and consequences beyond the school-information form. And parents who are savvy and know the code use proactive strategies to present their children and their family in a positive light.

A number of the parents did not feel that the school knew much about them. The forms of knowing they referred to ranged from the personal to the cultural. In Ramon's quote above we heard that the school had generalized knowledge but not much else. While some parents were OK with a census approach to school knowledge, LaShonda, an African American mother of five in the middle of a divorce put it most bluntly when we asked her what the school knows. In a disappointed tone she answered:

> Nothing. Other than that I have two at Roosevelt and two at Forward and one at home. I don't think they know anything else.

Claire, a White, married mother of three noted with exasperation:

> I always feel like they don't know anything about us . . . like I've often wondered if they know that I'm a professor of Classics. I mean, I don't know why that should be so important but I feel like I am an educator—*use me,* you know. Okay, I teach at the college level but I sometimes wonder if they even read those sheets that you fill out.

Feeling unrecognized by the school was unsettling to these mothers, in a general sense for LaShonda, and for Claire, because she felt she had resources that were untapped by the school.

Jaime, a Latino father of three, pointed to markers like language and involvement but did not feel that the school had specific knowledge about him or his family:

> They know we're Latino—we speak Spanish at home—they see that we try to get involved in activities when we need to and that is why the principal sometimes invites me . . . they know me and my wife are working hard. . . . They know we came here years ago, because my daughter went to Forward. They ask me where I'm from, but I don't think they know a lot about my background.

Jaime's response indicates that the school was scratching the surface in their getting to know his family. He had received invitations from the principal to participate, and school people had asked questions about his country of origin. But beyond that, knowledge was limited.

All of these responses are meaningful when juxtaposed with a question we also asked in our interviews. Parental perceptions about school knowledge are given meaning in relation to family desires for the school to have a particular type of knowledge about families. We turn to that next.

What Parents Want Schools to Know About Their Families

We asked parents to talk to us about what they wished school people knew about their families. Their responses focused on the personal and cultural. While most figured the school had the demographics covered, they wanted more contour to the knowledge. These contours ranged from intensely personal to social or cultural knowledge and values that shape action. And it was in their responses to this question that differences between families of English language learners and native English-speaking U.S. families came to light.

For the U.S. natives, the knowledge they wanted to impart to educators was personal or family-related. For example, Denise talked about how the whole school knew when her husband Don had cancer, their child's teacher had taught the class about chemotherapy and its effects on the body when a very frail Don was a regular volunteer in Alicia's classroom. This type of personal knowledge was important to Denise and represented the kind of relationship she wished for between home and school. On a less personal note, both Amy and Sally focused on making sure that the school understood their family values. In Amy's case their family did not participate in sports or watch much TV:

> Every year you're given a form to supposedly help with teacher
> choice and we all kind of fill it out with a smirk. But I make a point
> of filling out that form and I always tell them that we don't watch
> TV and we're not at all involved in organized sports. And those are
> values that we hold dear. Because I think there are some teachers
> that organized sports and TV are central to their curriculum and I
> really don't want that for my kids.

Sally wanted the school to know that they didn't want a lot of homework:

> I would want them to know that [I don't like homework] in a way
> that's not offensive or makes them feel that I feel they're not doing

a good job. I think they must not realize how much we just don't want that. And how much I just don't believe that it's right.

In contrast, Tong, a Hmong immigrant who spoke to us through his son who served as translator, focused on cultural rather than personal issues, connecting individuals in a family to practices rooted in history and culture:

> I think it would be great that teachers have knowledge of family's background. . . . Communication would be really helpful, if they communicate how the child is doing at school. It's hard for us because we don't have a formal education. . . . It's just we were waiting for the communication of problems from the school to us. [The school needs to know] some of the rituals, cultural practices that we do. . . . I think if they knew, it would be helpful. What I think they should know is for them to understand the reason why we are here . . . and just accept us as just another person in the community.

Tong's wide-ranging description of knowledge he would like schools to have includes what information he wanted from the school, but it was focused primarily on knowledge of culture—including markers of cultural affiliation, like rituals—and a sense of why they immigrated to the United States. This knowledge was connected in Tong's mind to acceptance.

Ramon articulated a parallel sense of knowing beyond the local education scene. He thought it would be good for teachers to see what the schools taught in Mexico:

> Maybe they should get a copy or guide from the public education in Mexico and see if there is anything that they can benefit from and make their program better by copying something that is done over there; and also maybe they should learn something more of the traditions of the culture and things that are important because maybe it might help the kids feel more like they belong and they hear those things being taught in school and they hear us talking about it at home and they are going to be more interested in those things.

While Tong is focused on acceptance, Ramon seems to explicitly say that if teachers had more knowledge of children's home cultures and cultural histories and then incorporated this knowledge into classroom instruction, children would be more interested in learning. Both responses focus on a form of engagement. In Tong's case, the engagement is related to tolerance, or even more, recognition of a group's presence and potential contribution to the community. For Ramon, the engagement sought is for his children, modeled through shared conversations between home and school.

Why There Are Differences in Parents' Responses

We posit that there are differences between White parents' responses and minority parents' responses, with White parents focusing on their individual family circumstances, values, and characteristics, and minority families on group or cultural ones. While the differences may be attributable to what has been identified a *collective* perspective as opposed to an *individual* one (Trumbull, Greenfield, Rothstein-Fisch, & Quiroz, 2001), they may also result from the fact that families from nonmainstream language and cultural backgrounds have experienced barriers to communications and connections that mainstream families have not. Middle-class White families share a common culture with schools: Not only do they look like the teachers and administrators, but they have rich and detailed understandings of how school works, how schools place value on families and children, what behaviors are expected, what parental involvement should look like, and the nature of academic practices. White, middle-class families and teachers take these for granted, enabling them to focus on individual concerns rooted in their wish to ensure the well-being of their children. Even so, school staff may perceive their attempts at involvement, meant to shape their children's education as they feel is best, as interference, thus creating a barrier to developing a partnership. Minority families also wish to support and protect their children but have different conceptions of how schools expect them to do so, and how their family structure, involvement strategies, and parenting may be perceived by schools. These differences in experiences and understandings, when paired with language and physical difference, get translated into deficits that also serve as barriers to collaboration for student learning. These barriers are invisible and therefore pernicious, formed through normative views of good parenting and teaching. Making the barriers visible is a first step in disabling them. But recognizing them is only the first step. Promoting action is the next. We spend the rest of the chapter on action that is responsive to families' desires and capacities to form relationships with schools.

RESPONSIVE ACTION FOR HOME-SCHOOL RELATIONS

There are many metaphors we could use to depict the connection between home and school. Within the metaphors are implied actions, scripts and roles for participants, and hoped-for results (Lakoff & Johnson, 1980). We think it is helpful to understand the metaphors that underlie practice as they say much about the assumptions we bring and the actions we ultimately undertake. We'll begin with a metaphor that shapes our work. One of us has an assessment background and it has shaped the way we think about information. From an assessment perspective, a guiding principle has always been that collecting information implies action, and that the data sought should always be linked to a question of interest and a potential action for improvement. Simple enough. If we go back to the quote that started this chapter, the teacher was right *not* to ask for information from families because if she did, she would have been answerable to their responses in some way. The information-action rule becomes more complicated when it is given an ethical twist. Whose needs should dictate what information is collected? And what potential good can be achieved? Let's look at several examples that allow us to play out the assessment metaphor and related ethical implications.

When the connection between home and school is portrayed as parent involvement, it is frequently a type of subcontracting or outsourcing, in which educators provide families with tasks to support the school. The idea is to engage families in education, as if it were possible that families could not already be involved. It requires good information on how to contact potential supporters and though sometimes it assesses capacity, it is most often undertaken with a mainstream model of appropriate participation. This can be done in terms of volunteering in the classroom, fund-raising for the school, supervising homework, and providing resources like healthy contexts (good nutrition, adequate sleep), classroom supplies (backpack, pencils, glue sticks, tissues, and so on) and supplementary resources (money for field trips, poster board for special projects, computers for a PowerPoint presentation).

All of these types of involvement contain a cost for families—flexibility of work schedules or alternate care for young children, financial resources, knowledge—and though they have potential to enrich family experience, that potential is secondary to the benefits derived by the school. Through this kind of involvement, schools benefit. They gain supplementary staffing, financial resources, and expertise. Recognition of school privilege in this approach is not easy as the normative power of mainstream involvement is incredibly strong. For parents, this form of involvement is sometimes in conflict with their family needs and values. For example, when Elizabeth asked Allan, a White, middle-class father, to talk about different ways parents could be involved in school, he answered:

> I've kind of chosen not to be in the classroom . . . in Alex's [son]
> case, that tended to be mostly because Natasha [daughter] was

home . . . I have a strong underlying feeling about giving my child an experience that is exclusive of parents. You know, not involving parents . . . I just think it's an independence thing . . . it's partly because I feel like once you start that kind of stuff, then there's an expectation and a level of involvement that they expect. And because we do other things. You know, like we do a long family vacation. . . We take our kids out of school for family vacations. We always attend their events like when Alex has piano recitals or Little League games. We're around enough that I feel like it's just one place where, let's don't do this thing.

Allan was finding this approach difficult to maintain with his second child, a daughter in kindergarten who regularly asked when her mom was going to come work in her classroom, where many other parents volunteered. While Allan focused on the classroom, Denise felt that traditional involvement through the Parent Teacher Organization (PTO) was often counterproductive:

I really don't see PTO participation as something that is—it's good for the school, but I don't know that it's good for the particular family and child. . . . I think it can be negative because. . . people use their position to get things that they think are good for their kids but aren't necessarily good for their kids, and they're less likely to give a teacher or a principal the benefit of the doubt I think . . . because they know everything, because they know this teacher, they know that, they know this. So they use their information in ways that are detrimental to their kids.

She recounted an experience where she had facilitated a parent group for a school improvement team and was surprised when an African American mom, who had been silent for the whole discussion session, talked her ear off at the very end. Denise was shocked by this burst of participation because it didn't follow the rules as she knew them. In this process-oriented setup, participants were expected to have conversations during a discussion period, not sit silently only to deliver a monologue at the end of the allotted time. What she first took as rudeness or naiveté was something else entirely. It finally dawned on Denise that the meeting genre of the PTO was White, middle-class culture:

This parent was obviously not socialized into that mode of communication . . . so [we need] more understanding of different ways that different people communicate. I mean, that's why the PTO is only attended by White upper-middle-class [parents]—they're using Roberts' rules of order!

STRUCTURAL SUPPORTS
FOR CULTURALLY RELEVANT INVOLVEMENT

This reticence was something we heard from almost all the mainstream parents, who were leery about being part of the official parent-teacher organizational channels. This reluctance was less pronounced among the parents of color. One reason this might be is that the school had developed subgroup organizations called Parent-Empowerment Groups (PEG) for African American, Latino, and Hmong families. These groups were designed around the particular needs and desires articulated by each subgroup and included teachers who helped make explicit links to school. Recognizing that different people needed different types of information and that the needs are not only individual but also cultural, members of the Forward and Roosevelt school communities formed these subgroups. The main premise of these groups was that all families have valuable knowledge to contribute to the school and alternate options to the PTO were necessary to create avenues for input and dissemination of information for minority families.

The school formed three groups representative of the population of the schools: Latino, Hmong, and African American. They used school resource staff and other liaisons—those who were insiders to the respective communities—to spread word of the meetings. They provided food, child care, transportation, and interpreters as needed by the families. At least two teachers volunteered to coordinate each subgroup (though all staff were always welcome), ensuring some consistency throughout the year. The first meeting was spent setting agendas, listening to questions and concerns of families, and learning what they wanted to know about and discuss.

The topics of the meetings addressed issues identified by the families as well as by school staff. For example, parents wanted information on conferences, saying that they didn't understand what they were for or what their role was. Staff met prior to the PEG meeting to discuss what to cover in the meeting, and discovered that conferences meant different things to different teachers. Ultimately, they used the meeting to model conferences, with sample interactions that everybody could discuss. Not only did parents better understand the conferences, it also resulted in deeper reflection by teachers on what conferences can and do accomplish. In another example, parents wanted to know more about special education—what it was, and why so many minority students were receiving these services. A meeting was devoted to special education, resulting in heightened staff and parent understandings that the practices of school are essentially cultural. Not knowing school practices is disadvantageous to certain children and their families and as a result lessens the ability of teachers to meet their needs.

Conversely, school staff wanted parents to understand issues surrounding homework, and devoted a meeting to discussions of how parents could support their children at home. They stressed, for example, that even if parents couldn't read English, they could have their children read to them or the younger children could do a "book walk" in their native language. *Book walks* use illustrations to infer meaning and are often done before read-alouds in early childhood classrooms. One particular project that resulted from this meeting was the creation of special backpacks that contained the identical book in English and the home language, plus a tape recording of the book in English, so that children could read with their parents. In another example, teachers wanted parents to understand the particular math curriculum the school used, which involved supporting a deep understanding of mathematics through reasoning, and made that the topic of one meeting.

These meetings had good rates of participation and families spoke highly of them. We offer them as an example of how that schools might go "outside the box" to create partnerships with parents. The meetings accomplished many things for both the teachers and the parents. For the parents, they served as an introduction to the "insider knowledge" that Sally displayed earlier, to the ways of thinking and knowing and the practices of the school that might otherwise be invisible. They brought parents, who may never have come to the school before, inside the building and began to familiarize them with the environment. They supported the creation of communities of parents, so that parents did not feel isolated but were part of a network, thus providing a real tool for empowerment. It sent a message that school staff wanted to hear what they had to say; that their voices matter here. For teachers, these meetings brought them closer to these communities. They broke down stereotypes around ethnic groups, so that teachers realized that all Latino or all Hmong or African American parents are not the same but have different interests, needs, and opinions. They enabled staff to have a deeper understanding of what it feels like to be "other." As one teacher said, "You know how it feels to go into a room and there's only three White people there. That's how they must feel all the time when they come to school." And they challenged teachers to rethink some of the taken-for-granted practices of school and their effects on diverse families.

The groups created a venue where teachers and staff could hear parents' voices and discuss concerns and issues; thus they began the creation of a partnership. They were not a panacea, however. While they did involve parents who otherwise did not come into the schools or attend meetings, they did not equalize the power differential among parents. The middle-class, mainstream parents still ran the PTO, and it was the PTO that sponsored events and fund-raisers, and thereby had the power and voice to make decisions and purchases based on their own perceptions of children's and parents' needs. The barriers between different groups of parents remained, as the Parent Empowerment Groups were not integrated with the PTO, nor with each other. In addition, all teachers were not involved in PEG meetings, thus limiting the powerful effects the interactions had on the teachers who were involved.

THE DEVELOPMENT OF
MEANINGFUL HOME-SCHOOL RELATIONSHIPS

As we have claimed in other work (Graue & Hawkins, 2005), all aspects of effective home-school partnerships are relational, and building good relationships takes not only effort, but a significant amount of time. The Parent-Empowerment Groups made great strides in establishing relationships with minority parents. The groups addressed some of the concerns articulated above by Tong and Ramon, as teachers began to learn about the cultures of the various ethnic groups, as well as their attitudes and values. Still unaddressed, however, were the concerns articulated by both minority and mainstream parents, who want teachers to know about their family's values, beliefs, and activities. And while the Parent-Empowerment Groups were set up deliberately to address relationships with the groups that the school perceived to be marginalized, no such efforts were made to establish relationships or collaborate with mainstream families. Indeed, we amply documented a culture of protection against such families, as evidenced by the opening quote.

A one-way relationship isn't much of a relationship at all. Limiting ourselves to telling families what we want or what they should do does not take advantage of the rich experiences and knowledge that every family brings with them to their children's education. Nor does it respond to what all families need and want from schools to create partnerships that effectively support children's learning. We acknowledge that the work involved in building meaningful, productive relationships with parents is sensitive, difficult, and time-consuming, especially when the diversity among families creates divergent desires and needs. Yet we agree with Karen Mapp (2003) that the result is worth the work:

> When school personnel initiate and engage in practices that welcome parents to the school, honor their contributions, and connect them to the school community through an emphasis on the children, these practices then cultivate and sustain respectful, caring, and meaningful relationships between parents and school staff. . . . these relationships enhance [parents'] desire to be involved and influence how they participate in their children's educational development. (p. 35)

Trustful relationships are, indeed, the key to effective partnerships. It is up to schools to reenvision what collaborative relationships might look like given the power relations between home and school. Taking an approach that assumes families have assets that contribute to schooling, that the home is an important educational context that can and should be complementary to the classroom, opens up collaborative opportunities that have the potential to enrich everyone's experience.

Discussion Questions

1. What have been your experiences with home-school relations? What models of the role of home and school are enacted in your experience?
2. Equitable home-school relations utilize the expertise of both families and educators. What are some of the forms of knowledge each brings to schooling? How can they be used to enrich children's educational experiences?
3. Brainstorm strategies that allow diverse families and educators to teach each other about the goals, resources, and values that support the children they share.

REFERENCES

Graue, M. E., & Hawkins, M. (2005). Relations, refractions, and reflections in research with children. In L. D. Soto & B. B. Swadener (Eds.), *Power and voice in research with children* (pp. 45–54). New York: Peter Lang.

Hanafin, J., & Lynch, A. (2002). Peripheral voices: Parental involvement, social class, and educational disadvantage. *British Journal of Sociology of Education*, 23(1), 35–49.

Lakoff, G., & Johnson, M. (1980). *Metaphors we live by*. Chicago: University of Chicago Press.

Mapp, K. (2003). Having their say: Parents describe why and how they are engaged in their children's learning. *School Community Journal, 13*(1), 35–64.

Miller, B. (2003). Critical hours: Afterschool programs and educational success. Quincy, MA: Nellie Mae Education Foundation. Retrieved October 11, 2006, from http://www.nmefdn.org/uploads/Critical_Hours.pdf

Trumbull, E., Greenfield, P. M., Rothstein-Fisch, C., & Quiroz, B. (2001). *Bridging cultures between home and school: A guide for teachers*. Mahwah, NJ: Erlbaum.

CHAPTER 8

Debunking the Myths About the Urban Family: A Constructed Conversation

Rochelle Brock

Dear Reader,

Why are you reading this chapter? Are you interested in learning more about the myths of urban families? Are you curious as to how to debunk these myths? Are you committed to social justice in education and therefore reading everything you find to help you in that quest? Or are you reading this chapter because it was assigned to you by a professor at your university somewhere in the United States? That's okay—as long as you are honest I can work with you. I believe if you are reading this chapter, then you care about urban families.

As a future teacher, your goal should be, first, to understand the myths about the urban family, and second, to understand how these myths (if left unchecked) color how you see and interact with urban families and urban students. The subliminal messages within this chapter—"You will care" and "You will be a seeker-of-knowledge"—are designed to put you on the path to becoming a teacher-scholar committed to change and dedicated to the education of all children. It is this dedication that will foster in you the Socratic method: questioning, leading to answers, leading to more questions. When we question, we unearth deeper meanings, find bigger truths, and ultimately embark on a journey toward becoming a great teacher. Being a great teacher entails becoming an intellectual, a researcher, a social worker, a parent, and a community activist.

What do we need to ask ourselves as we prepare to become an urban teacher? What assumptions do we hold about urban families prior to entering a classroom? What happens when these assumptions go un-

checked? How do these assumptions affect our interactions with an urban family or an urban student? Realizing that we all hold certain assumptions and biases, it is important that we continuously seek the knowledge
needed to debunk these myths and assumptions.

I speak from a place of understanding; I know the biases and assumptions we all hold. When I first moved to Gary, Indiana, I came with certain
assumptions based on what I had been told and what I had read about
my new home: crime, drugs, violence, poor schools, and the list goes on.
Instead I found a place filled with promise and hope; people working to
make the best life for themselves and their children.

You might be surprised to learn that we have had a "Four-Star" school
in Gary for the past 16 years. Banneker Achievement Center—98% of the
students are African American and 40% get free or reduced-price lunch—
flew in the face of everything I had read about Gary. Although test scores
are not the only assessment of how well a school is doing, Banneker's
test scores are indicative of a successful school. The third-grade students'
passing scores in English/Language Arts (99%) and Mathematics (94%)
were the highest scores obtained among all third graders in the entire
state of Indiana. Like Banneker's third graders, its fourth-, fifth-, and sixth-
grade classes were also listed among the "Best Performing Schools" in
the Northwest Indiana Region, with 93–98% of those students passing
both tests. (For specific grade percentages, see www.garycsc.k12.in.us/
Banneker/html/history.html.)

Banneker is a gifted-only magnet school that draws from many schools
in Gary. It is important to note that not only are the children at Banneker successful at taking and passing standardized tests, they also are
involved in music and dance, making them more well-rounded children.
The teachers, the parents, and the principal of Banneker Achievement
Center will tell you that the key to their success is parent/grandparent
involvement. In contrast to the myth that poor, inner-city parents do not
care about their children, in Gary we have a shining example of what can
happen when teachers understand, respect, and work to involve parents
in their child's education.

After a brief introduction to the theory and methodology behind my
work, you will find below an in-depth discussion of the myths and realities
of urban parents and students in the form of a fictional constructed conversation with my preservice teachers during the first day of the course
titled Schools and Families in Urban Education.

Sincerely,

Rochelle

BLACK FEMINIST THEORY AND CRITICAL PEDAGOGY

A very basic definition of *theory* is "something that helps us make sense of the world." When we attempt to understand any problem, it is necessary to use as many theories as we need. For my purposes, I use Black feminist theory and critical pedagogy as ways to demythologize the urban family. When used separately, each theory helps me ask the right questions and when used together, they help me understand the answers I receive. Black feminist thought is a useful tool in framing this chapter because it furnishes the space for voice by challenging the prevailing approaches to studying oppressed groups (Collins, 1991). *Voice* equals the words, thoughts, and spirit of "the people." "The people" equals those whose words, thoughts, and spirits have been silenced, ignored, and subjugated. A false notion exists that the oppressed identify with the powerful and are therefore seen as less human and less intellectual, and thus less-capable of interpreting their oppression. A feminist perspective allows a language of critique to be both developed and utilized that questions this assumption. This language of critique is developed through an epistemological framework, which is useful in understanding the urban family. *Epistemology*, the study of how knowledge is constructed, lets us construct the questions to delve more deeply into the realities of the urban family. Moreover, we are better able to understand the answers we receive from those questions.

Critical pedagogy frames schooling and teaching within a critical dynamic that affords students an ability to name their world, to critically reflect on self and society, and to have the agency to act for change (Giroux, 1997; Kincheloe, 2004; McLaren, 2000; Pozo, 2003; Wink, 1997). This ability changes the student from an object to be constructed to a subject in the construction of their own knowledge. As such, critical pedagogy speaks to issues of power, of how power is distributed to some and kept from others, and of what influence it has on schooling. Critical pedagogy forces the student and the teacher to view the world critically, taking nothing for granted but instead questioning the reason behind various systems of domination. Critical pedagogy is the framing tool that provides a language of critique to question the structures of the education system in general and classroom pedagogy in particular. According to Giroux and Simon (1989), *critical pedagogy* is "a deliberate attempt to influence how and what knowledge and identities are produced within and among particular sets of social relations" (p. 239). From this statement you can see the connection of critical pedagogy to the study of epistemology I've explained above.

USING CONSTRUCTED CONVERSATION
TO ASSESS URBAN-FAMILY MYTHS

The essence of the *constructed conversation* is the "use of dialogue in assessing knowledge claims," which is an important characteristic of a Black feminist epistemology (Collins, 1991, pp. 212–215). A constructed conversation is based on the group-conversation method, which is a culturally relevant, qualitative ethnographic strategy used by King and Mitchell (1995) in *Black Mother To Sons*. They state that the group-conversation method developed by DuBois and Li (1971) to "reduce social tensions," was revised and adapted by them to "help participants identify shared experiences and to facilitate the discussion of highly personal or deeply felt emotional issues" (King & Mitchell, 1995, p. 3). Taking the group-conversation method one step further, the constructed conversation is based on the tenets of Black feminist thought and allows a fictional dialogue to personalize the subject by creating a connectedness between the words (Brock, 2005). A constructed conversation asks you to momentarily suspend reality.

Hooks (1989), asserts that *dialogue* implies talk between two subjects, not the speech of subject and object. According to Collins (1991), "a primary epistemological assumption underlying the use of dialogue in assessing knowledge claims is that connectedness rather than separation is an essential component of the knowledge-validation process" (p. 212). Hill Collins further states that people become human and empowered only in the context of a community, and only when they "become seekers of the type of connections, interactions, and meetings that lead to harmony" (p. 185). Dialogue allows this to happen.

Dialogue presupposes that we talk *with* each other, not *at* each other. In addition, dialogue is an important aspect of both African American and Latino(a) language; understanding that language is more than words and cannot be a singular event, as in one-sided talk. As the word *dialogue* denotes, a feminist epistemology demands discourse. In order for ideas to be tested and validated, everyone in the group must participate. As in the first characteristic, which speaks of the importance of community as well as knowledge and wisdom, dialogue occurs within a community of individuals.

The use of dialogue in assessing knowledge claims supports the methodology of constructed conversation. The method of constructed conversation is "in tune with" the African American and Latino tradition of dialogue within a community setting. In addition, the constructed conversation methodology allows research to be presented in a more realistic format.

A CONSTRUCTED CONVERSATION:
SCHOOLS AND FAMILIES IN URBAN EDUCATION, DAY 1

Characters: Dr. Brock—professor, Black
Valerie—student, Black, working-class
Ben—student, White, working-class
Charlotte—student, Black, middle-class
Bob—student, White, lower-class

Setting: It is 3:30 on a Thursday afternoon. Dr. Brock sits in her office staring at the clock on her desk. In 20 minutes class will begin. The thoughts are whirling through her mind—the first day of a new semester is always a hopeful time, as well as a time of apprehension. Who will her students be? What knowledge will they bring into class? What are their assumptions that she, as the professor, will need to fight? How can she make sure that by the semester's end these students are on the right road to understanding all of the intricacies of urban students? With no more time for reflecting, Dr. Brock gathers her materials for class and walks down the long hallway to room 400.

What's This Class About?

Dr. Brock: Welcome to Schools and Families in Urban Education. In this class we will discuss and analyze the multitude of factors that affect schools and families. Teaching is the best profession you could have chosen, and I promise this will be the best class you will take as you prepare to teach. I may be somewhat biased in this assertion, but I believe it nevertheless. By the semester's end, I want each of you to understand the various assumptions and realities of families in urban America. More important, I want you to begin to view schools as a central part of the community, and understand that our job as educators is to create the linkage between "socially marginalized groups and the school" (Grinberg & Goldfarb, 1998. p. 135). I need to warn you from the start that to get as much as possible from this class, you cannot be afraid to talk about race. Typically when we talk about the urban family, we are talking about people of color, specifically African American and Latino. Therefore we have to talk about race, stereotypes, racism, sexism, and inequality; all of the subjects we as a nation have a difficult time addressing. This class is your safe space to tackle these delicate issues: Like Vegas, what happens in this class stays in this class.

As prospective teachers, you "need to receive . . . information about the histories, contributions, and current status of the various racial, ethnic, and cultural groups that comprise our society" (Zeichner et al., 1996, p. 9). It is important that you understand the impact of the social, historical, and economic changes on urban families and the relationship these changes have on the nature of schooling for children. Knowing the connection between school and family is extremely important for you to accept as a future teacher.

Now, let me give you a clue to my pedagogy: It's through—and with—constant dialogue that learning takes place. Remember we are not just talking; we are digging deep so as to ferret out the various aspects of the urban family. Throughout the semester, discussion will be the focus of this class, and it will be through honest discussion that is grounded in research that we will come to truly understand the relationship of families and urban schools. So let's start the dialogue from the beginning. What do we know about the urban family?

Myth and Assumptions About Urban Families

Charlotte: When I hear *urban*, I immediately think low-income.

Dr. Brock: So *urban* is synonymous with *poor*?

Ben: Yeah, I agree with Charlotte and I hate it, but typically when I hear *urban*, I think minorities who are poor and do drugs—you know crime and gangs.

Dr. Brock: Let's go with that. Two things: Why and Who? Why do we immediately think low-income when discussing urban, and whom do we hear it from?

Charlotte: News. News stories constantly show urban neighborhoods as poor, decaying, crime-ridden, welfare-fraud, full of drugs . . .

Ben: Yeah, but they are not making up the news—I mean they are not fabricating stories. That stuff really happens.

Dr. Brock: I want everyone to keep a glossary of new words and concepts, and here are your first two terms: *hyperreality* and *reified*. When we discuss *hyperreality* in relation to the media's portrayal of urban environments, we are talking about their portrayal as being exaggerated in relation to reality. In other words, all you see and hear is the negative and nothing else, so you come to believe the negative without information to refute it. Now that brings us to our second term, *reified*: when an abstract concept is regarded as concrete. In our mind, urban and poverty become inextricably linked. Not only do we link urban with poverty, but also we instantly juxtapose urban, poor, and dysfunctional, making them one married concept. Words carry a great deal of power and are the perfect medium through which miscommunication occurs. They carry with them a set of baggage, or preconceived notions. These preconceptions, or emotive-sensation words, that become instilled in us are based in part on subjective interpretations. We experience language and that experience gives meaning to the word. Our definition comes from what the word represents and how it fits into our individual ideology. With this in mind, what does *poor* mean? What do we visualize when we hear that word?

Valerie: I visualize someone on welfare. You know, food stamps, WIC, government cheese—not that I know anything about government cheese.

Dr. Brock: Good, the emotive sensation behind the word *poor* makes us immediately jump to certain conclusions. When you become aware of this, you can easily see that what we visualize might be negative, problematic, pathological. First, I can tell you that government cheese makes the best grilled-cheese sandwiches—something about the way it melts. Second, we assume certain things about urban areas without any statistics to back up these assumptions. You might be surprised to know that according to a 2004 study from the Urban Institute only "5% of all low-income families with a full-time, full-year worker receive Temporary Assistance for Needy Families benefits" (2005, p. 1). Despite this fact, the myth persists that a majority of urban families are on the government dole.

If we believe that urban families are on welfare, it goes without saying that they are not working or refuse to work. To understand the inaccuracies in this belief, we first must understand that even before the recession of 2008–09, labor markets had significantly decreased, which means fewer jobs, higher unemployment, and lower incomes. Although "the vast majority of low-income parents today are working, [they are] still struggling to make ends meet: struggling to find and keep a toehold in a changing labor market, to keep up with their bills, to pay the spiraling costs of essentials like health-care and housing, and to raise children with a chance of future success" (Urban Institute, 2005, p. 1). Although parents and children in low-income families are more financially vulnerable than those in higher income families, as with any family, urban parents are attempting to balance work and family life (Goldfarb, 2004; Urban Institute, 2005).

Poverty is still a blot on America's conscience. Let me give you some statistics:

In 2004, there were 37 million Americans—12.7 percent of the population—who lived in poverty. One-third of America's poor are White, with a 10.5 percent poverty rate. The rate for African-Americans and Hispanics is twice that of Whites, at more than 20 percent. Black and Hispanic median family income is 38 percent below the median income of White families. Nationally, one out of six children—12.9 million children—live in poverty. One out of every three Black and Hispanic children lives in poverty. Many poor people are people who work full-time, year-round but don't earn enough to lift themselves and their families out of poverty. Of 9.3 million people in poverty whom did some work in 2004, there were 2.8 million on the job full-time, year-round. Another 6.5 million worked full-time for part of the year but remained in poverty (Ginsberg, 2006, pp. 4–5).

The causes and effects of poverty are much more intricate and interrelated than sound bites about urban poverty. In order to even begin to understand what is taking place with urban families, we need to contextualize our discussion. When we decontextualize a family living in poverty, we fail to see the multitude of circumstances that have placed them there because we are viewing them separate from the world they inhabit. For example, poverty is maintained in large part through the low hourly wages of the working poor. According to the Urban Institute (2005), a low-income family receives their income from low-paying jobs. It is extremely difficult to move to a higher income level when the hourly wage grows at such an insignificant rate.

We have research from the Urban Institute that refutes the assumptions about urban families, yet these and other negative assumptions persist. As a society, we falsely believe that there is an overrepresentation of Black single women having children out of wedlock. In accordance with this, Anderson (1990) states, "in this way, persistent poverty affects norms of the ghetto-culture, such as the high value placed on children" (p. 127). The thought is that for low-income Black women having children is a form of status and a rite of passage into adulthood. He goes on to say that "it may be less a question of whether the girl is going to have children than of when, for she may see herself as having little to lose and something to gain by becoming pregnant" (p. 127).

Unfortunately, this myth is widely believed and serves to construct single female-headed households as both monolithic and dysfunctional. In addition, despite the fact that welfare policies have changed (McKernan & Ratcliffe, 2006), there is still the belief that minority women have children to receive some form of welfare. Since children are capital and a status symbol, they therefore cannot be loved and nurtured in the same way as children from traditional middle-class families. As in the other assumptions we have discussed, this, too, can be easily dismissed with some basic facts. In reality, over the last 3 decades the birthrates among Black women has fallen by 13%. In contrast, during the same period the birthrates for single White women increased (McKernan & Ratcliffe, 2006).

Charlotte: I don't get it. If all of this is true then why do we constantly hear reports from the media that support what is false.

Valerie: I think because that is what they want us to think.

Dr. Brock: Here are three interrelated concepts for your notes: *pathologization, demonization,* and *ideology.* The pathologization of urban families shows them as morally impoverished, and therefore unable to instill in their children the values needed to be productive members of society. As such, the urban family can be blamed for their predicament based on their perceived moral depravity. The systemic problems that force urban families into their predicament are pushed under the rug, thereby mystifying their real causes. Urban families are blamed for urban problems, which relieves society from addressing the real problems of unemployment, racism, decaying economic infrastructure, underfunded schools, and so on. As long as the urban family is framed as pathological, then we can blame them for the school failure of their children rather than doing what is needed to make schools work. Because of their assumed pathology, urban families are *demonized* as wicked and violent criminals, who do not deserve our time and energy because nothing we do will make a difference. All of this is able to occur because of *ideology*, which blurs and mystifies the social, economic, and political causes of the problems that exist in urban environments.

Ideology Smoke Screens

Dr. Brock: Specifically, Bruce Hare postulates that the current "endangered status" of Black youth is precipitated by the structural inequality of the American educational systems (Hare, 1987, cited in Hale-Benson, 1989, p. 83). He suggests that ideas about the biological and cultural inferiority of Black people serve to justify race, class, and gender inequalities found in American society. He further states that the myth of equal opportunity serves as a smoke screen through which the losers will be led to blame themselves and be seen by others as getting what they deserve. This is how ideology works.

Ben: Don't you put any of the fault on them? It sounds like you are saying
   this ideology thing makes us believe something that is not real. I can't
   buy that when everything I see tells me otherwise.

Dr. Brock: I want you to start questioning what you see. Yes, ideology
   does make us believe what is not real because we stop asking
   questions. Ideology is how society thinks of itself, how it knows
   itself. When we discuss the concept of ideology, we are talking about
   social consciousness. It is the framework people use to make sense
   of the world, to understand their culture, to know what to believe
   in, and then to act on that belief (Brock, 2005). Ideology allows and
   encourages the constructions of what we know about urban families
   to be taken for granted and implies some natural state, because what
   is forgotten and ignored is that images of urban families are faulty
   constructions of reality, created by dominant thought as much as they
   create dominant thought. Ideology allows society to believe that the
   constructed images of urban families are valid. This allows for visions
   of urban families as abnormal through dichotomous thinking, which
   categorizes based on difference and an accepted norm. Urban, minority,
   low-income families are placed in opposition to middle-class White
   families and consistently fall short. Again we stop questioning and
   merely accept.

   King (1994) asserts that "Dysconscious racism is a form of racism
   that tacitly accepts dominant White norms and privileges" and "is an
   uncritical habit of mind (including perceptions, attitudes, and beliefs)
   that justify inequality and exploitation by accepting the existing order
   of things as given" (p. 338). When a teacher views urban families as
   monolithic and does not take the time to truly learn about the families
   of her students, the teacher is practicing dysconscious racism. In this
   case, the teacher is creating a monolithic view of urban families by
   viewing them as undimensional. They do not see the complexities
   of urban families or the intersection of race/class/gender on specific
   realities of specific people. Worse, the teacher does not want to see; it is
   easier (perhaps even safer) to hold onto a narrow view of the "other."
   According to King, when people do not have a critical consciousness, it
   "involves an ethical judgment about the social order"; those involved
   in dysconscious racism accept the social order uncritically (p. 338).

Charlotte: I don't get it. Hey, is anybody else lost besides me?

Dr. Brock: Okay, let me go a little deeper. Earlier I talked about the power
   of words. When discussing ideology and how it can construct what we
   think and see, it is important to understand that it can also determine
   how the person or group view themselves. At the same time that they

reject the stereotypes and images, they also buy into them. Ladson-Billings and Tate (1995) contend that a "factor contributing to the demoralization of marginalized groups is self-condemnation. Members of minority groups internalize the stereotypic images that certain elements of society have constructed in order to maintain their power" (p. 57).

The importance of self-definition cannot be stressed enough as it relates to empowerment. To name something is to have power over that thing. We become the definition others place on us. For example, the concept of *self-fulfilling prophecy* is well-known and accepted in the field of teaching: The labels that teachers apply to children can influence that child's performance. Likewise, the labels and definitions we adhere to people and groups is a determining factor in how others view them, as well as how the group views themselves. This imposed definition manifests itself in the conscious and subconscious images used to represent the group. The insistence on self-definition reframes the entire dialogue from one of protesting the technical accuracy of an image, to one stressing the power dynamics underlying the very process of definitions. This act of insisting on self-definition validates people's power as human subjects. We are no longer objects placed outside the world or the thoughts of others, but instead we are subjects acting in sync with the world.

Urban families operating under an imposed definition are not in control of who they are, what they want to be, or where they are going. Instead the locus-of-control is external, in full view and easy reach to be used by others. What is needed is an internal locus of control, an internal self-definition versus a definition given by the dominant group. In this way they are usurping the power others attempt to have over their lives.

Valerie: But education is important, and I have read articles in other education classes that say urban children are at a disadvantage when compared to children from the middle class due to the lack of education of their parents. You know, those who have an education place a higher value on education and then instill it in their kids.

Dr. Brock: Okay, now we are talking about the politics of knowledge. We need to broaden our definition of what it means to be educated. Earlier I talked about Black feminist epistemology (Collins, 1991). Who remembers, or at least took notes and can tell me, what *epistemology* means?

Ben: A study of knowledge—whatever that means.

Dr. Brock: Ah, Ben, I can already see that you are going to add so much laughter to this class. But seriously, when we talk about epistemology, we are talking about how knowledge is constructed—the how and why we believe what we do. For example, when we think of education only in terms of "book" knowledge, we are denying all other forms of knowledge and these other forms are also important. One of the characteristics of Black feminist epistemology is "concrete experience as a criterion of meaning," which defines two types of knowing: wisdom and knowledge. This distinction between knowledge and wisdom has been instrumental in the survival of people living in low-income environments. It is wisdom that helps them pay bills with a limited income, find ways to maneuver a violent environment, and deal with health care for self and children without medical insurance. As teachers, when we understand the wisdom of our students' parents we are better able to develop strategies that include parents in their child's education.

Valerie: I see what you mean. I also think when we not only understand but accept wisdom as real knowledge, we as teachers stop looking down on urban parents. And y'all know that's what teachers do.

Dr. Brock: You are right. Some teachers look down on urban families because of their preconceived notion of those parents. And at the same time some urban families have preconceived notions of teachers.

Ben: Okay, but as long as parents don't care, what can I do as a teacher? And as a teacher, I only have so much power over the lives of my students, especially when you compare my role as just-their-teacher to the role of their parents.

Dr. Brock: Are you asking a question or making a statement? Either way you are parroting the view of conservative ideology. As long as we can ask that question, we are relieved of trying to do anything to help urban children. So the myth persists and with the myth comes the school's failure of children. For example, Moreno and Valencia (2002) discuss the myth that Mexican American families do not value the education of their children. They state that according to the literature, these parents "fail to inculcate . . . [a value in education] . . . in their children via academic socialization, and seldom participate in parental-involvement activities in their home or in the school. As a consequence, the myth contends, Mexican-American children perform poorly in school" (p. 228).

Let's answer your statement in a different way, based on what we have been discussing in class so far. Perhaps urban parents do not attend certain school activities because of the time at which they are held. For example, parent conferences are usually held on weeknights after school, a time when skilled labor is working second shift; and as we discussed earlier, those living in urban environments are typically working at low-paying skilled jobs. Instead, what would happen if a parent-teacher conference was held on a Saturday or Sunday afternoon? How many parents would be able to attend during that time? Of course I don't have the definitive answer to that question, but isn't it worth trying? Another reason urban parents do not always attend school activities is based, in part, on the negative treatment they themselves may have received as children in school from teachers. So why don't we have in-service training for teachers that specifically addresses this issue to help teachers develop a positive relation with the parents of their students? We have to begin to think outside of the box when talking about working with urban families and dismantling urban myths.

Valerie: See, Ben, that's why I have a problem with what you just said. Okay, how many people sitting here remember a great teacher they had in school? What about a bad teacher? I think—no, I know—as teachers we have the power to change the lives of our students. If not, why go into teaching in the first place?

Dr. Brock: We do have power, and Ben, that is what I want you to see by the end of the semester. When we fail to deconstruct the myth that urban parents do not care about their child's education, we cannot see or acknowledge the forces and conditions that shape how minority parents view schools. For instance, when discussing the education of Black students, Roslyn Mickelson (1990) argues that the paradox between stated and achieved goals is caused by a divergence in the beliefs about education that Black students hold. On the one hand, each person holds abstract beliefs regarding the value of education. These are shaped by the dominant value system that believes education is the means to the "American Dream." Concrete attitudes, on the other hand, "reflect the diverse empirical realities that people experience with respect to returns on education from the opportunity structure" (p. 50). A student develops concrete attitudes based on her life experience in which educational credentials may be fairly rewarded by the opportunity structure. Mickelson further claims that "In this society, minorities, women, and members of the working class often fail to receive the same wages, jobs, and promotions that middle-class White men receive for similar educational credentials" (p. 45). Concrete attitudes, according to Mickelson, offer insights into how class, race, and gender differences in the opportunity structure shape students' efforts in school and are expressions of lived culture.

According to Mickelson, the roots of the paradox are inadequate conceptualizations and measurements of students' attitudes toward education. Black students simultaneously possess a positive perception of education and hold concrete attitudes that are shaped by their actual observations of society. Racism is still alive; and based on their observations, they see that the rewards of academic perseverance do not always match the promise. This realization often results in disillusionment and academic underachievement.

Charlotte: I can see that. My mom drilled into my head that I had to get an education, that it was the one thing "they" couldn't take from me. But at the same time, I see an episode of *Dateline* that shows two people, one Black and one White, attempting to transact different forms of business. Despite the fact that they present the same credentials to the rental agent or bank loan officer, the Black man is always turned away. Oh yeah, and then there is the research that examines how people will discriminate based on the name of a person, if that name sounds like it belongs to a person of color. What's a sista to do?

Dr. Brock: Mickelson believes that the paradox will cease to exist when the gulf between abstract and concrete goals is diminished. So when we focus on the relationship between urban students and their environment, we begin to view their existence from a holistic perspective. The individual is affected by, and affects, the community. This interdependency, asserts Mickelson, requires that fundamental changes be made in the larger opportunity structure. Until that time, the underachievement of minority and poor students will persist, despite other educational efforts. If reform movements do not confront societal inequalities and work to bridge the gulf between abstract and concrete goals, their results will be hollow. Mickelson adds that the paradox will not cease until Black children see the benefits of education played out in their community. This goes back to Valerie's earlier statement. Although I agree with much of Mickelson's theory, I cannot agree with the last part. If I did then, what's the use of teaching this class on urban education? I might as well just throw up my hands in defeat. When we teach in urban schools, we can never give up, despite whatever obstacles are in our way. We can overcome the paradox Mickelson discusses by truly engaging in what I call radical education. *Radical education* is simply a form of education that seeks to find and then speak the truth.

When we attempt to understand urban families, we must become true intellectuals, which means we do not take anything at face value; rather, we dig through the layers to find the answer.

The Whole Child in the Urban Classroom

Dr. Brock: What does all of this tell us? Charlotte?

Charlotte: I don't know. I mean right now I am feeling mad! But mad at myself for not questioning anything and just believing what I'm told.

And what makes it even worse, I'm believing the worst about my own people—hell, I'm Black!

Dr. Brock: What you are experiencing, Charlotte, is what happens when we finally examine our assumptions. We are angry, we feel duped, and we are not sure whom to blame. To get past our anger, we just need to become aware. Awareness leads us to our personal transformation, and then we can begin to make our students aware.

Valerie: Our conversation so far has been interesting, but I don't see how this is going to help me teach. I mean what does all this have to do with what I do in the classroom. I need you to tell me what to do in my future classroom. How do I really affect these various issues positively?

Dr. Brock: I cannot give you a recipe; one doesn't exist. Instead, I hope to teach you how to think, how to question, how to know yourself as a person and as a teacher. Once you begin to do those things, then you will know how to find the answers you need. Remember the awareness—your awareness as a teacher. Your job as a teacher encompasses so much more than developing lesson plans on a specific subject or topic. In order to truly teach, you must be aware of the realities of the students you serve. Teaching the whole child is a concept that I want each of you to grab hold of. When we teach the whole child, we understand the importance of every aspect of the child's world. The relationship between the child, the community, the family, and the school is made evident in everything we perform. "Urban teachers often work detached from the community and family resources that would help them to understand their students' lives, needs, and interests; a problem compounded by procedures and regulations designed to make education impersonal and anonymous" (Weiner, 2000, p. 371). For learning to take place teachers must embrace the lives of the children they teach.

It is an accepted fact that schools operate with a White, middle-class cultural norm and often don't see the inequalities of power relationships between teachers and parents. Instead these power relationships are hidden within the way schools operate (Hamovitch, 1996). Teachers must understand the importance of parents and the community and use both as resources for their students' education. Moreover, they need to see the constructions of both as valuable to help them improve the academic achievement of the student.

Grinberg and Goldfarb (1998) convincingly state that "the obstacle that multicultural teacher education faces is how to incorporate family studies as a regular component in preservice education, within the constraints of state regulations, university policies, and colleges of education territorial politics" (p. 135). In a discussion on effective teaching of Black students, Foster (1994) posits that it was apparent that a teacher's philosophy and pedagogy was "influenced by" and "grounded in" the "social and cultural experiences" of the Black community (p. 137). Family involvement is paramount to student success. Shartrand, Kreider, and Erickson-Warfield (1994) state that "research has shown that when parents are involved in schools, children achieve more academically, parents become empowered, teacher attitudes improve, and school and community environments improve" (p. 4).

Ben: I agree with that. In all of the education classes I have taken, we never even discussed the family of the children we will teach one day. I guess, because of that, I haven't given the family much thought. You know, I thought that learning how to be a teacher was all about lesson planning and classroom management. I mean, I have been living for the day when I could finally start my student teaching. Based on some of the things I have said in class today that you've called me on, I can sort of see where my education is lacking. And what is funny or sad is that until today I didn't think I was lacking; I thought I was ready to teach and now I don't know.

Dr. Brock: Ben, the fact that you don't know means you will be a good teacher because you are learning to question what you think you know. Earlier you gave me the definition of *epistemology* as the study of knowledge. You ended your answer with, "whatever that means." Tell me, what do you think it means now, based on our discussion in this class?

Ben: Now I understand epistemology, not completely, but it's more than just a big word. In all of my education classes we never talked about the whole life of the child. It's like the student was taken out of his or her environment, as if the environment isn't important.

Dr. Brock: That's called *decontextualization*.

Ben: And if we don't contextualize the student, then we don't know the student; and if we don't really know the student, then we cannot teach the student. It's like everything we have been talking about today is linked to epistemology, or why we know what we know and why we don't know certain things. Why isn't there a class on the family? This class is an elective and I only took it because I heard you were a great teacher, but this class should be required for all preservice teachers.

Charlotte: I agree with Ben. If the research says that the family is important to understand, then why don't we learn more about the family—and not just the family, but everything to do with the life of a student? This is so important, especially if we are teaching in a school with students who are different from us. I mean, I know about growing up Black in a suburban, middle-class family, but now I realize that I hold some of the same assumptions about urban families as other people. And if I go into the classroom with these assumptions, then how can I adequately teach my children. If my assumptions are negative, there is a good chance that I will view those children negatively and from a deficit perspective.

Valerie: You go, girl! We studied deficit theory in another class and just from our discussion so far, I really see how it applies to urban students and urban families. Before I said that when I think about urban families, I think of someone on welfare; and then you gave us statistics disproving that. If I, as the teacher, understand the life of my students outside of school, then it stands to reason that I know better how to motivate them in school. But I also see that studying the urban family is important, based on what Ben said earlier. It's the influence of the family that motivates a child to achieve in school. So if we want to influence the child, teachers must be willing to not only understand but design meaningful interaction with parents and families.

Dr. Brock: To me it is common sense that, as teachers, we must be concerned with, and work to better understand, the families of the children we teach. In order to educate the whole child, we have to be part of a community of learners that includes the family of that child. When we understand that, then we can begin to work at developing educational programs that do not deny what those closest to the child have to offer. We can develop the climate in our classrooms that embraces parents rather than shuns them.

For the first day of class we have discussed quite a bit. Of course we have just scratched the surface of what we will be talking about and learning for the rest of the semester. I only ask that you come into this class each time with an open mind and be as honest as you have been today. Don't forget to do your reading, and I will see you next week.

Reflection: Class was over. As the students began to leave, Dr. Brock noticed several were still debating what had been discussed in class. That was good. Let the debates and the learning continue. Perhaps by the semester's end, these soon-to-be teachers would be a step closer to being the type of educator we so badly need in urban schools. Dr. Brock gathers her materials and leaves room 400, heading back to her office.

Discussion Questions

1. What are the assumptions the students held about urban families?
2. Where do these assumptions originate? Why?

3. What is the relationship between school and family? Why is it important?
4. Why do you think most teacher education classes do not discuss the family, or if they do, provide only a cursory view of the family?
5. Explain Mickelson's theory about abstract and concrete goals? How does an understanding of this theory benefit you as a teacher?

REFERENCES

Anderson, E. (1990). *Streetwise: Race, class and change in an urban community.* Chicago: University of Chicago Press.

Brock, R. (2005). *Sista talk: The personal and the pedagogical.* New York: Peter Lang.

Banneker Achievement Center. (n.d.). *School History.* Retrieved June 3, 2008, from http://www.garycsc.k12.in.us/Banneker/html/history.html

Collins, P. H. (1991). *Black feminist thought: Knowledge, consciousness, and the politics of empowerment.* New York: Routledge.

DuBois, R., & Li, M. (1971). *Reducing social tension and conflict: The group conversation method.* New York: Association Press.

Foster, M. (1994). The power to know one thing is never the power to know all things: Methodological notes on two studies of Black American teachers. In A. Gitlin (Ed.), *Power and method: Political activism and educational research* (pp. 129–146). New York: Routledge.

Ginsburg, W. (2006, January). *Income and inequality: Millions left behind.* (5th ed.). Washington, DC: Americans for Democratic Action Education Fund.

Giroux, H. (1997). *Pedagogy and the politics of hope: Theory, culture, and schooling.* Boulder, CO: Westview Press.

Giroux, H., & Simon, R. (1989). Popular culture and critical pedagogy: Everyday life as a basis for curriculum knowledge. In H. Giroux & P. McLaren (Eds.), *Critical pedagogy, the state and cultural struggle* (pp. 236–252). Albany: State University of New York Press.

Goldfarb, K. (2004). Who is included in the urban family? In S. Steinberg & J. Kincheloe (Eds.), *19 urban questions: Teaching in the city* (pp. 373–381). New York: Peter Lang.

Grinberg. J., & Goldfarb. K. P. (1998, Spring). Moving teacher education in/to the community. Preparing teachers for cultural diversity [Special issue]. *Theory Into Practice, 37*(2), 131–139. Retrieved April 22, 2008, from www.jstor.org/stable/1477294

Hale-Benson, J. (1989). *Black children: Their roots, culture, and learning styles.* Baltimore: John Hopkins Press

Hamovitch, B. (1996). Socialization without voice: An ideology of hope for at- risk students. *Teachers College Record, 98*(2), 286–306.

Hooks, Bell (1989). *Talking back: Thinking feminist, thinking black.* Toronto: Between the Lines.

Kincheloe, J. (1991). *Teacher as researchers: Qualitative inquiry as a path to empowerment.* New York: Falmer Press.

Kincheloe, J. (2004). *Critical pedagogy primer.* New York: Peter Lang.

King, J. E. (1994). Dysconscious racism: Ideology, identity, and miseducation of teachers. In L. Stone (Ed.), *The education feminism reader* (pp. 336–348). New York: Routledge.

King, J. E., & Mitchell, C. A. (1995). *Black mothers to sons: Juxtaposing African American literature with social practice.* New York: Peter Lang.

Ladson-Billings, G., & Tate, W. F. (1995, Fall). Toward a critical race theory of education. *Teachers College Record, 97*(1), 47–68.

MacLeod, J. (1987). *Ain't no makin' it: Leveled aspirations in a low-income neighborhood.* Boulder CO: Westview Press.

McKernan, S. M., & Ratcliffe, C. (2006, May 23). *The effect of specific welfare policies on poverty.* Retrieved June 4, 2009, from http://www.urban.org/url.cfm?ID=411334

McLaren, P. (2000). *Che Guevara, Paulo Freire, and the pedagogy of revolution.* Lanham, MO: Rowan & Littlefield.

Mickelson, R. (1990). The attitude-achievement paradox among black adolescents. *Sociology of Education, 63,* 54–84.

Moreno, R. P., & Valencia, R. R. (2002). Chicano families and schools: Myths, knowledge, and future directions for understandings. In R. R. Valencia (Ed.), *Chicano school failure and success: Past, present, and future.* (pp. 227–249). New York: Routledge/Falmer.

Pozo, M. (2003). Towards a critical revolutionary pedagogy: An interview with Peter McLaren. *St. John's University Humanities Review, 2*(1). Retrieved April 4, 2004, from facpub.stjohns.edu/~ganterg/sjureview/vol2-1/mclaren.html

Ramirez, L., & Gallardo, O. M. (2001). *Portraits of teachers in multicultural settings: A critical approach.* Needham Heights, MA: Allyn & Bacon.

Shartrand, A., Kreider, H., & Erikson-Warfield, M. (1994). *Preparing teachers to involve parents: A national survey of teacher education programs.* Cambridge, MA: Harvard Family Research Project.

Urban Institute. (2005, August 25). Low-income working families: Facts and figures. Retrieved April 22, 2008 from www.urban.org/url.cfm?ID=900832

Weiner, L. (2000). Research in the 90s: Implications for urban teacher preparation. *Review of Educational Research, 70*(3), 369–406

Wink, J. (1997). *Critical pedagogy: Notes from the real world.* New York: Longman.

Zeichner, K., Grant, C., Gay, G., Gillette, M., Valli, L., & Villegas, A. M. (1996, February). A research-informed vision of good practice in multicultural teacher education. Paper presented at the annual meeting of the American Association of Colleges for Teacher Education, Chicago.

CHAPTER 9

Reaching Native American Families to Increase School Involvement

Angela Jaime
Caskey Russell

American Indian parenting communities have spoken. Their voices tell of their concerns and desire for involvement in the education of their children. They have spoken loudly of the need to preserve and value their cultures as integral to that learning, and not to allow education to become a vehicle for cultural genocide.
—Carol Robinson Zañartu and Juanita Majel Dixon, "Parent Voices," p. 48

In the mid-1990s a Bureau of Indian Affairs (BIA) high school on a reservation in the Pacific Northwest was having trouble getting parents and family members actively involved in school activities. The school hosted a parent-teacher night and not a single parent showed up. The school board decided to host a second parent-teacher night and to insure a high turnout of parents, they paid for three door prizes to be given away in a raffle with the main prize being an all-expenses-paid trip within the United States. Even with the lure of such a prize only two parents showed up.

This sad story, related to us by a former teacher at the tribal school in question, may sound familiar to researchers and teachers involved in Indian education. According to findings by Robinson-Zañartu and Majel-Dixon (1996), on-site parental involvement in tribal schools remains "dramatically low" in spite of legislation, such as Title IX, the Johnson-O'Malley Act of 1934, and Goals 2000, mandating that federally funded schools actively promote and support parental involvement. For instance, Goal number eight of Goals 2000 states: "Every school will promote partnerships that will increase parental involvement and participation in promoting the social, emotional, and academic growth of children" (Goals, 2000). Our findings from one-on-one interviews and various interactions with the Native community suggest similar patterns of low on-site parental involvement in American Indian education (discussed later in this chapter).

In 1983 the National Education Association (NEA) conducted a study on the state of American Indian and Alaskan Native education. This report gave the following assessment of parental involvement:

> The lack of involvement of [American Indian/Alaskan Native] parents is often misinterpreted to mean disinterest in the education of their children. A more accurate assessment of their behavior is that they lack experience in interacting with school staffs; feel they do not have the expertise warranted to speak to the curriculum or counseling needs of their children; and are doubtful about how their input, once given, will be received or instituted. Not wishing to feel intimidated or appear foolish, they remain inactive but not disinterested. (p. 31)

Even though there is legislation mandating that schools promote active parental involvement, there still remains a demand from Native parents and educators for strategies to overcome those barriers noted by the NEA 25 years ago.

In this chapter, we highlight key concerns gleaned from interviews with parents and teachers at various tribal schools. We also make recommendations about how school teachers and administrators can foster active parental involvement and overcome the hostilities that put American Indian parents and students at odds with local tribal schools, and subsequently lead to the high dropout rates that currently plague Native communities.

THE AUTHORS' INVOLVEMENT IN
AMERICAN INDIAN EDUCATION

As researchers in the field of American Indian education, we are interested in parental involvement in American Indian and Alaskan Native education and its relation to academic success and achievement. One of the biggest predictors of academic success is the level of parental involvement in education (Demmert 2001; Kamehameha Early Education Program, 1974). Though American Indian dropout rates are hard to track, research findings suggest American Indians have the highest dropout rate percentages of any ethnic group in America (Ledlow, 1992; Reyhner, 1992). A 2004–2005 National Center for Education Statistics (NCES) survey also found that the dropout rate for American Indian/Alaskan Native high school students was the highest of any ethnic group in America, nearly double the national average (NCES, 2008). It therefore behooves us in the field of American Indian education to examine ways of improving parental involvement and support in tribal schools and, perhaps more important to listen to concerns that American Indian parents have regarding their children's education.

We are both enrolled tribal members and have done previous work in the area of American Indian education (Jaime, 2003; Jaime & Rios, 2006; Russell, 2002). Our role as American Indian educators is, in a sense, neither traditional nor unidirectional: We are expected to expose students at a predominately White institution to the histories, cultures, and lives of American Indians; we also have the opportunity to develop a relationship with the local reservation community, which includes a commitment to students, parents, and teachers in tribal schools on that reservation.

As we see it, a main component of our relationship with the local tribal schools is listening to the concerns that American Indian parents have about their children's education and aiding them in their dialogue with tribal school teachers and administrators in order to ensure greater academic success and achievement. We would never presume to speak for those parents, nor do we consider ourselves experts in what is best academically for their children; rather, our position as university faculty allows us to act as outside mediators between parents, teachers, and administrators and to present a forum in which the concerns of parents and teachers can be heard.

There are two main types of reservation schools: those operated by the tribe and others operated by the Bureau of Indian Affairs (BIA), a federal department housed in the Department of Interior. Robinson-Zañartu and Majel-Dixon (1996) found that American Indian parents are more dissatisfied with BIA schools than with tribally operated schools. We have conducted interviews to elicit the views of teachers and parents at both BIA and tribally operated reservation schools. Our research finds that parents and teachers in both types of schools recognize benefits and deficits in contemporary American Indian education.

THE BOARDING SCHOOL LEGACY

As educators, we are reminded that events and tragedies in the past can be and have been repeated if not studied to prevent reoccurrence. We therefore include a review of the Indian boarding school experience for two reasons: (1) Teachers need to know the past before they can teach for the future, and (2) an understanding of the boarding school experience provides needed information in gaining perspective on the mistrust many American Indian families have toward the educational system.

The History

American Indian communities still suffer from the legacy of Indian boarding schools, which created intergenerational cycles of mistrust toward education systems, cycles that still affect the performance of today's Indian students (Butterfield & Pepper, 1991). What is now recognized as the boarding school era began in 1879 with the opening of the U.S. Training and Industrial School at Carlisle, Pennsylvania. The mission of the boarding school was to eradicate all facets of Indian culture (language, religion, dress, history, and so on) and to assimilate Indians into mainstream White America. In an 1892 speech, Richard Pratt, the founder of the Carlisle boarding school, stated:

> A great general has said that the only good Indian is a dead one, and that high sanction of his destruction has been an enormous factor in promoting Indian massacres. In a sense, I agree with the sentiment, but only in this: that all the Indian there is in the race should be dead. Kill the Indian in him, and save the man. ("Official Report of the Nineteenth Annual Conference of Charities and Correction," 1892/1973, p. 4)

That now-famous last line encapsulates the main purpose of education at American Indian boarding schools, which was to eradicate Native cultures for the supposed good of Indian people. Because of the schools' remote locations from Indian populations, Indian families had little recourse in addressing the situation in boarding schools. Boarding schools instructed Indian children in standard curricula, such as reading and writing English and basic arithmetic, and they also provided occupational and military training. Pratt's famous line contains the tacit equating of education with liberation and equating of Native cultures with a type of bondage from which it is necessary to free Indian children in order that they may succeed in the non-Indian world. Except for a limited number of students, the promise of the boarding school was a lie: The damage done to the identities and self-images of many students outweighed any benefits of the boarding schools. Moreover, boarding schools were training Indian students to supposedly succeed in a country that was racist and almost totally averse to accepting Indians as equals.

Within a decade of the founding of the school at Carlisle, there were 26 off-reservation U.S. government boarding schools for Indians (as well as many more on-reservation government-run boarding schools), and by 1893 Congress authorized the Commissioner of Indian Affairs to compel all American Indian children of appropriate age to attend these schools—even if it took withholding food rations and annuity payments from the children's families to do so (Calloway, 2004). The boarding school era began its decline in the 1930s due to the closure of many schools for financial reasons and because of certain governmental reports and legislations, such as the Merriam Report of 1928 and the Indian Reorganization Act of 1934, aimed at mitigating the deficiencies found in those schools; however, the boarding school era didn't really end until the 1960s with the growing Red Power and Self-Determination movements (Calloway, 2004). In 1969 a Senate subcommittee report delineated the appalling state of contemporary Indian education. The subcommittee called their findings "shocking," and their report signaled the end of the kill-the-Indian-save-the-man boarding school policies (Josephy, Nagel, & Johnson, 1991; U.S. Senate Special Subcommittee, 1969).

The Effects of that Legacy Today

American Indian children still hear horror stories from older relatives who either witnessed or were victims of the abuses of boarding schools. Stories of sexual and physical abuse by school staff, stories of punishment for speaking Native languages, stories of homesickness and the desire to escape, and stories of students who died either through disease or suicide permeate American Indian communities. The damage done to American Indian nations by the boarding schools is hard to quantify when assessing the long-lasting impacts of the boarding schools: the loss of Native language, the loss of traditional religions and ways-of-knowing, the creation of cycles of dysfunctional behavior and relationships, and the furthering of the distrust of institutions and structures of authority. An equally important, though less well known, impact of the boarding schools is the disruption of parenting skills within American Indian communities—and the dysfunctions created by that disruption. Hirshberg and Sharp (2005) noted this impact in their research on the legacy of the boarding schools within Alaskan Native communities. One Native interviewee in their study responded:

> we missed out in having the opportunity to observe our parents raise kids our age . . . we missed out the guidance that we could have received from them. . . . So when I see parents not doing anything with their children, not talking to their children, not disciplining their children, parents that are my age, I think about that. Because when I look at the parents, I see they've gone to St. Mary's or Bethel or Edgecumbe or to Chemawa, Oregon, Chilocco, Oklahoma, all those boarding schools that were popular at that time, they're the parents that went away. And I really think that had an effect on how we parent today. (p. 20)

This lack of parental guidance for former boarding school attendees needs to be acknowledged. Throughout the boarding school era, the input and advice of Native parents was neither sought nor allowed; rather, it was purposely devalued and ignored. However, in the post–boarding school era, we now decry the lack of parental input, support, and involvement in Native education. Moreover, that input, support, and involvement is now sought from the victims of boarding schools, who had little or no parental guidance while they were students. This particular insight, then, is of great importance when researching parental support in Indian education. Boarding schools disrupted traditional modes of parenting, and Native parents are in a sense relearning ways to support their children's education.

PARENTAL INVOLVEMENT AND SUPPORT IN EDUCATION

As the research of Robinson-Zañartu and Majel-Dixon (1996) suggests, Native parents desire to support their children's education and become involved in on-site school activities, and they desire to do so in ways that promote traditional values. Yet, the lingering effects of the boarding schools make any current promise of liberation through education suspect in the eyes of many Native families. We even find a mistrust of the university and its intentions in the minds of many Native people on the nearby reservation. Native parents and students alike recognize the benefits a college degree can provide, but are concerned lest Native students assimilate too deeply into the non-Native worldviews promoted by the university's pedagogies and structures. Parents desire pedagogies and practices that allow Native students to enhance their own unique tribal identities while obtaining the tools that will enable them to succeed on their own terms in both Native and non-Native worlds.

Distinguishing Involvement from Support

Again, it must be stressed that the lack of such involvement does not automatically denote a general noninterest in education. There are a number of reasons why American Indian parents do not become actively involved in on-site school functions. In assessing this particular dilemma, it is helpful to follow the pattern set by Butterfield and Pepper (1991), whose work distinguishes between parental involvement and parental support. "Parental support includes such activities as sending children to school, attending parent-teacher conferences, encouraging the completion of homework, doing math games, or reading to children. Parental involvement not only supports the educational process of each individual child, but it includes additional activities which impact school systems" (p. 2). Those additional activities include serving on committees—both educational and tribal—and serving on state school boards, as well as regional educational and/or Native associations (Butterfield & Pepper, 1991). Butterfield and Pepper further note that parental support is not only possible for all Native parents, but also "has the greatest impact on the achievement, behavior, and attitudes of students" (p. 2).

Lack of Parental Involvement

Although the meanings of the two terms overlap, separating parental support from parental involvement allows researchers, teachers, and parents greater focus in creating and implementing policy change. As such, it may be easier to understand the lack of parental involvement rather than the lack of parental support. Due to the historical disempowerment of Native parents in educational systems (Butterfield & Pepper, 1991), as well as to the social ills (poverty especially) that still haunt tribal communities, Native parental involvement with school boards and larger educational associations remains limited. In working with tribal schools and talking with parents about parental involvement in education, we found that many of the conclusions the NEA reported in its 1983 assessment of parental involvement in Indian education are still relevant today. Native parents do not feel their input is welcome nor will be implemented if given; and Native parents feel they lack the experience necessary to meet with tribal school teachers and administrators on an equal footing to cocreate tribally responsive pedagogy. Such issues still affect parental involvement in Indian education.

Lack of Parental Support

The lack of parental support, however, is more puzzling. It is helpful here to further qualify the term *parental support* to include a more indigenous understanding of the role that grandparents, aunts, uncles, and familial relatives, especially elders, have in transmitting cultural values and educating American Indian children. Whereas in mainstream America parental support denotes the role of a child's immediate parents, whether biological or adoptive, in American Indian communities the role of parenting often includes larger familial and clan structures. Often American Indian children are raised by, and live with, relatives who may not be their biological parents. "In an Indian community, kinship is identified with even the most remote family tie. All clan members are considered relatives" (Gilliland, 1999, p. 28). Therefore, it is important to expand our understanding of parental support when dealing with American Indian communities. Combined with the impediments to parental involvement, the social ills of the reservation often preclude active parental support in tribal-school education. We examine this issue in some detail later in the chapter, and offer suggestions for teachers to enhance parental support.

Equally as interesting was the response from teachers that we keep in mind that parental support has both positive and negative elements. At times, too much support from certain parents can affect a child's academic performance in negative ways. One tribal-school teacher believed some of the students did better without the active support of the parents; rather, it was the students' connection and comfortableness with the teacher in a safe environment and with the materials presented in the classroom that led to better academic outcomes.

INDIGENOUS FORMS OF EDUCATION

As with recognizing the difference between parental involvement and support, it is also important to recognize that there are different forms and avenues for education. American Indian families play a major role in transmitting cultural and tribal education to their children. Native children are educated by their elders in clan stories, songs, dances, traditional foods, and ceremonies, as well as tribal-specific histories and lineages. This form of education solidifies a sense of community and tribal identity in Native children. Though tribal schools often try to incorporate traditional elements of Native cultures within their pedagogies and practices, most of the tribal and cultural education still takes place outside the confines of the classroom or school. This type of tribal-specific education should also be considered when assessing the level of parental support, not just educational achievement.

Teacher Perspectives

As we said early on, we sought out the expertise of parents and teachers in Native communities. In April and May 2008 we interviewed three tribal-school teachers (two Native, one non-Native), asking specific questions about the level of parental involvement and support they witness in their classrooms.

Ronnie is a Native teacher at a western reservation school. For the past 2 years her primary role with the school has been literacy coordinator; before that, she was a fourth-grade teacher. Her perspective is unique in that she is both a parent and educator of Native children on the reservation. When asked about improving parent interaction and involvement in the classroom, she responded:

Getting Native parents involved is difficult. Some of the challenges are the parent's constraint of time, the intimidation of the school environment, lack of child care for other children at home, lack of transportation, lack of trust of the system, and lack of formal education of the parents. Parents are overwhelmed by the lack of time they have in any given day, so accommodating parents and their needs will help ensure parents have what they need to attend teacher conferences and become involved in classroom activities.

Linda, a non-Native, was an English teacher for 2 years at a reservation tribal high school in the Pacific Northwest. When asked about parental involvement in her tribal-school classroom, she responded:

Parental involvement exists on a variety of levels, not all of which I witnessed. It can range from anywhere between collecting school information in the mailbox to participation/attendance at school events. Parental involvement includes positive as well as negative interactions with school personnel and with the student about school issues. As with most schools, there was a range of involvement. We had parents volunteer to teach the students how to do totem-pole and canoe carvings, come in to tell stories, do brushing ceremonies, cook the food for the community dinners, and so on. We also had some parents who were silent, or were actually hindering the education of the students. . . . Parental involvement was minimal from my point of view. Very few parents would show up for conferences or school events. No one would answer the phone if I called. Discipline issues were handled within the school, or with the police. We were very lucky to have a cultural teacher on staff to handle the niceties of the community events. She had the connections with the community and could pull in the talent when needed.

Linda also recalled facing obstacles at both the classroom and administrative levels:

Honestly, most of the students at my tribal school were kicked out of the regular school system. There were a few students whose parents wanted them to have a strong cultural experience, but for many of them, we were the next chance. I felt that I had to do the best I could with the students with or without parental involvement, and sometimes I had to acknowledge that the parental involvement would not be a positive thing for all students. There is a difference in the performance of children whose parents are actively involved, but it isn't necessarily a causal relationship. In other words, even if we could cause more parental involvement, we may not necessarily improve the student performance. My interactions with the students during class time made the biggest difference in performance.

Linda also succinctly delineated the barriers to parental support in her classroom:

Interest, availability, transportation, babysitters, feelings of intimidation, lack of positive experiences with the schools in the past, feeling uncomfortable/unsure, students not wanting the parents to come, sense that the time would not be well spent, or that they didn't have anything to contribute.

One of the teachers we interviewed was an elder for a tribe in a western state. Lillian is 88, a culture and language teacher in a reservation school, and also a parent of five. She has had little formal teacher training but works with a coteacher in developing curriculum for the culture and language program in her school. Lillian shared a powerful piece of advice about being a Native parent and teacher:

It is a constant struggle to sustain our culture and language with the kids at our schools. The parents at home are hardworking or having a really hard time making ends meet every month. School is important to our people but survival is the priority; even when our education suffers. Teachers must use the knowledge of us elders so we can pass on our stories to the next generations and make sure history doesn't repeat itself.

Parent Perspectives

In April and May 2008 we also interviewed three parents, all of whom are American Indian, asking questions similar to those we posed to the teachers regarding levels of parental support and/or involvement in education, as well as the barriers to it.

Joan is a Native, a single mother of four, and a college graduate. She lives with her children on a reservation in a western state. When asked to describe her experiences in the classroom as a parent, she replied:

I feel pretty comfortable in the classrooms of my kids, but I'm always wondering what the teacher is thinking about my kids or the

way I raise them. I wonder if she is criticizing me for living on the
reservation and not moving to make a better living. I know I could
move to a big city and make a lot more money and not struggle, but
our culture is so important and that is why it is important to live
on the reservation and be close to the elders and community. Most,
if not all, the teachers my kids have had in school have been White
and not interested in getting to know the community or the importance of ceremony or place. I am concerned my children are not
being taught about their culture in the classroom and that bothers
me—we live on the rez, it should be a priority.

Roxy, a Native and a single mother of one, has similar views of the
school system in the rural town off-reservation where she lives. Since Roxy
is a college student in a teacher education program for elementary education, she has a great deal of school observation and practicum experience,
as both are requirements of her program. When asked about her role as a
parent of a Native student, she expressed concerns regarding her own self-
esteem, as well as her son's perception of native culture as influenced by the
curriculum and classroom materials used by his school.

I feel intimidated when I go to parent-teacher conferences or need
to speak to the teacher about my kid. It seems as though I should
feel comfortable in the classroom; I mean I'm going to be a teacher,
right? But every time I step foot in the classroom, where my kid
goes every day, I get anxious. I know I shouldn't, but most of the
reports I get about my child are negative, and the teacher seems to
never have a solution for the classroom environment; but instead
they look at me and ask what I'm going to do about the problem.
I am also constantly reminded that the classroom is not an inviting
place for our culture. I walk into the classroom and there are never
pictures of people who look like my son. I never see positive images of native culture; instead I see Thanksgiving stereotypes of the
pilgrim and the "Indians" during the month of November—always
makes me cringe and want to scream.

Like Roxy, Dan also expresses his frustration with the stereotypes of
Native people in his son's classroom. Dan, who is Native and works on a
university campus in a western state, is married and has two young children.
Dan explains that as an educator he realizes that his frustration has to pro-
duce positive action in order to see change in the classroom:

My son was 3 years old when he started at the local day care for
the university I worked at. It was late October and the classroom

he was assigned to was having a Halloween party. During the party
the kids were given packets of images to color. One of the pages
contained a princess, dragon, batman, and a stereotypical American
Indian image with the buckskin-looking dress and the headband-
braids and feather. It was disturbing, but all too common in my
daily life. I have come to learn that by saying something without a
solution or alternative, the teacher shrugs it off and doesn't think
twice about it. I always try to give the teacher alternatives and
donate my time and materials to the classroom for their use. This
particular time I took several alternative images, posters with positive images of Native children for the walls in the classroom, and
a couple of current books for the classroom. I approached the
[non-Native] teacher and explained to her my concern and then
provided her with the items I brought. She seemed receptive; yet I
never saw the posters on the wall, she never asked for me to come
into the classroom and share my culture, and the books appeared
on the shelves with little use. My frustration doesn't just come from
the fact that I see these images everywhere in education, but more
than anything my frustration is rooted in the fact that I see teachers
making little effort, if any at all, to be culturally responsive or ask
parents for help. As a professor in the college of education, I have
resources and offer them to the teachers and few take me up on the
offer.

Dan has a valid point regarding the reluctance of many teachers to accept
help from parents. If a parent expresses a concern regarding culturally in-
sensitive materials in the classrooms or aspects of the curriculum, teachers
must be receptive to those concerns and be willing to actively seek out a
solution. To not do so creates the sense of frustration noted above by Dan.

RECOMMENDATIONS FOR TEACHERS

As teachers we have to strive consciously to create a classroom of inclusion
for both children and parents. Texts like *Culturally Responsive Pedagogy*
by Geneva Gay (2000) can aid teachers in understanding the importance
of integrating the non-dominant cultures within the classroom, especially
if their students represent some of those cultures. This text and others like
it can provide the teacher with techniques for incorporating culturally responsive pedagogy and curriculum into the classroom. Another helpful text
is *Beyond Heroes and Holidays* (Lee, Menkart, & Okazawa-Rey, 2002). As
the title implies, this text can aid teachers in incorporating culturally diverse
materials into their classroom throughout the entire school year, rather than

relegating that information to a handful of holidays and single units on famous historical figures.

The parents and teachers who provided input for our research had many
suggestions for improving the involvement of parents in the classroom. The
following are a few synthesized suggestions from our interviews and research to aid teachers in increasing and enhancing parental support and
involvement in the classroom.

Student-Led Conferences

Students could create a portfolio, which they walk their parents and
teacher through during the conference meeting; the student becomes the
leader and expert on his or her own learning. The student also becomes
a part of the conversation. Parents are encouraged to ask questions about
work in the portfolio and within the classroom. Teachers could include such
components as: student firsts, as a baseline of learning (first essay, first research paper, and so on); a reading journal with responses to in-class readings; learning logs with responses to lessons in class using KWL writing
activities (Know, Want-to-know, and Learned-after-the-lesson); writing
samples; audiotapes or videotapes of presentations or group projects; a list
of the books the student has read; and most important, student reflections of
their own learning, which could be typed by the teacher or handwritten by
the student himself (Clemmons, Laase, Cooper, Areglado, & Dill, 1993).

Parent-Teacher Conferences

Holding parent-teacher conferences at a location outside the school may
encourage parents to attend the conference. Entering a school or classroom
may be overwhelming to Native parents. Identifying a few locations for
parents to choose from may ease the anxiety: a cultural center, coffee shop,
place of employment, public library, or even within the home are all places
Native parents may feel more comfortable meeting with teachers. Moreover,
allowing parents to select the venue for parent-teacher conferences may cut
the risk of cancellation due to scheduling conflicts, tribal- or work-related
events, or transportation problems.

Sending Home Positive Notes

Teachers are constantly criticized for contacting home only when something bad has happened. The theory here is to make a constant effort to send
notes home with the student reporting positive feedback about the child. It
is important for students to report home with the many good things they
accomplish at school. Even students who frequently demonstrate less-than-

good behavior should have constructive notes and positive feedback sent along home when they exhibit improvement in behavior and performance.

Literacy Breakfasts and Lunches

Providing refreshments for the parents when they drop their kids off in the morning is an inviting way to get parents into the classroom. Ronnie called her literacy breakfasts Donuts for Dads and Muffins for Moms. Parents were encouraged to read books with their child for 20 minutes first thing in the morning. During literacy lunches, Ronnie would provide a light lunch or have parents go to the lunch room with their kids, return with their lunches, and read books to their children in the classroom during the lunch break. This provided a forum for Native parents to spend time with their children in the classroom under minimal pressure.

Parent Trainings

Providing parent-training seminars to acquaint Native parents with the curriculum being presented to their children allows parents the opportunity to become involved in their children's education. During the training, high school students or other teachers can provide child care for the parents attending the session. While in the session, the teacher reviews the curriculum used in the classroom and activities the students are currently involved in, as well as the future units the teacher is preparing.

Teacher Education

Teachers at tribal schools need to be involved in the local Native community. Tenured teachers need to facilitate the relationship between new teachers and community members. The hope is that relationships developed within the Native community will facilitate, for the teacher, a better awareness of the Native culture, especially in regard to how the Native culture differs from the dominant culture. For instance, the Native student who appears to not be paying attention but to be listening to his or her peers before responding, or who does not look the teacher in the eye because it is viewed as a sign of disrespect is exhibiting a cultural difference that could easily be misread by a teacher unaware of Native cultural codes.

Teachers must have an understanding of the familial situations of their students, the involvement of the extended family in raising children in Native communities, and the traditional responsibilities of the students' family members (Klug & Whitfield, 2003). Teachers should consider themselves to be lifelong learners: The continuous gathering of knowledge and information about culturally responsible curriculum and pedagogy for American Indian children is a must.

Native parents, the tribal school, teachers, and elders could collaborate to create and update a comprehensive teachers manual. This manual would instruct new teachers about the community and the culture in which they are employed, as well as provide vital, culturally relevant information to aid them in the classroom. Such a manual would also house resources available to the teacher in the school, on the Internet, and in the community. There are Web sites and resources available that sell classroom materials that focus on Native communities.

If Native parents are concerned about the content being taught in the classroom, teachers must be receptive to their ideas, ask for suggestions as to how to improve the curriculum, and encourage them to become actively involved in culturally sensitive curriculum decisions. Teachers must offer an invitation to the parents and extended family to visit the classroom as well as to help out with classroom projects and activities. Such steps, when taken by the teacher, will demonstrate to Native parents that their input and involvement is valued (Klug & Whitfield, 2003).

To increase parental involvement and support, school administrations must encourage teachers to take the initiatives mentioned above. School administrations can also provide transportation for parents on parent-teacher conference days, open house and back-to-school nights, and school-sponsored activities. Lastly, both teachers and administrators must realize that not being involved in on-site school activities doesn't necessarily mean a parent is not concerned about their child's education; going to school functions such as parent-teacher night is just one of the many ways that parents can support their child's education.

FINAL THOUGHTS

Over the course of writing this chapter we have reflected on our own practices, both as teachers and as parents, and have come to some conclusions about what teachers can do to improve the positive involvement and support of Native parents in education. We both spend a great deal of time in our children's classrooms—reading books to the class, attending field trips, visiting at lunchtime, and asking the teachers what they need from us. Due to our exposure to the dominant culture through higher education and having lived in multiple locations in the country, we understand the importance of being actively involved in education. Native parents on reservations and in border towns across the country also understand the importance of being actively involved in education, yet barriers to that involvement still exist.

Native families need to be cared for by teachers in unique ways. Teachers of Native students need to talk to the parents, grandparents, and family members. They need to know the people in the community and the culture, and take the time to visit with the elders and tribal leaders. As a current or future teacher of Native children, make it known to the community that you are willing to learn and do whatever it takes to make the experiences of Native children beneficial and positive. They are the future—treat them as such.

Discussion Questions

1. What responsibility does the teacher have in reassuring Native parents that their children's culture is a priority in the classroom?
2. How can teachers work to be more open-minded about inclusion of Native culture and community in the classroom?
3. Beyond the suggestions in this chapter, what can teachers do to encourage Native parents to be involved in the classroom?

REFERENCES

Butterfield, R., & Pepper, F. (1991). Improving parental participation in elementary and secondary education for American Indian and Alaska Native students. In *Indian nations at risk task force commissioned papers* (No. 10). Washington, DC: U.S. Department of Education. (ERIC Documents Reproduction Services ED343763)

Calloway, C. (2004). *First Peoples: A documentary survey of American Indian history* (2nd ed.). Boston, MA: Bedford/St. Martin's Press.

Clemmons, J., Laase, L., Cooper, D., Areglado, N., & Dill, M. (1993). *Portfolios in the classroom: A teacher's source book.* New York: Scholastic Professional Books.

Demmert, W. (2001). *Improving academic performance among Native American students: A review of the research literature.* Washington, DC: U.S. Department of Education, Office of Educational Research and Improvement. (ERIC Documents Reproduction Services ED463917)

Gay, G. (2000). *Culturally responsive pedagogy: Theory, research, and practice.* New York: Teachers College Press.

Gilliland, H. (1999). *Teaching the Native American* (4th ed.). Dubuque, Iowa: Kendall/Hunt.

Goals 2000, Educate America Act. (1994). Retrieved May 3, 2008, from www.ed.gov/legislation/GOALS2000/TheAct/index.html

Hirshberg, D., & Sharp, S. (2005). *Thirty years later: The long-term effect of boarding schools on Alaska Natives and their communities.* Anchorage: Institute of Social and Economic Research, University of Alaska Anchorage.

Jaime, A. M. (2003). A room without a view from within the ivory towers. *American Indian Quarterly, 27,* (1/2), 252–263.

Jaime, A., & Rios, F. (2006, Fall-Winter). Negotiation and resistance amidst the overwhelming presence of Whiteness: A Native American faculty and student perspective. *Taboo: Journal of Culture and Negotiation, 10*(2).

Josephy, A., Nagel, J., & Johnson, T. (1999). *Red power: The American Indians' fight for freedom.* Lincoln: University of Nebraska Press.

Kamehameha Early Education Program. (1974). *Major KEEP findings, 1971–1975.* Honolulu, Hawaii: Kamehameha Schools. (ERIC Document Reproduction Service No. ED158869)

Klug, B. J. & Whitfield, P. T. (2003). *Widening the circle: Culturally relevant pedagogy for American Indian children.* New York: Routledge Falmer.

Ledlow, S. (1992). Is cultural discontinuity an adequate explanation for dropping out? *Journal of American Indian Education, 31*(3), 20–36.

Lee, E., Menkart, D., & Okazawa-Rey, M. (2002). *Beyond heroes and holidays: A practical guide to K–12 antiracist, multicultural education and staff development.* Washington, DC: Teaching for Change.

National Education Association, Human and Civil Rights Division. (1983). *American Indian/Alaska Native education: Quality in the classroom.* Washington, DC: Author.

National Center for Education Statistics (NCES). (2008). *Dropout rates in grades 9–12, by race/ethnicity and state or jurisdiction: School year 2004–05.* Retrieved May 3, 2008, from http://nces.ed.gov/pub2008/hsdropouts/xis/table_6.xls

Official Report of the Nineteenth Annual Conference of Charities and Correction. (1892). Reprinted in Pratt, R. H. (1973), "The Advantages of Mingling Indians with Whites," *Americanizing the American Indians: Writings by the "Friends of the Indian," 1880–1900* (pp. 260–271). Cambridge, MA: Harvard University Press. Retrieved May 3, 2008, from socrates.bmcc.cuny.edu/bfriedheim/pratt.htm

Reyhner, J. (1992). American Indians out of school: A review of school-based causes and solutions. *Journal of American Indian Education, 31*(3), 37–56.

Robinson-Zañartu, C., & Majel-Dixon, J. (1996). Parent voices: American Indian relationships with schools. *Journal of American Indian Education, 36*(1), 33–53.

Russell, C. (2002). Language, violence, and Indian mis-education. *American Indian Culture and Research Journal, 26*(4), 97–112.

U.S. Senate Special Subcommittee on Indian Education. (1969). *Indian education: A national tragedy—A national challenge.* Senate Report No. 91-501.

CHAPTER 10

Social Class, Culture, and "Good Parenting": Voices of Low-SES Families

Guofang Li

Imagine you are an immigrant parent with six children living in an inner-city neighborhood. You can't speak English well, and you have a factory job that pays minimal wage. You have to work longer hours and different shifts to make enough money to feed the family. Though you have limited time with your children, you seize all the moments you have to teach them good values and supervise their homework. You are happy that your children can go to school every day and come home to food on the table. You hope that they will learn English and excel in school so they can do better than you when they grow up. However, you are called to school often because your kids are failing, missing homework, or misbehaving. The teachers have told you that you have to do more at home, be more responsible, and become more involved with their homework. You are torn: You cannot afford to miss any work as you need to provide for a big family; but if you don't, the teachers will think that you don't care. You don't know what to do and you wish that the teachers could understand your situation and hear your voice.

This is the situation faced by millions of immigrant and minority families with low socioeconomic status (SES) in America's inner cities, whose children are overlooked and underserved in the public schools (Ruiz-de-Velasco & Fix, 2001). In the past few decades the number of families who are in similar situations has shown steady increase along with the rising poverty rates among the immigrant and minority groups and widening achievement gaps among the middle-class and low-SES children. Despite an unprecedented period of economic growth in the 1980s and 1990s, poverty persists in the United States, especially among immigrant groups. Among the immigrant population, in 1970, poverty rates were lower than among children of the native-born populations: 11.6% versus 14.1%. But by 1980, only 10 years later, this pattern had reversed itself with poverty rates for immigrant and nonimmigrant populations being 16.7% versus 14.7%. In 2000, poverty rates among children of immigrants rose to 21.6%, with 14.7% for the nonimmigrant population (Hook, 2003). By 2004, roughly one in four poor persons was an immigrant or member of an immigrant's family.

Along with the growing poverty rates, the achievement gaps between high-SES and low-SES groups have also increased or remained consistent over the years. According to assessments by the National Assessment of Educational Progress (NAEP), the 2003, 2005, and 2007 results in reading and math indicate that students who are eligible for a free or reduced-price lunch program (high poverty) and those who are not (low poverty) turn out to have substantial differences in their achievement. In fact, low-SES students' average scores have been consistently lower than their higher SES peers since the 1990s.

The fact that achievement gaps persisted despite over 50 years of racial desegregation and billions of dollars of funding allocated to schools in poor districts in recent years, many educators began to argue that school reform alone is insufficient since it leaves class-based disparities untouched. In fact, Rothstein (2004) argues that the achievement gap results not from failed policies, poor school quality, or ineffective schools, but from social-class disparities between students of different racial backgrounds. Therefore, there is a need to go beyond the school context to examine factors outside school that are equally significant to low-SES children's academic development.

While we know much about the overall impact of poverty on immigrant and minority students' educational achievement, we know little about how poverty is lived by low-SES families in their daily lives and experienced in their interactions with the public schools. Sitting at the bottom of the richest country in the world, they are often depicted as "the *cause* of national problems" and "the *reason* for the rise in urban crime" as embodying the *necessity* for welfare reform, and of sitting at the *heart* of moral decay (Fine & Weis, 1998, p. 1; italics original). Yet this group, especially the foreign-born immigrants and refugees, are often excluded in national conversations and ignored in the policy-making processes—their voices are often not heard and their experiences remain foreign to their middle-class neighbors and to the general public (Fine & Weis, 1998). In this chapter, drawing on data from an ethnographic study, I bring the voices and experiences of this group, especially the foreign born, from the margins to the center by examining how their SES status impacts the families' parenting practices and involvement in their children's schooling in their daily lives.

SOCIAL CLASS AND PARENTING PRACTICES

Parenting practices take many forms and include parental involvement at home and in school. The practices commonly accepted as "good parenting" practices at home include: providing a secure and stable environment, intellectual stimulation, parent-child discussion, good models of constructive social and educational values, high aspirations relating to personal fulfillment and good citizenship, and involvement with their children in learning activities and homework. Parental involvement in school events include: communication and interaction with schools to share information, and volunteering and participating in school events, such as PTA/PTO, school councils, committees, and other parent organizations (Epstein, 2001).

The extent to which parents can realize these "good parenting" practices, however, is heavily influenced by a family's social-class background. Social class, traditionally defined by parental occupation, education, income, and private ownership, is believed to influence parents' ways of raising and educating a child, which in turn affects the child's sociocognitive and academic development. For example, middle-class parents (mostly White Americans) are reported to be more responsive to their children's needs, more communicative with their children at home, and are more likely to use inductive reasoning and authoritative parenting (setting clear standards and firm enforcement of rules, encouragement of independence and individuality, and so on) than their working-class and low-income counterparts. They often engage in a process of concerted cultivation in which children's talents are refined early on in life through organized activities, such as music lessons and sports; this concerted, deliberate cultivation usually fosters a sense of entitlement, which helps negotiate more class advantages when interacting with schools (Lareau, 2003). In addition, middle-class parents are also reported to be more involved in their children's education in school and at home than low-SES parents. In Lareau's (2000) study, for example, the upper-middle-class parents influence their children's school programs through requests for teachers and placement in specialized programs and through direct intervention in classroom instructional practices in subjects, such as spelling and math. They also take a more assertive role than working-class parents in shaping the promotion and retention decisions (Lareau, 2000, 2003).

Social class of the community and school context in which the family resides is another significant factor in mediating parenting practices. Working-class and poor immigrants and/or minority families tend to settle in impoverished inner-city neighborhoods while middle-class families often choose to stay in suburbs. It is common knowledge that communities with higher socioeconomic status tend to have better schools than those of poor neighborhoods. High-SES schools and communities possess more physical capital—they attract better qualified teachers, receive more resources and funding, are better equipped with technology, and are generally in a safer and more orderly environment. On the contrary, schools and communities that serve low-income students receive fewer resources, experience greater difficulties attracting qualified teachers, face many more challenges in addressing students' needs, are usually located in neighborhoods troubled by drugs, prostitution, and gangs; and often focus on survival rather than learning (Lee & Burkan, 2002; Suárez-Orozco & Suárez-Orozco, 2001). These social and physical characteristics of communities and schools often contribute to the decisions parents make about the way they structure, regulate, and monitor their children's activities (Beyers, Bates, Pettit, & Dodge, 2003; Kotchick & Forehand, 2002). Gutman, McLoyd, and Tokoyawa (2005) suggest that neighborhood characteristics are important mediators between economic hardship and parent-child behavior. Higher neighborhood stresses often lessen parents' ability to share positive activities with their children or to be actively involved in their children's learning at home.

In addition to these influences on parental involvement in school and at home, social class also interacts with sociocultural factors, such as ethnicity and culture, to influence parenting practices (Kotchick & Forehand, 2002). In terms of culture and ethnicity, it is widely accepted that culturally determined child and adult characteristics drive parenting behavior and hence the way of educating their children (Kotchick & Forehand, 2002; Ogbu, 1982). Though research on culture-specific parenting styles among different ethnic groups has not been conclusive, some generalizations can be made about child-rearing values and specific parenting strategies. For example, different from Latinos and White parents, Asian immigrant mothers have been found to place greater value on individual academic achievement and prefer to use a more direct intervention approach (e.g., through teaching and tutoring at home) to their children's schooling and learning and convey a much stronger belief that they can play a significant role in their children's school success (Chao, 1996; Li, 2006). These culture-specific child rearing practices are sometimes in conflict with school practices that are often based on the values and beliefs of middle-class White Americans.

These varied influences on parenting practices suggest that parenting is not a straightforward issue for low-SES families. Instead, it is mediated by a myriad of socioeconomic and sociocultural factors that can become impediments to their children's learning.

CASE STUDIES: PARENTING PRACTICES IN THE FOUR FAMILIES

The families described here are two Sudanese families and two Vietnamese-refugee families. They were selected through a local international elementary school designated for refugees and were part of a larger study on school and home literacy connections of fourth-grade students. All the families were formally and informally interviewed during May 2004 and July 2006 (see Li, 2008, for more details). This section presents the themes about their parenting practices that emerged from these interviews.

All parents in the four families had high expectations for their children and were dedicated to their children's well-being and schooling. They all recognized the importance of being involved in their children's schooling at home and in school, and all of them tried their best to meet the schools' increasing demands for their active engagement in their children's school work. However, several factors, namely, time, income, culture, language, and the sociocontextual factors of school and community became serious barriers to their parenting practices.

"Good Parenting" May Not be Possible: The Time and Financial Factors

All the case study families were employed in low-wage jobs in factories (such as meat or hat factories) or the service sector (such as hair salons or grocery shops). Like many immigrant families, most of the families had experienced a drop in terms of their occupation status when they immigrated to the United States (Li, 2007). For example, several of the parents had university degrees and had been white-collar professionals in their native country (such as lawyers, teachers, accountants, and engineers). These prior experiences, however, were often not considered or counted in their resettlement process in America, and they had now become factory workers here. The husbands in the refugee families all had a short period of job training upon entry into the United States. The Sudanese men, Tifa Torkeri and Mahdi Myer, for example, both received about 6 weeks of training and each got a factory job. Tifa Torkeri became a welder and Mahdi Myer became a meat slicer. The women attended only a few weeks of English training. Several stayed home at first and later managed to find low-wage jobs as well. Mahdi's wife, Gloria, for example, eventually found a job in a food factory an hour away from their house. Tifa's wife Anne had more trouble finding a steady job. She found a parent-liaison position at an Even Start Program shortly after her arrival in the United States but was later laid off. After staying home for a while, she found a factory job through some friends. Similar situations were also found in the two Vietnamese families.

There were considerable variations across the families with regard to the number of children they had. While the Vietnamese families each had two or three children, the Sudanese families each had six children ranging from 8 months old to 17 years old. Most families had difficulty supporting a large family with their low-wage jobs and were often on welfare support. They also had to work extra-long hours or find a second job to make ends meet. Even though the families tried hard to be actively involved, time and financial burdens often made it impossible for the families to spend quality time with the children at home and become actively involved in their school activities.

The Myer family's situation well illustrates some of the time and financial issues faced by the families. For Mahdi, the most important thing was to have a job that enabled him to pay for the house and to support the children. He went to work from 4:00 p.m. to 2:30 a.m. every day except Saturday. He slept about 2 to 3 hours when he came home from work, then got up around 5:00 a.m. to drive Gloria to work. When he returned from Gloria's workplace, he drove the children to school. After that, he attended a community college where he took courses in business administration. Upon completion of the day's classes at 2:00 p.m., he rushed to a computer lab to do his homework before he went to work. Sometimes he went home to check the children's homework or to take a quick nap before going to work. On Saturdays, he shopped for the family groceries in the morning and took the children along to the laundromat in the afternoon. On Sunday mornings the whole family attended church. In the afternoon, Mahdi had a couple of hours to run errands or catch up with his own school work before going to work. For Gloria, the change has been even greater. In Sudan, her job as an Arabic teacher was neither stressful nor physically demanding. At home, she had relatives to help with house chores so she did not have to do anything. Now she has to get up at 4:00 a.m. every morning to get the children's meals ready before going to work at the food factory. In the afternoon, she takes the bus home and is often so exhausted that she can barely move, but still she has to make sure that the children have completed their homework and prepare dinner for them.

Contrary to the stereotypical notion that low-SES families are not involved or do not care about their children's education, the Myer family was actively involved in their children's school work at home. Their efforts, however, were constantly thwarted by their work and financial demands. Since two of their children constantly had problems at school, Mahdi and Gloria really wanted them to do better, utilizing all kinds of methods to help them overcome the language barrier, such as borrowing some language tapes from a school teacher. But Mahdi soon realized that his own limited English was not enough to help the children successfully complete their school work, which made him decide to go to school himself: "I started to learn English so that I can help my kids." After he gained enough English, he decided to attend a local community college with the assistance of a government subsidy. His original intention was to show his children in a direct way that one could learn at any age, especially his eldest son Rahman, who was seriously behind in all subjects.

Juggling his work and studies, Mahdi had even less time to be with the children. He joked that he did not have much time to read with the children or help them with their homework because "I need somebody to help me work." Since he was so busy, Gloria took up the daily responsibility of checking the children's homework. Because she could not read English, she could only supervise the completion of the homework. After she came home from work, she told the children to "come and sit there, and everyone have to open his book . . . even if you don't have homework, you have to read. No play." Since Gloria could not help, the children sometimes helped one another, especially with math and English. However, despite his efforts at home, the children often misbehaved in school and Mahdi had been frequently called to the school to meet with teachers, which meant he often had to take time off work to attend those meetings.

A similar scenario is also found in the home of the Vietnamese Phan family. The Phans have two children, 16-year-old Hanh, in 10th grade, and her 11-year-old brother Chinh who was born in the United States, in 5th grade and struggling with English and math. The Phan family was originally from South Vietnam. Like many refugee families, they had a difficult immigration experience. Fleeing from the communist regime in Vietnam, the Phan parents took different paths to enter the United States. Mom Lynne Phan went first to the Philippines to learn English for 6 months and gave birth to Hanh there in 1987. In 1988 mother and child came to Texas as refugees. Dad Dao Phan first immigrated to Halifax, Canada, in 1987 and then reunited with his wife and daughter in Lake City, Texas, in 1996. In order to support her family and help her extended family in Vietnam, Lynne Phan worked multiple jobs in factories and nail salons. After Dao Phan joined the family again and was able to find work, Lynne had to work only one job in a nail salon.

Since both Phan parents worked long hours, they did not have much time to read or spend time with the children at home. Dao Phan worked about 70 hours a week including Saturdays. His work schedule went from 6:00 a.m. to 2:00 p.m. and then 5:00 p.m. to 10:00 p.m., except Tuesdays when he worked only 8 hours. On weekdays, after he came home from work at 2:00 p.m., he went to pick up Chinh from school at 3:15 p.m. and spent an hour or so with Chinh while he did his homework before he went back to work for his night shift. Like Dao, Lynne also had little time to spend with the children at home. Her daily routine was to get Hanh and Chinh ready in the morning and drive them to school before she went to work at 10 a.m. After work at 9:30 p.m., she usually took care of house chores and prepared the next day's food for the family. Hanh painfully recounted her experiences growing up without her parents' active involvement at home or school:

> I was left alone a lot. And I don't feel like I needed anybody's help. And I never expect my parents to take any time off for anything for me, like when I was little. I don't need them to come to bake sales. I don't need them to come to my graduation. I don't need that. So, I never expect my parents to take any time off for me. So, even for my little brother, like I wish they'll take time off for him because he seems like he needs it. But I wouldn't ask them to do that. So, I'm really accepting of them not spending too much time, to take time off. So I accept that.

The Phans thought that since they both worked a lot and did not have much time for Chinh, if they paid money for the school, the school would do a better job for their son than the public school that was free. One year prior to the interview with the family in 2004, the Phans paid about $3,000 to enroll Chinh in a Catholic school to see whether the demands on parents were different. However, to their surprise, the Catholic school required even more of their involvement at home. As Hanh explained for her father,

> Most kids going to Catholic school come from better off families. So [the parents] have more time at home to take care of the children, be more involved in the work they do. But we don't have that kind of time. We tried. So we can't always [be there to teach Chinh]. We're happy to want to teach him new things. They should be mostly teachers [to take care of his school work].

Since Chinh did not get enough help from home with the increased amount of homework in the Catholic school, he cried a lot because he just could not handle it. Eventually, they withdrew him from the Catholic school and sent him back to the international school, where he felt much happier because there was much less homework and the homework was less demanding.

As the Myer and Phan families' experiences illustrate, family socioeconomic status is a significant factor in determining the available time parents have to spend with their children at home or to participate in school activities. Since they had limited time with the children at home, most of the families did not participate in school events unless they were called in because the children misbehaved. Therefore, for these families, unless there was substantial improvement in their SES, the kind of "good parenting" that demands a lot of time and financial resources was usually difficult for them to realize in the host society.

"Good Parenting" May Not be the Same to all Families: The Culture Factor

In addition to the time and financial factors, culturally different understandings of parenting practices is another barrier to parenting in a cross-cultural context. All the families believed that there was too much freedom in the American society, which made it hard to raise their children in their own cultural ways, with emphasis on obedience to elders and strict discipline such as corporal punishment.

In the Ton family, for example, Lo and Cam Ton found it extremely hard to raise their three children (two boys, ages 14 and 12, and daughter, 8) "according to the Vietnamese ways." In their view, American culture is too open and gives too much freedom to children, which makes them disobedient to parents and elders. Lo noted, "In Vietnam, they listen to us more. They scare. . . . Like I said, in America, it's . . . more open." As a result, when Lo talked to his eldest child, Mien, about safety in the neighborhood and about going to the best high school, conflicts often arose as Mien would not always listen. Since corporal punishment is not allowed in America, Lo was frustrated about not being able to discipline Mien: "For example, Mien [did] wrong to me, I just *talk* to him [emphasis his]. But like he make me mad . . . I can do nothing. If he in Vietnam, I beat him something like that. . . But here, I cannot. I worry about that. That's like . . . do nothing. That scare me too. . . . He know that. That's why he don't worry because sometimes he mad at me, I just *talk* louder [emphasis his]."

Similarly, Mahdi Myer explained his frustration with not being able to discipline his children in the Sudanese ways because physical punishment is not allowed in the United States. "If you hit your child, they call police. What can you do?" Mahdi further explained,

> In Sudan, by law, teacher can beat the child. But here, no . . . If the teacher . . . is going to punish that child by his hand, and [parents] also have to punish your child by doing so. . . . You have to punish him because . . . the child believe if in the school, teacher is going to beat him and then when they come back home, the parents are going to beat them, so there is no initiative . . . you have to accept what the teacher [does], you have to accept what a parent [does].

> But here . . . I don't want do [the same] value, they may call police
> and police may take my child away from me.

Since they could not discipline the children in the same way as in Sudan,
they now tried to "talk to them" like the Tons, which they thought was
ineffective most of the time.

Another concern for the families was raising their daughters in America. Lo Ton commented, "We had a worry about girl in Vietnam [but] not
like in America." He believed that because of frequent exposures to TV,
girls in America "experience a lot" more than those in Vietnam. Since it
was so open, parents could "say nothing." Lo preferred that "they follow
the Vietnamese way." Since there were many things that were out of their
control in America, Lo was not confident that he could raise his daughter
in the Vietnamese way: "I wonder right now. I don't know how. . . [In]
a couple of year, I don't know." This concern had forced the Vietnamese
families to enforce more control over the girls at home. The Ton family
(as well as the Phan family) rarely let their daughters go out and socialize
with their peers, their ethnic friends, or even their cousins although the
boys were free to do so.

This differential treatment had resulted in a lot of psychosocial stress
among the girls, who struggled to understand their parents' cultural ways of
parenting. Hanh Phan explained:

> I was raised by my mother, and she is very careful about how she
> raises me. I'm not allowed to go outside much. . . . I'm not allowed
> to date, to do lots of things. . . . She let my brother, you can go out-
> side with little friends whatever, but I can't do that because I am a
> girl. . . . I stay home 24 hours a day unless I'm going grocery shop-
> ping with my mother. I haven't, I won't go outside for like [a walk]
> . . . During that time, I was really angry and acting out a lot. I had
> a counselor who suggested to my mother that she come and talk to
> me about the situations, like maybe she can give me some time off
> to be with my friends. Obviously that was out of the question, it
> never happened.

The stories above suggest that immigrant families' cultural traditions
shape which and how much parents adjust their child-rearing practices
in the host culture. Though the parents made adjustments in some practices, such as corporal punishment, their parenting practices, especially
with regard to their daughters, were highly influenced by their cultural
backgrounds.

"Good Parenting" May Not be Doable:
The Language Factor

Although all the parents had the desire to be more involved with their children's homework at home and with school events, one of the consistent barriers had been the language difficulty that they experienced. As noted earlier, most of the families only had minimum language training upon their arrival in the United States. According to them, the training was not enough for finding a good job or becoming truly involved in their children's studies in the United States.

In the two Sudanese families, since the fathers worked most of the time, the responsibility of checking the children's homework was usually taken on by the mothers, whose English language proficiency was often even more limited. Anne Torkeri checked the children's homework every day and tried to follow the teachers' instructions to read with her younger children. However, with limited English and a limited understanding of the American school system, it was a tremendously difficult task for her. She noted:

Although I know that there are some subjects, they have difficulties. But I try my best to help them. If there is something that I could help, then, I will help. But if there is something that is very difficult, I cannot. Sometimes I called the teachers and I said, if there is an example, so that I may follow the example. Maybe I can help them. Like math, it's very difficult. And I had difficulty with math when I was in school, too.

In the two Vietnamese families, the parents' lack of English language proficiency had severely limited their ability to help their children who were struggling in school. Dao Phan tried to help his son, Chinh, with his homework when he had some time between his shifts. He bought a workbook for Chinh to practice his math. However, it was difficult for Dao to help because both of them had limited English proficiency and Chinh was not proficient in Vietnamese either. As Hanh explained, "[My father] did try, but his English is very poor and he can't help that much. Like he is good at math . . . but when you are trying to explain it to someone, you need to be able to articulate it and neither of us can speak [English] very well, so we can't take a book and help each other."

Their accents were another factor that affected the parents' decision whether to be involved in the children's homework, especially in reading. Like many immigrant parents who were not confident about their oral English, Dao normally did not read to Chinh. He believed that his accent had influenced Chinh's oral language development. "We found when we get book from most English. You know like pronunciation something like that . . . so Chinh learn from English from me, too . . . like really accent, and big accent, something like that. So he pick up from dad and he go school, and when he speak English, the teacher [think] Chinh get problem with English."

In the Ton household, their youngest son Dan was seriously behind academically in the second grade. Lo and Cam were very worried and decided to try their best to help him at home even though they knew their English was not good. Lo's English had affected his ability to communicate with the teachers about his concerns. He explained, "Very hard sometimes. I don't speak [English] very well, I don't know how to talk to the teacher." They decided to try their best by reading the words to Dan and asking him to repeat after them. They also asked Dan to copy the words to help him memorize. Lo expressed his feelings, "me and my wife just try make them better and better, but I cannot do nothing, because he's slow." Lo also admitted that he was not sure how to help his son improve his math or express his concerns to his teacher, "I don't know how to teach math. I try help him. How I want to say to teacher?"

"Good Parenting" May Not Be Enough: The Contextual Factors

The data also suggested that the families' parenting practices were constantly thwarted by the sociocontextual factors, such as the school and neighborhood conditions. All the parents expressed concerns about their children's safety due to rampant drug use and alcohol abuse in the schools and in the community.

Mahdi Myer, for example, was concerned that "in this country, there is no control in the school. Children play bad things in the school." His "big fear" was that his children might be involved in drugs and alcohol and the teachers did not care. He explained in length:

> In America, it's a country of freedom, teacher is free to do anything, like I see accident [fights] from here sometimes between teachers and students. . . . The teacher should respect themselves, respect that job, because respect got us to respect them. . . . That's why my child learn the bad way, to talk in bad way. . . . That's why drug use in school is very common. Because teachers are not care enough. . . . [when] I went [to school], sometimes they smoking inside school, [kids] learn with somebody, they get the children [learn] that.

Similarly, Anne and Tifa Torkeri were also concerned about their children's safety and learning in the school. They were shocked to learn that "even in the primary schools here, they have a lot of crimes." Anne commented, "This is more advanced country. But still there is a lot of crime because there are other crimes that I have never seen in my country. So when it happened here, I'm not happy. When they are at school and just playing, let them come back safely. And I can't keep on taking them to school, [wondering whether they will come back home] and all this stuff, because I have a lot to do." The biggest concern for them was the safety issue in school. Like the Myers, they attributed the crime to the lack of discipline in American schools. Tifa explained, "In the country I came from, the way how they discipline kids is different from here. Here they allow kids even to say bad words about their teachers. . . . Because of the system here, sometimes it happens. . . . In the class, students sometimes when the teacher is teaching, and students are talking, doing different things than paying attention to the teacher."

The declining neighborhood condition is another important factor that influences the parents' parenting practices. The neighborhood in which the families reside had once been a nice neighborhood with mostly middle- and working-class Italian residents. Over the years, the widespread drug and violence problem had made the neighborhood a notorious "war zone" for gangs. It had also become a very transient place where the population was in constant flux. This transient nature had, to some degree, made the neighborhood a dangerous place to live. As a site-facilitator for some urban-school initiatives in the district explained, "High crime, a lot of gang activity, a lot of drugs, a lot of gun-running, that sort of thing. It comes out of [this neighborhood]. The kids grow up in this sort of environment." The families all witnessed fights and violence almost every day from their doorsteps. Once, the Torkeri children saw a murder scene on their way from school. Other kids watched a police drug raid from their front porch and heard bullets fly by. As another parent in the larger study described, it was like "watching a movie, except it's happening right outside [our] house in my neighborhood. My kids are *sitting right there!*"

All the families realized that they needed to find a safer place to live. However, due to their financial situations, none of them could afford to live in a better neighborhood. As housing in this neighborhood was much cheaper than others, three of the families (the Tons, the Myers, and the Phans) were able to afford small houses in the neighborhood. For the Torkeris, with their six children, the second-floor, two-bedroom apartment in an unkempt two-story house was all they could afford in rent.

Unable to move out, the school and community conditions had forced the families to monitor their children's whereabouts more closely. They rarely let their children go out to play. As Anne commented, "Oh my goodness, these neighbors . . . all out drinking; people coming in and out . . . I don't want my kids to go out and play." Because they were concerned that they might join in gang activities, the Sudanese parents also forbade their children to join many of the after-school activities. As a result, the children were confined to their homes most of the time, playing alone or watching TV.

CONCLUSIONS AND IMPLICATIONS

The stories above demonstrate that though all parents want to be involved in their children's education, a complex of factors outside school within the family milieu affect what parents can or cannot do to facilitate their children's learning. The findings suggest that school teachers and administrators must have a contextualized understanding of the immigrant and minority children's social realities outside school. They must recognize the real obstacles many parents have in helping their children with homework and school activities and be sensitive to the wide-ranging circumstances of these students and families who often come from diverse cultures and low-SES backgrounds.

To understand students' social realities, teachers in low-SES schools must take a culturally reciprocal approach (Li, 2006) in minority education, by which teachers and families mutually learn each other's cultural knowledge. Teachers and educators must find effective ways to collect student social and cultural information outside school (such as family practices, beliefs, family strengths, as well as language and socioeconomic barriers in their lives) as we cannot teach when we do not know who we are teaching. In effect, direct contact with and systematic study of students' families and communities should become the basis for instructional planning. This information collection process will not only help teachers recognize the cultural differences and values in "good parenting" between home and school but also enable them to understand the real obstacles surrounding their students' lives.

Once they have a solid understanding of the children's lives outside school, teachers in low-SES schools must also be proactive in exploring effective strategies to help parents overcome the barriers in their lives. As Goodwin and King (2002) argue, diverse cultural backgrounds of families demand new strategies to encourage parental involvement. The narratives of the four families given above suggest that conventional ways of communicating (such as parent-teacher conferencing and report cards in English) with parents who are from different cultural backgrounds and who do not speak English may not work. They must use a variety of nonconventional

channels to work with parents of diverse backgrounds. First, since time and
financial factors constrain low-SES parents' involvement in school activities,
it is necessary that schools change parental participation in school from un-
paid volunteer work to paid participation or seek innovative ways to involve
parents. This suggestion can be controversial, but it is important to take into
consideration the social realities of many parents who cannot afford to take
time off from work or other daily chores. Consideration must also be given
in terms of transportation and the time of such activities. For example, some
schools have laundry machines that parents can use when they come for
consultations concerning their children. This simple accommodation is an
important gesture by the schools to recognize difficulties for active parental
involvement faced by some families. Second, since language is a major barrier to the parents' involvement at home and in school, school activities and
communication with parents must provide interpreters or language support
for these parents. Schools can also set up family literacy programs that encourage parents to learn the English language together with their children
or as a social support group. Since culture is a factor, schools can organize
informal meetings with parents (again with financial and language support)
and teachers to discuss different cultural beliefs and practices as a way to
understand and bridge the differences. Schools can also involve parents in
joint planning about ways to improve the school and neighborhood culture
and environment. In sum, through creative problem solving, teachers and
schools can establish a reciprocal cultural exchange and work with parents
as collaborators to best facilitate learners' educational needs.

In conclusion, teachers and administrators of low-SES schools can create
a variety of new strategies and initiatives to understand and address the real
obstacles in the children's lives outside school. These strategies and initiatives will help both teachers and parents learn from each other and build
strong and genuine parent-school partnerships in which low-SES parents'
voice is both present and heard.

Discussion Questions

1. How does poverty influence minority children's educational
   experiences?
2. What is considered as "good parenting"? By whom?
3. What are the barriers to "good parenting" practices in low-SES
   families?
4. How does the school play a role in addressing these barriers?
5. What can teachers do to help address social-class issues through
   their daily instructional practices?

REFERENCES

Beyers, J. M., Bates J. E., Pettit, G. S., & Dodge, K. A. (2003). Neighborhood structure, parenting processes, and the development of youths' externalizing behaviors: A multilevel analysis. *American Journal of Community Psychology*, 31(1/2), 35–53.

Chao, R. K. (1996). Chinese and European American mothers' beliefs about the role of parenting in children's school success. *Journal of Cross-Cultural Psychology*, 27(4), 403–423.

Epstein, J. L. (2001). *School, family, and community partnerships: Preparing educators and improving schools*. Boulder, CO: Westview Press.

Fine, M., & Weis, L. (1998). *The unknown city: Lives of poor and working-class young adults*. Boston: Beacon Press.

Goodwin, A. L., & King, S. H. (2002). *Culturally responsive parental involvement: Concrete understandings and basic strategies*. Washington, DC: American Association of Colleges for Teacher Education. (ERIC Document Reproduction Service No. ED472940)

Gutman, L. M., McLoyd, V. C., & Tokoyawa, T. (2005). Financial strain, neighborhood stress, parenting behaviors, and adolescent adjustment in urban African American families. *Journal of Research on Adolescence*, 15(4), 425–449.

Hook, J. V. (2003). Poverty grows among children of immigrants in U. S. Washington, DC: Migration Policy Institute. Retrieved August 4, 2008, from http://www.migrationinformation.org/USfocus/display.cfm?ID=188

Kotchick, B. A., & Forehand, R. (2002). Putting parenting in perspective: A discussion of the contextual factors that shape parenting practices. *Journal of Child and Family Studies*, 11(30), 255–269.

Lareau, A. (2000). *Home advantage: Social class and parental intervention in elementary education* (2nd ed.). New York: Rowman & Littlefield.

Lareau, A. (2003). *Unequal childhoods: Class, race, and family life*. Berkeley: University of California Press.

Lee, E. V., & Burkam, D. T. (2002). *Inequality at the starting gate: Social background differences in achievement as children begin school*. Washington, DC: Economic Policy Institute.

Li, G. (2006). *Culturally contested pedagogy: Battles of literacy and schooling between mainstream teachers and Asian immigrant parents*. Albany: State University of New York Press.

Li, G. (2007). Parenting practices and schooling: The way class works for new immigrant groups. In L. Weis (Ed.), *The way class works: Readings of school, family and the economy* (pp. 149–166). New York: Routledge.

Li, G. (2008). *Culturally contested literacies: America's "rainbow underclass" and urban schools*. New York: Routledge.

NAEP. (2007). The nation's report card. Retrieved November 13, 2008, from http://nces.ed.gov/NationsReport Card/

Ogbu, J. U. (1982). Cultural discontinuities and schooling. *Anthropology & Education Quarterly* 13(4), 290–307.

Rothstein, R. (2004). *Class and schools: Using social, economic, and educational reform to close the Black–White achievement gap*. Washington, DC: Economic Policy Institute.

Ruiz-de-Velasco, J., & Fix, M. (2001). *Overlooked and underserved: Immigrant children in U.S. secondary schools*. Washington, DC: Urban Institute.

Suárez-Orozco, C., & Suárez-Orozco, M. M. (2001). *Children of immigration*. Cambridge, MA: Harvard University Press.

CHAPTER 11

The Interwoven Stories of Teachers, Families, and Children in Curriculum Making

Simmee Chung
D. Jean Clandinin

Human lives are not pieces of string that can be separated out from a knot of others and laid out straight. Families are webs. Impossible to touch one part of it without seeing the rest vibrating. Impossible to understand one part without having the sense of the whole.

—Diane Setterfield, *The Thirteenth Tale*, p. 59

Setterfield's quotation calls us to consider the complex interconnections when lives meet and become interwoven. As teachers and researchers in schools, we see our lives and our families' lives as interwoven with the lives of our students and their families, as well as other teachers and administrators. These intertwined and fluid sets of lives seem to ripple and shift as they bump against social, cultural, and institutional narratives. Setterfield's words illuminate a frame for this narrative inquiry of how curriculum can reflect the lives of all those it affects.

We began this narrative inquiry (Clandinin et al., 2006) with research puzzles around children's experiences both in and out of school. As we attended to children's lives we necessarily attended to the stories they lived and told (Clandinin & Connelly, 1992). We wondered about how teachers experienced making curriculum attentive to the diverse lives of children within achievement-focused stories of school.

During our inquiry we became aware of some of our assumptions about the lives of children and their families. We became attentive to the gaps and silences in children's and families' "lived" and "told" stories of school as they bumped against our teacher stories (Clandinin et al., 2006). Considering ourselves in relation with children and families helped us see how they often experienced school and classroom landscapes as places of tension.

In this chapter we focus our research on one child, newly arrived to Canada, and her mother's lived and told stories. We consider how these stories shaped in-classroom curriculum making as well as how the in-classroom curriculum making shaped the lives of this child and her mother. The elementary school in which the study was undertaken was in an urban, upper middle-class community composed of children from multicultural backgrounds. In the 2006–07 school year we lived our lives alongside children from a Grade-3 classroom, a year when the children have their first set of provincially mandated standardized tests.

Our research puzzles became a journey of unknowing and knowing (Vinz, 1997) through which we became aware of the need to consider the diverse voices and lives of families, too often absent in schools. Vinz (1997) suggests the practice of "shifting valances of dispositioning" (p. 145) in which educators move between "unknowing, giving up present understandings (positions) of our teaching, to "not knowing" to acknowledge ambiguity and uncertainty (p. 139). Vinz's concept of dispositioning became important to us as we were dispositioned from attending to "planned" curriculum, attending that blurred our vision of the "living" curriculum (Clandinin & Connelly, 1992; Aoki, 1993). We wondered how children's and families' stories were given space in curriculum making in schools.

In our view, we are a "living" curriculum, not a curriculum laid out by mandates and plans, but rather one composed of lived and told experiences. This view of curriculum, as composed of children's and teachers' lives, allows us to notice complexities that are not otherwise visible as they meet in the nested milieu of classrooms, schools, and communities around particular subject matters.

If children and teachers are cocomposing curricula of lives in schools and classrooms, in what ways does the story of each child's family become part of this cocomposition? By listening more closely to each child's and each family's lived and told stories, might we better understand the tensions children and families experience in curriculum making? Our work is situated with Clandinin and Connelly's (1995) understanding of school landscapes that include both in-classroom and out-of-classroom places. We imagine landscapes, not as static sites in which people's "stories to live by" (Connelly & Clandinin, 1999)—their identities—are fixed, but rather as temporal places that shape and are reshaped by those who live within them.

VIBRATIONS ON THE FAMILY WEB:
A NARRATIVE INQUIRY METHODOLOGY

Entomologists tell us that a spider feels every vibration on its web (Mason, 1999). Revisiting Setterfield's metaphor, we imagine a child and her family as a web, and we realize that when we touch one part of a child's life, we set off vibrations in the rest of the family. By the same token, when the family touches its child, the child's life vibrates into classroom curriculum making. In this view, we see the place of families in curriculum making in new ways.

Too often when we think of curriculum making, we think about only the visible lives of the children and the teacher. Setterfield's notion of family webs helps us think about what is invisible. Could it be that even though we do not usually know about families' stories, they create vibrations in our classroom curriculum making? We wonder if, like a spider, a child feels every spiraling vibration from her family web, then conversely, do the vibrations that bounce off a child shake the family web to its core? By being attentive to our unfolding, narrative inquiry research puzzles, we became aware of the importance of seeking out and listening more closely to not only children's and teachers' stories but to families' stories as well.

Clandinin and Connelly (2000) describe narrative inquiry in terms of a three-dimensional inquiry space with dimensions of sociality, temporality, and place. By inward, they mean toward the internal conditions, such as feelings, hopes, aesthetic reactions, and moral dispositions. By outward, they mean toward the existential conditions, the environment. By backward and forward, they refer to temporality past, present, and future. Narrative inquiry consists of being in the field, writing field texts (data), and composing research texts. A variety of field texts were constructed and collected for this study: oral histories, memory-box items, photographs, student- and teacher-generated documents, transcripts of individual conversations with children, parents, and teachers, and field notes.

By considering family stories, we focus in on how one mother's lived and told stories shape her relationship with her child both in and out of the classroom and out of school altogether. Setterfield (2006) wrote, "I shall start at the beginning. Though of course the beginning is never where you think it is. . . . Our lives at the start are not really our own, but only the continuation of someone else's story" (pp. 58–59). Setterfield draws attention to how we are always in the midst of living and telling the stories of our lives and that our lives are always composed in relation to family and cultural stories. As we worked together in the move from field texts to research texts, we composed fragments of a child's story and her family stories as they vibrated against each other without clear beginnings or ends, but rather as story fragments "lived and told." We selected six story fragments from our field texts to show how we have come to understand the ways that vibrations, as stories bump together, can touch the child's life, her family's life, the teacher's life, and other children's lives in the classroom.

Story Fragment 1: So Korean

As Simmee Chung engaged in conversation with Elizabeth's mother in the fall of 2006, Mrs. Han, who had begun to feel comfortable with telling stories to Simmee, told stories of Elizabeth as well as stories of her own uncertainties. Mrs. Han fiddled with her hands as she nervously spoke through our translator (Dr. Ji-Sook Yeom):

> I don't know if you want to listen to this story or not. . . . Elizabeth had a bit of a problem with a friend in her classroom. This child gave Elizabeth a hard time on how she dresses, talks, and how she behaves, all kinds of things.

The friend, also Korean, was born in Canada, whereas Elizabeth had immigrated to Canada. Mrs. Han described how Elizabeth came home crying that day as the other child told her that she "talked funny" and that she should not act "so Korean" but more like everyone else. Through telling the story, which had strained their family, Mrs. Han began to fill in gaps in Simmee's ways of knowing this family. Simmee realized that Elizabeth was now dressing more like the other children. Rather than wearing her unique clothing from Korea, Elizabeth now wore clothing purchased locally. Intrigued by Elizabeth's new style choices, Simmee asked her why she wore her jeans with one pant leg rolled up. Elizabeth shrugged as she stated she did not know why, only that she had seen others wearing their pants like that. Simmee now understood why Elizabeth had given her a "cover story"—that is, a story that she composed and told to help her fit into dominant stories of school (Clandinin & Connelly, 1995).

Mrs. Han's voice was barely audible as she described how she confronted the other child's mother, who responded, "This is Canada, but same in Korea." The other child's mother explained that, similar to Korea, teachers and families see the children differently according to how much money the family has. She said people judge others by "how they dress," and said that she agreed with her daughter's advice to Elizabeth, as they, too, being Korean in a predominately affluent White community, were also learning to fit in. Her daughter was helping Elizabeth fit in. Still shaken, Mrs. Han wondered if her Korean friend was right. She asked Chung if this was true in Canada. For Elizabeth and her mother, what Elizabeth was experiencing in school, that is, her living curriculum, was at the forefront.

What could have been overlooked or seen as small vibrations between her and her friend marked an important moment of tension for Elizabeth as she questioned who she was, and perhaps who she could be, while she negotiated her living curriculum alongside her peers. These vibrations gained momentum as they touched those she loved. Attending to the vibrations in these family stories, we began to see the threads that connect the two mother's stories. Elizabeth is told how to dress and behave in school by another child. She then tells her mother who speaks to the other child's mother. These family stories, in turn, vibrate forward to the children and their stories of who they are. The children's stories vibrate onward and shake the classroom's living curriculum.

If we look at children and families as part of their own family webs and as possibly threaded together with other children's families' webs, we imagine how strong these collective vibrations might be within families and between families. As we trace through the threads of stories, traveling forward and backward among a child's stories, her mother's stories and the family stories of another mother and child, these vibrations become visible.

Story Fragment 2: A Bouquet of Flowers

It was the week of Thanksgiving when Elizabeth secretly handed Simmee a gift with a card attached. The card, with no words on the cover, was illustrated with a beautiful bouquet of flowers. Elizabeth shyly told Simmee it was from her mother.

Dear Teacher,

I appreciate that you always look after my daughter, Elizabeth, with love. Since the first day of school she has enjoyed everything with pleasure. Because she has come to Canada not even a year ago. She would have some problems with English and with Canadian Culture. Please understand that and Elizabeth and I will do our best to help her to get along with it well. I always hope to see you at school someday, but due to my lack of English, my cares weigh heavily on my chest. I feel sorry that although I'd like to see you at school, my lack of English makes me worried. I wonder if Elizabeth doesn't bother you during classes.

When Simmee finished reading the card, Elizabeth explained how her mother had asked a Korean neighbor to translate and write this letter in English. Simmee began to understand how important it was for Mrs. Han to connect with her, the teacher, to share her fears and hopes for her daughter. Simmee found herself shifting backwards and forwards between the stories she had initially "told" of Elizabeth and her mother. Simmee was surprised to hear that Mrs. Han felt tension about who she and her daughter were on the school landscape. For Simmee this contradicted her story of seeing Mrs. Han on the first day of school. Before dropping Elizabeth off in the classroom, she smiled at Simmee and they bowed politely to one another. Now Mrs. Han's words on the card interrupted Simmee's first stories of Elizabeth as she began to wonder more deeply about the other stories Elizabeth and her mother lived by.

Simmee felt compelled to respond to Mrs. Han, a mother who cared so deeply about her child. She realized Mrs. Han wanted to be visible in composing the classroom curriculum.

Dearest Mrs. Han,

I am so touched by your words and acts of kindness. You are too generous and do not need to give me anything as the best gift is having Elizabeth in my class. Elizabeth is doing so well in Grade 3, you do not need to worry about her. Elizabeth is an excellent student. She is loving, helpful, hardworking, and kind. I could not ask for a more thoughtful student as Elizabeth always puts a smile on my face. I wish I could speak Korean because you are so lovely. Thank you again for your gift. Have a wonderful Thanksgiving and Chusok day. Elizabeth told us all about this special holiday.

Always,
Simmee

Story Fragment 3: Living a Presence of Being Korean

When Simmee first met Elizabeth, her thoughts were ones in which she admired Elizabeth's strength. Simmee recalled the first day of school when Elizabeth bounded into class holding her mother's hand. Elizabeth excitedly waved good-bye to her mother. Simmee was struck by how grown-up Elizabeth was in a tailor-made coat covering a plaid dress. Simmee remembered commenting on her outfit and Elizabeth confidently responded that her outfit was from Korea, where she was from. As Simmee got to know her, she marveled at how she took the initiative to bring in various collections of Korean dictionaries and information books that complemented classroom resources. In the first month of school Elizabeth even participated in a schoolwide writing task about traditions and wrote two pages about a special Korean moon festival called Chusok celebrated every October. She volunteered to read it aloud to her classmates.

Elizabeth explained to the class that she and her mother wrote it together. Her mother described the tradition and Elizabeth translated it into English. Elizabeth told Simmee they wanted other people to learn about their Korean traditions. Simmee continued to be fascinated by what she saw as Elizabeth's courage. Once, on a field trip, Elizabeth offered Simmee a homemade Korean sushi roll that she brought as lunch. As they ate together, Simmee noticed other children staring at Elizabeth's lunch. Elizabeth munched happily on her seaweed snack and didn't seem to notice the stares. Simmee wondered how Elizabeth and she were so different: When she was a little girl, Simmee hid her culture and heritage. She did not dare eat authentic "smelly" Chinese food at school, nor did she choose to share her heritage with her classmates.

During one art lesson as the children studied Van Gogh, Elizabeth brought in a Korean version of a book about Van Gogh and excitedly translated the book to English so her classmates could understand. A classmate asked if Elizabeth could read it aloud in Korean and she did. Some classmates were in awe as she read. Simmee thought she and Elizabeth lived out very different stories as children who immigrated to Canada. Elizabeth seemed to be a confident, carefree child with little tension and few worries in her life.

During one snowy recess Simmee began to see herself in Elizabeth's lived stories. Elizabeth asked if she could read an information book about space, the topic of study in language arts, outside. Simmee thought it a strange request to bring a book outside when it was so cold; most children opted to make snow angels. Elizabeth explained she wanted to get an A in language arts so she was learning as much as she could about space. Simmee agreed to Elizabeth's request and later, when Simmee was outside walking with the children, she noticed Elizabeth sitting by herself, clutching the book in her bare hands. Concerned, Simmee asked another student to bring Elizabeth some gloves. As she looked at Elizabeth with her nose pressed against the book, she began to retrace her own memories of herself as a little girl. She wondered if there could be multiple and more complex plotlines in Elizabeth's life. Simmee recalled how she, too, had wanted to belong, to fit in, to not stand out. As a child, she had found solace by immersing herself in books, imagining herself in other worlds, imagining what could be otherwise. Simmee began to see how Elizabeth and she were not so different after all.

Story Fragment 4: Tensions on the Family Web

As we listened to children's stories, teachers' stories, and family stories, we began to understand the importance of attending to tensions that may impact a child's and her family's lives.

Around Christmastime, the children composed letters to Santa Claus. Simmee found herself traveling back to a familiar childhood landscape as she read Elizabeth's letter. Elizabeth wrote:

> I don't know what I want. But the first thing that I want is for my family to come to Canada because everybody in my class has their family in Canada.

Simmee reflected on the landscape on which Elizabeth lived, a landscape similar to her own. Simmee and her family, too, once had to leave a homeplace. She could feel Elizabeth's words in her letter. She began to listen more closely in the classroom as Elizabeth revealed many stories about aging grandparents, cousins, and close friends who still lived in Korea. Elizabeth longed for her extended family to be living in Canada. Simmee understood how Elizabeth felt for she, too, had once longed for her extended family to be close by. Elizabeth wrote the following letter to Simmee at Christmas:

> Thank you Ms. Chung for teaching me and loving me. I want to be like you because you are smart. Have a Happy Christmas! Ask Santa if he has a good present for you. P. S. Be healthy. Your Friend, Elizabeth

Simmee was surprised as she read that Elizabeth wanted to be like her for she wished she had been as brave as Elizabeth when she was a little girl. Revisiting Setterfield's words, "Impossible to understand one part without having the sense of the whole" (2006, p. 59), we are reminded that we cannot fully understand a child without listening to the interconnected vibrations of her life in the context of her family. Simmee found herself thinking about their stories lived and told as immigrant children, as well as the stories of her own mother; her mother had also felt the vibrations as they bumped against stories of school and school stories. When Simmee was 4, her family immigrated to Canada from England in the hope for greater opportunity. During her childhood, her family transitioned to three small rural communities, each time opening and closing a Chinese restaurant. In every town, Simmee remembers being the only Chinese family. She remembers moments of tension in her childhood as she struggled to fit in and make sense of who she was. She recalls her mother's anxieties and worries for her. Now, recollecting her childhood stories and her mother's stories, Simmee wondered if the tensions in her family web were similar to the ones Elizabeth and her mother were feeling.

Story Fragment 5: Naming the Tensions on the Family Web

Simmee gathered the children in the classroom sharing corner. Acknowledging the diversity within her classroom, Simmee read the children her latest favorite book, *The Name Jar* (Choi, 2003). On the cover is a picture of a Korean girl staring into a jar filled with names written on pieces of paper. The story began with a little girl, Unhei, reluctantly saying good-bye to her grandparents at the airport in Korea as she leaves for North America. Wiping away Unhei's tears, her grandmother gives her a tiny pouch, which held a wooden block carved with a Korean character. "Your name is inside," her grandmother tells her. As Simmee read the book, Elizabeth inched closer, at one point even reaching out to touch a page. Afterwards, Simmee and the children engaged in a discussion about whether the main character should have kept her Korean name—a name others found difficult to pronounce— or taken a common English name.

Many stories about belonging were told by the children that day. Elizabeth revealed her name was not Elizabeth at all, it was Ji-Sook. Shortly after reading the book, Elizabeth wrote a note to Simmee: "Well, I didn't pick my English name so I just want to be called my Korean name (Ji-Sook). Ji-Sook proudly shared that, on her mom's side of the family, all children's names end in Sook and their last name goes in the front. As Elizabeth explained this, Simmee recalled that she wondered when she first saw Elizabeth's report card with the name Ji-Sook. When we learned of the significance of Elizabeth's Korean name, we began to use her English name and Korean name interchangeably in the classroom. Simmee had not questioned why Ji-Sook went by an English name as her own parents had also changed their names in order to belong in Canada. Accepting the silence at that time, Simmee had not thought to ask why, making assumptions as she forwarded her own stories of belonging.

The day after reading the book, Simmee had another research conversation with Mrs. Han. She asked Mrs. Han if she had heard about Elizabeth wanting to use her Korean name. Mrs. Han told Simmee that when Elizabeth came home the day before she said, "Oh mom, I just don't like my name, Elizabeth." In response, Mrs. Han firmly told her daughter that everybody wants that name; she was named after English royalty. As Elizabeth debated with her mother, Mrs. Han stated, "So that's a good name and you'll be a good person. I think about it a lot when I give you that name." Elizabeth settled by agreeing with her mother.

After listening to Mrs. Han's account of the conversation, Simmee asked how she would feel if Elizabeth still wanted to use her Korean name. Mrs. Han said she wanted her daughter to be "common" and "the same as other children." Simmee and Mrs. Han shared more stories as they wondered about what "belonging" could mean. Mrs. Han began to realize how brave and strong her daughter was to want to use her Korean name. She wondered if it connected Ji-Sook to their culture. Simmee shared her experiences of inclusion as a child immigrating to Canada and how she once felt that belonging meant being like everyone else. Simmee and Mrs. Han came to a shared appreciation of Ji-Sook's strength as she struggled to hold onto her Korean name, a name that gave a story of who she was. Simmee told Mrs. Han that Ji-Sook was a special little girl who stood out. Standing out, being different, is good. As Simmee said this, Mrs. Han smiled and nodded.

Simmee later spoke to Ji-Sook while they were playfully making outfits for Ji-Sook's teddy bears. Not knowing the earlier conversation Simmee had had with her mother, Ji-Sook shared that she felt very sad when she arrived home after thinking about *The Name Jar*. The book reminded Ji-Sook of leaving Korea and her family. She felt particularly sad about the airport scene at the beginning of the book. Simmee asked Ji-Sook if she wanted everyone to call her by her Korean name,

Ji-Sook: I don't care what I'll be called. Uh just, it doesn't really care for me.
Simmee: So a name isn't really important to you? So how come yesterday you told me that you wanted them to call you Ji-Sook?

As Simmee reflected, she understood the tensions Ji-Sook was experiencing around using her Korean name. Although Ji-Sook previously shared with her classmates the tensions around her name, Simmee wondered if Ji-Sook would feel comfortable sharing the tensions that occurred between her and her mother around the name.

We wonder if it is possible or necessary to pinpoint where vibrations first begin, for the vibrations in a web reverberate strongly to every thread, in every direction. As curriculum makers attentive to children's and families' lives, we know, regardless of where vibrations begin, we need to attend to them all. By attending closely to negotiating a curriculum of lives in the classroom, there are safe spaces for the children to engage in inquiry into their stories to live by. However, the vibrations that began through reading the book and engaging in the discussion left lasting imprints on Ji-Sook's life, vibrating onwards, touching the story of who Ji-Sook is and may become. As Ji-Sook wondered about who she was becoming in choosing to use her Korean name, she bumped against a story her mother wanted for her.

Simmee: Do you think that your mom wants you to use an English name?
Ji-Sook: Yeah.

Simmee: What do you want?

Ji-Sook: I can't just . . . my mom. We don't like to be or disagree.

Simmee: You said some of the other kids were calling you your Korean name today? Did you like that?

Ji-Sook: Yeah. Kind of they're learning from me and I'll try to learn their names in Chinese or like lots of stuff. So I'm trying to memorize all of them so I can like work on other languages.

Ji-Sook's words stayed with us, "I can't just . . . my mom. We don't like to be or disagree." Although the vibrations were first noticed in the classroom as Ji-Sook identified with the book, these vibrations traveled to touch Ji-Sook's story of who she was and who she wanted to become. Reverberating from her family web of stories to the classroom curriculum making, the vibrations of stories lived and told, inevitably lingered, touching webs of lives.

As spaces were opened in the conversation between Simmee and Ji-Sook, Ji-Sook once again began to share stories where she imagined herself and others to be otherwise. Although her story of "being otherwise" bumped against her mother's story of who Ji-Sook was, Ji-Sook revealed she loved her Korean name and wanted to use it more. While she feared that some people would have difficulty pronouncing Ji-Sook, her Korean name was important to her and she was determined to use it.

Over the year, we saw Ji-Sook waver between using her English and Korean names. She signed her name Ji-Sook or Elizabeth, depending on how familiar a friend was to her. Ji-Sook was mainly used for those who were closer to her and Elizabeth for those who still called her Elizabeth. Ji-Sook continued to struggle with what name to use. One day she ripped up a beautiful butterfly title page on which she had written "by Elizabeth." She redid the entire assignment, writing instead "by Ji-Sook." Ji-Sook frequently chose to reread *The Name Jar* during independent reading time. Each time we saw Ji-Sook with *The Name Jar* in hand, we wondered about the impact it had on her life and her mother's.

At the end of the year, Simmee gave Ji-Sook her own copy of *The Name Jar* as a gift, inscribed:

Dearest Ji-Sook (Elizabeth),

Ji-Sook, thank you for teaching me about following your dreams and how to be strong. You make me smile every day with your warm heart. I have learned so much about your special Korean culture and I think you are a brave little girl. I think you will change the world with your kindness—you already do. You remind me of this special girl in this book. When you write the book about your life one day, I want to be one of the first people to read it. You and your mother have special stories to tell. Keep dreaming and imagining. . . . Thank you for making everyone feel like they, too, belong.

Love always,
Ms. Chung

Story Fragment 6: Gaps and Silences In and Between Webs

"While I wash dishes, I cry."

—Mrs. Han, 2007

Mrs. Han's voice quavered as she described her part-time job at a fast-food restaurant. In Korea she was a vice principal of a kindergarten. In Canada, she worked as a dishwasher and sandwich maker. We sensed sadness in Mrs. Han's voice as she shared her and her husband's hopes for their daughter. They came to Canada so Ji-Sook would learn more English. Mrs. Han's eyes lit up as she described how she hoped, one day, to return to Korea where Ji-Sook would attend university and then, eventually, a university in the United States. She wondered about their decision to come to Canada. She wondered if Korean families do too much for their children. She wondered if she was putting too much stress and pressure on Ji-Sook to succeed.

As Simmee listened, she realized how little she really knew about this family. Mrs. Han continued to fill in the gaps as she described firmly telling Ji-Sook, "Although you work very, very hard there is discrimination because we are strangers in this society." She shared that Ji-Sook cried when she said this and responded, "I can do very well. I will do my best!" Ji-Sook shared her dream of attending Harvard University. Mrs. Han, surprised at her daughter's knowledge, asked how she knew of Harvard. Ji-Sook replied, "That is the best university in the world. You trust me, I will work very hard to get into Harvard University."

In our inquiry into the tightly interwoven stories in this family web, we saw how each thread vibrated and, inevitably, touched other threads. Simmee found herself returning to the image of Ji-Sook reading a science book outside on a cold winter day. Attending to all of the story fragments, we began to better understand how the family's web of stories was, in part, threaded around dreams of Ji-Sook's academic achievement.

We felt the vibrations, the tensions, as Simmee apologized for not being able to talk much to Mrs. Han during the Grade 3 parent information session. This session, given by teachers, was intended to alleviate parents' and children's anxieties around provincial achievement tests. Mrs. Han shared how she had not wanted to go to the session because of her lack of English. However, Ji-Sook begged and pleaded, saying "Mom, if you don't come, I won't be able to graduate my Grade 3." Mrs. Han gave in. Ji-Sook was worried that she would "lose information or miss something that other children might know." Although Mrs. Han would not understand what was being said at the session, she agreed to attend as she wanted to help her daughter find success in a foreign school landscape.

Mrs. Han shared that at first she did not think these government tests were important, but her Korean friend told her that usually only the "elite" are well-educated people and are known to do better at these "tests." Resonating in Mrs. Han's mind were her friend's words: "This is the same kind of society as Korea. In Korea we have a lot of gap between the poor families and the rich families. The higher scores are from the 'elite' [rich], they are known as the well-educated people." Mrs. Han's fears were cemented as the other Korean mother told her that the results of these "tests" in Grade 3 determined children's placement in junior high. As Mrs. Han shared this story of tension, Simmee shared her stories of growing up with limited financial resources. Moving through a series of small towns, the last place she remembered living with her parents was above their restaurant in a place they would eventually see as a home. Simmee's story brought forth tension for her as an educator for she hoped that teachers, like families, would not be judged by their financial status. As Simmee and Mrs. Han continued to share their stories, their journey of knowing and not knowing connected their lives.

As we understand family stories as intergenerational and interwoven, we realized it was important to inquire into Mrs. Han's stories of her experiences of school as a child. More silences were revealed. When Simmee asked Mrs. Han about her experiences in elementary school and her relationship with her mother, Mrs. Han began to cry as she traveled back to her childhood experiences.

Mrs. Han spoke of her stories, which ultimately shaped her daughter's curriculum of life.

> I grew up in a small country. There was not much competition in academic areas, so if somebody is doing really better than other children, that person is really stands, stands out. When I look at my mother's younger face, my mother is like me. The relationship between my mother and me is like the relationship between me and Ji-Sook. I want my daughter to stand out and my mother was like that to me.

Mrs. Han tearfully explained that she wished her mother had pushed her more academically because she felt she missed out on opportunities, having only gone to a two-year college rather than a four-year University. "I tell Ji-Sook to work hard and then later you choose what you want to be and that's your choice. . . I don't want her to blame me later."

As Mrs. Han opened up to tell her childhood stories, she became mindful of how they were affecting her daughter's life:

> One day Ji-Sook came home and then she sighed, "oh tomorrow is reading test." I told her to not worry and just be comfortable and you can do your best. Then that night, Ji-Sook threw up everything.

Although Mrs. Han had come to new ways of knowing during our time with her, a knowing where she tried to put less stress on Ji-Sook, Ji-Sook still put pressure on herself to succeed. Family stories appear to be so deeply and tightly woven that, even when we try to loosen the strands, each story in the web continues to reverberate through each child's curriculum of life. We wondered about how the stories of assessment shaped and reverberated through each family's web. We wondered about possibilities in our stories as we shared our hopes. In our conversation with Mrs. Han on the last day of school, she reaffirmed the need for spaces in our lives to reimagine new possibilities for ourselves and for our children.

Simmee: What are your hopes for your daughter?
Mrs. Han: Respect. If people don't listen to you, you cannot have . . . but
   if you have reputation or respect then other people will listen to you.
Simmee: Is that how you can make a difference?
Mrs. Han: Yes.
Simmee: My last question. What are your hopes for yourself?
Mrs. Han: I didn't think about that. Here in this country, in this situation,
   I do not have any room or any energy to think about that hope

A SENSE OF THE WHOLE:
CREATING SPACES FOR FAMILIES IN CURRICULUM MAKING

Relational knowing is a primary aspect of narrative inquiry (Clandinin & Connelly, 2000). In our inquiry we became aware of the importance of listening to family stories as they influenced their child's interactions with the mandated curriculum as well as their unfolding life curriculum. We realized that we needed to be intentional about creating spaces where the interwoven personal stories of children existing within their family stories could be told and retold through shared narrative inquiries. In the classroom we worked together with the children and their families to create what became known as a project in citizenship education. In this 7-month-long narrative inquiry project, children composed annals and took photographs of places and people where, and with whom, they belonged. They also took photographs of objects that symbolized "belonging" in their lives and made collages of who they were and who they were becoming. Working in small-group and whole-class response groups, the children and we became aware of the ways family stories were present in classroom curriculum making.

Through attending more closely to one child's story, her mother's story, and other family stories, we learned more about making spaces to cocompose a curriculum of lives. For example, we wondered about the stories of achievement testing that are shaping stories of school. As we heard in Ji-Sook's and her mother's stories, vibrations from these stories can travel backwards to parents' earlier experiences of assessment. In turn, these earlier experiences may vibrate forward to a child's life. We wondered how often parents are caught in their own spaces of tension and thus live out their stories through, and with, their children. We wondered about how we could more intentionally create spaces for such stories to be told so that we could understand how assessment could be shifted from assessment of learning to assessment for learning and assessment as learning (Adamson, 2008). These latter ways of thinking about assessment fit more seamlessly within our view of curriculum making.

We remain hopeful that school landscapes can be otherwise as we attend to family stories and begin to make spaces for cocomposing a curriculum of lives alongside children, families, and teachers. As Mrs. Han and Simmee continued to imagine otherwise with one another, Simmee responded, "Yes, I think that hope is all we have." To create change in our ways of knowing, we need to attend to all vibrations, especially those that are invisible upon first glance. By listening to the voices of families, we can acknowledge and appreciate the diversity in our classroom webs and in our webs of lives.

By attending to family vibrations lived and told, we can begin to interrupt and rewrite dominant stories of school (Clandinin et al., 2006). Through listening closely to vibrations within these intergenerational webs of lives, we can cocompose a curriculum in schools where all involved feel like they belong. Simmee's conversation with Ji-Sook on the last day of school reminds us of the importance of creating spaces in schools where families can tell, retell, and compose their stories in the most important curriculum of all, a curriculum of lives:

Simmee: What are you looking up?

Ji-Sook: *Belonging.* [She reads the definition in the dictionary.] I don't get it. It's too hard the words for me. Just that it takes a long time to think what really belonging means. Like you can't use the dictionary that you could see what belonging means. Can you just figure out what belonging means. Feels like I'm a crazy dictionary.

Simmee: Do you think we might just have to figure out what belonging means ourselves?

Ji-Sook: Yeah. [She sighs, slowly closing the dictionary.]

Discussion Questions

1. In what ways do stories such as those told in this chapter create disruptions in how each of us use our knowledge in our teaching practice?
2. What challenges do you imagine educators will face as they adhere to the planned/mandated curriculum but also try to integrate stories from their students' lives into the curriculum?
3. How can teachers work with parents and children to make lives (children's, families', and teacher's lives) more visible in classrooms?

REFERENCES

Adamson, D. G. (2008). *Shifting the professional landscape: Professional development and assessment for learning.* Unpublished doctoral dissertation, University of Alberta, Edmonton, AB, Canada.

Aoki, T. (1993). Legitimating lived curriculum: Towards a curricular landscape of multiplicity. *Journal of Curriculum and Supervision, 8*(3), 255–268.

Choi, Y. (2003). *The name jar.* New York: Dell Dragonfly Books.

Clandinin, D. J., & Connelly, F. M. (1992). Teacher as curriculum maker. In P. Jackson (Ed.), *Handbook of research on curriculum* (pp. 363–401). Toronto: Macmillan.

Clandinin, D. J., & Connelly, F. M. (1995). *Teachers' professional knowledge landscapes.* New York: Teachers College Press.

Clandinin, D. J., & Connelly, F. M. (2000). *Narrative inquiry: Experience and story in qualitative research.* San Francisco: Josey-Bass.

Clandinin, D. J., Huber, J., Huber, M., Murphy, S., Orr, A. M., Pearce, M., & Steeves, P. (2006). *Composing diverse identities: Narrative inquiries into the interwoven lives of children and teachers.* New York: Routledge.

Connelly, F. M., & Clandinin, D. J. (1999). *Shaping a professional identity: Stories of educational practice.* New York: Teachers College Press.

Mason, A. (1999). *The world of the spider.* San Francisco: Sierra Club Books.

Preston-Mafham, R. (1991). *Spiders*. London: New Burlington Books.

Setterfield, D. (2006). *The thirteenth tale*. Toronto: Bond Street Books.

Vinz, R. (1997). Capturing a moving form: Becoming as teachers. *English Education, 29*(2), 137–146.

Zabludoff, M. (2006). *Spiders*. New York: Marshall Cavendish Benchmark.

About the Editors
and the Contributors

Monica Miller Marsh, PhD, is an associate professor of education at De-Sales University. She is interested in teacher education, early childhood and elementary education, and issues of diversity. Her work has been published in various journals including *Curriculum Inquiry, International Journal of Qualitative Research in Education* and *Reflective Practice.* Her most recent book, *Other Kinds of Families: Embracing Diversity in Schools* (also published by Teachers College Press) was coedited with Tammy Turner-Vorbeck. She has recently cofounded with Tammy Turner-Vorbeck the Family Diversity Education Council, a nonprofit organization.

Tammy Turner-Vorbeck, PhD, an adjunct professor of education at Purdue University, focuses on multiculturalism and diversity, curriculum theory, and sociology of teaching. Her work has appeared in *Curriculum Inquiry* and *Multicultural Education,* as well as in several edited books She also coedited (with Monica Miller Marsh) the recently published book, *Other Kinds of Families: Embracing Diversity in Schools.* She speaks at educational conferences and presents workshops on issues of family diversity and representations of family in school curricula and classrooms. She has recently cofounded with Monica Miller Marsh the Family Diversity Education Council, a nonprofit organization.

Rochelle Brock, PhD, is the executive director of the Urban Teacher Education Program at Indiana University, Northwest. Her areas of research are Black feminist pedagogy, spirituality, and identity, as well as urban education. In addition to several articles and book chapters on identity and spirituality, she has written a book, *Sista Talk: The Personal and the Pedagogical* (2005), which is an inquiry into the questions of how Black women define their existence and move toward the liberation of their minds and souls from ideological domination.

Simmee Chung is a graduate student at the University of Alberta in Edmonton. Her works in progress focus on narrative matters in teacher education, conceptualizations of student engagement, and a narrative inquiry into the interwoven, intergenerational stories of immigrant children and their mothers. She has taught in elementary school for 11 years and won an Excellence in Teaching Award in 2008 from the province of Alberta.

D. Jean Clandinin, PhD, began her career in education as a teacher and school counselor in elementary school. She is currently a professor in elementary education and director of the Centre for Research for Teacher Education and Development at the University of Alberta. She has received several prestigious awards and has written many books and chapters, the latest of which is the edited volume *Handbook of Narrative Inquiry: Mapping a Methodology* (2007). The main focus of her research has been narrative inquiry.

Deborah Graham is the primary–12 program coordinator for the Strait Regional School Board and president and newsletter/journal editor of the Primary Elementary Teachers Association of Nova Scotia. During her 30 years as an educator she has been a secondary and elementary classroom teacher, consultant, and literacy coach, as well as a part-time instructor at St. Francis Xavier University in Antigonish, Nova Scotia. At the present time she is completing a doctorate of education at the University of Nottingham.

Elizabeth Graue, PhD, is professor of early childhood education in the Department of Curriculum and Instruction at the University of Wisconsin-Madison and the director of Graduate Training at the Wisconsin Center for Education Research. Her areas of interest include readiness, class size reduction, preparing teachers for inclusive home-school relations, and qualitative research methods. Her work has appeared in *Educational Policy, Teachers College Record,* and *Harvard Educational Review.*

Margaret Hawkins, PhD, is an associate professor of English as a second language in the Department of Curriculum and Instruction at the University of Wisconsin–Madison. Her areas of interest include language, teacher education, and sociocultural and sociopolitical approaches to language and literacies. She has published in such journals as *Educational Researcher* and *Teaching Education.*

Janice Huber is an associate professor in preservice and graduate teacher education at the University of Regina in Regina, Saskatchewan. She recently coauthored with D. Jean Clandinin and others the book *Composing Di-*

verse Identities: Narrative Inquiries into the Interwoven Lives of Children and Teachers (2006). A former elementary teacher and teacher researcher, her research interests include narrative understandings of identity in relation with Aboriginal teachers and elders in Canada, assessment, curriculum making, and diversity.

Angela Jaime, PhD, is an assistant professor of education at the University of Wyoming. Dr. Jaime's tribal affiliations include enrolled membership in the Pit River and Valley Maidu of northern California. Her expertise is in ethnic studies and curriculum studies, and she specializes in American Indian education, the study of Native women and their experiences in higher education, multicultural education, and women's studies.

Guofang Li, PhD, is an associate professor in the Department of Teacher Education at Michigan State University and specializes in ESL/ELL education, family and community literacy, and Asian American education. She has received distinguished awards from the American Educational Research Association, the National Reading Conference, McGill Journal of Education, and the University of Buffalo. In addition she has published several edited volumes and has written three books, *East is East, West is West?: Home Literacy, Culture and Schooling* (2002); *Culturally Contested Pedagogy: Battles of Literacy and Schooling Between Mainstream Teachers and Asian Immigrant Parents* (2006); and *Culturally Contested Literacies: America's Rainbow Underclass and Urban Schools* (2008).

Tamara P. Lindsey, PhD, is professor and graduate coordinator in the Department of Curriculum and Instruction at the University of Wisconsin–Eau Claire. Her research interests include caring in the classroom, culturally relevant pedagogy, and children's literature. She has published several chapters and articles and received the Teaching Excellence Award at her institution.

Gerardo R. López, PhD, is an associate professor of educational leadership at Indiana University. He teaches courses in school-community relations, critical differences in educational leadership, and inquiry methodology. His research intersects critical race theory, migrant education, and parental involvement, and directly challenges the taken-for-granted assumptions surrounding the role of parents in educational matters.

Anne Murray Orr, PhD, is an associate professor in preservice and graduate teacher education at St. Francis Xavier University in Nova Scotia. She coauthored with D. Jean Clandinin and Debbie Pushor the article called

"Navigating Sites for Narrative Inquiry," published in 2007 in the *Journal of Teacher Education*. Narrative inquiries into how teachers, children, families, and administrators experience life in schools, specifically around topics such as assessment, cultural diversity, and identity making, are the focus of Anne's research.

Linda T. Parsons, PhD, is an assistant professor at the Ohio State University–Marion. She teaches middle childhood literacy and young adult literature courses in the College of Education and Human Ecology, School of Teaching and Learning. Her work has appeared in various journals including *Language Arts, Reading Teacher,* and *Children's Literature in Education.*

Debbie Pushor, PhD, is an associate professor in the Department of Curriculum Studies at the University of Saskatchewan in Canada. She is engaged in narrative inquiries into parent knowledge and into parent engagement and leadership. In her undergraduate and graduate teaching she makes visible and central an often-absent conversation in teacher education about the positioning of parents in relation to school landscapes.

Nathalie Reid has a Masters degree in education from St. Francis Xavier University, Antigonish, Nova Scotia. Currently a high school teacher in Bonnyville, Alberta, she has taught high school in three Canadian provinces, as well as at St. Francis Xavier University and the Northern Albertan Institute of Technology. She works with two social action groups through her school, H.O.P.E. (Helping Our Peers Everywhere) and the Street Team (a group aimed at facilitating the transition of ninth-grade and new students into the school).

Caskey Russell, PhD, is an assistant professor in English and American Indian studies at the University of Wyoming. Originally from the state of Washington, he earned his doctorate at the University of Oregon in 2001. He has published in such journals as *American Indian Culture and Research Journal* and *Studies in American Indian Literature*. He is an enrolled member of the Tlingit Indian tribe of Alaska.

Shirley Steinberg, PhD, is an associate professor in the Department of Integrated Studies in Education and the Director of the Paulo and Nita Freire International Project for Critical Pedagogy at McGill University. She is the author and editor of more than 20 books and numerous articles, including *Kinderculture: The Corporate Construction of Childhood* (with Joe Kincheloe) and *The Encyclopedia of Contemporary Youth Culture* (with Priya Parmar and Birgit Richard).

Kent Stoelting, was an elementary school for 10 years prior to becoming a school principal He also worked as an educational consultant for the Indiana Department of Studies at Indiana University–Bloomington. He is currently a doctoral candidate in the area of educational leadership policy studies at Indiana University–Bloomington. His research interests surround parental involvement in the Latino community.

Index